MASTER
MEDIA
LIMITED

MasterMedia books are available at a discount with bulk purchase for educational, group, premium or sales promotion use. For information, please write to:

Special Sales Department
MasterMedia Limited
333 West 52nd Street
Suite 306
New York, NY 10019

# AGING PARENTS AND YOU

by Eugenia
Anderson-Ellis
and
Marsha Dryan

MASTER
MEDIA
LIMITED

*New York*

Published by MasterMedia Limited.

MASTERMEDIA and colophon are registered trademarks of MasterMedia Limited.

Library of Congress Cataloging-in-Publication Data

Anderson-Ellis, Eugenia.
  Aging parents and you.

  1. Parents, Aged—Care—United States.   2. Parents,
Aged—United States—Family relationships.   3. Adult
children—United States—Psychology.   4. Parents,
Aged—United States—Life skills guides.   I. Dryan,
Marsha.   II. Title.
HQ1063.6.A53   1988      646.7'8        88-12283
ISBN 0-942361-05-9 (pbk.)

Designed by Irving Perkins Associates
Manufactured in the United States of America

10   9   8   7   6   5   4   3   2   1

# Acknowledgments

The writing of such an informative and diverse book could not have been accomplished without help from many sources. Our special thanks go to the hundreds of caretakers, our contemporaries and our friends, who shared their successes and their failures with us in our focus groups, and to their parents, who helped us to understand. Our gratitude goes to the countless health care workers who, in spite of their overwhelming work loads, continuously nourished and supported us, and to the experts in the field—doctors, lawyers, and academicians—who directed our research and confirmed our information. Our respect goes to the numerous organizations, associations, support groups, and corporations who serve the communities across this country, and whose help to us was invaluable.

And a heartfelt "Thank you" to: Carole Lewis Anderson, who opened the door; Ruth Anderson Coggeshall, who added valuable support; Max Goody, for his inspiration; Susan Schiffer Stautberg, our publisher, who made it possible; Susan Victor, our editor, who showed us how.

# Contents

# AGING PARENTS AND YOU

*Chapter 1*

# Adult Children— Who Are We?

Tears filled my eyes as the bus pulled out of the station in Stroudsburg, Pennsylvania, leaving my strong, independent mother looking so alone and vulnerable as she waved to me from the curb. I was on my way home to San Francisco, almost three thousand miles away, but my mother, Ros, did not cry, and if she felt vulnerable, she had not admitted it.

I had been visiting my parents for five days. It was not a holiday, nor was there any crisis. Business had brought me close enough to their home to make it possible to spend some time with them. I had been feeling guilty about not being able to contribute as much time and energy to my parents' well-being as my sisters had, who lived closer, but the primary motivation for this visit was a desire to be with my parents.

I am a long-distance caregiver, full of conflicting and ever-changing emotions toward my aging parents. In the past, I resented the fact that my father demanded so much of my mother in terms of attention and care. I wished Mother could be freer to travel, as in the past, and, selfishly, I wanted her to spend more time with us and our children. Daddy, who had been the center of attention for years, had had a full life. It was Mother's turn. Without him, I reasoned, she would stay young much longer and have time to develop a fuller life of her own. Now, as my father continues to need so much of Ros's time, I see a big change in the relationship. Mother, at eighty-four, is feeling more needed and less used. Daddy, at ninety-seven, is gentle and more appreciative of favors. We have arranged good daytime help, and so the time Mother spends with him during those hours is by her choice.

I am frightened by the realization that the time has passed when my father's death would provide any relief to my mother. Maybe that was never true. What I do know is that now she will be left with an enormous void when he dies, and I want to protect her.

As the bus rolled on, I thought about the pain I was creating for myself, and I forced myself to reflect, instead, on the brilliant foliage we were passing, and how extremely lucky Mother and Daddy were to have yet another autumn on their own property in such a beautiful part of the country. Probably the greatest lesson I have learned over the years of visiting my parents and the repeated pain of saying good-bye is that what we expect to happen rarely does, and that finding solutions to problems that do not yet exist is the greatest exercise in futility we can practice. And yet we do it all the time. Learning to block thoughts of those things that we cannot change will leave us much more energy to concentrate on those we can.

Blocking is a skill caregivers for any age need to develop. I had had ample opportunity to use this skill during my visit to my parents. No sooner had I left San Francisco, with all apparently under control there, than one daughter experienced an earthquake during her first week at school in Los Angeles, and the other developed strep throat in San Francisco. The distance that magnifies my parents' problems was now working in reverse on my children in my absence. My immediate reaction was that I needed to be cloned! I assessed Nicole's strep-throat situation, confirming medical treatment with local advice, but spent no time worrying about Erin. What good would it do? I assumed that she was fine, blocking thoughts of any concern until I heard from her. I did not allow the worried inquiries from my parents' friends, who had heard about the earthquake, to sabotage my block.

Thanks to good friends and the early return of my husband

from his business trip, all was well at home, which brings us to a second skill. We try so hard to be all things to all people that sometimes we begin to believe that we are the only ones who can do the job, not allowing others to develop their contributing skills. As our caregiving chores intensify, we need a larger and larger network of friends and resources to draw upon for help. Asking for help and knowing when and whom to ask are important skills caretakers need to develop. *Aging Parents and You* will show you how.

By the time the bus was passing through the Delaware Water Gap, my mother had headed home to rejoin my father, and my thoughts turned to him and our last five days together. Trot is a dear, ornery man who, at ninety-seven and without clear diction, can still set his heels and let his will be known. My father and I have always argued. Lacking my sisters' diplomacy, I never gave up a good point just for the sake of peace. Some say that I am too much like him. If I thought they meant his brilliant mind or his charm, I would be delighted, but I think they mean his stubborn streak. As Daddy aged and mellowed, so did our relationship, but I have never allowed myself to falsely agree with him. That, I feel, would be patronizing and disrespectful.

That, in part, is what this book is all about—how to respond to the physical needs of our parents in an efficient and practical way without being disrespectful, and how to manage the psychological support without being patronizing.

First, however, we need to take a clear look at who we are.

## Our Background

We are the grown children of traditional families, the products of homes where divorce was unusual and single parenting even more rare. We were raised in families where the father went out to earn the living and the mother, unless there were pressing financial needs, stayed home and tended the house and the children. If our mothers went to college, it was more with the anticipation of meeting a husband than preparing for a career in the workplace. A woman's learned conversational and educational skills were viewed primarily as assets to her husband's career. Our fathers rarely held crying babies, and few ever tried to master the triangle fold of a diaper. The physical caring for others was definitely woman's work.

As families, we did things together. Many of us had lots of extended family nearby: aunts, uncles, cousins, and grandparents were a real part of our childhood—and each family member was definitely responsible for the other. We generally had one television, which we all watched, compromising on what was seen, or living with the dictates of the house. We had strict curfews, and our parents always knew where we were. We also had very specific chores, usually based on our sex. The boys took out the garbage and mowed the lawn and the girls helped with the house and kitchen. The jobs were important to the smooth running of the household, and they were not negotiable. We played together, we worked together, and we prayed together—at church or synagogue at least once a week.

Despite our "togetherness," communication was not key to family life. There were adults and there were children, each with very specific roles to play, and there was never any hint that someday it would be different. When a parental request was questioned, the explanation might simply be "Because I say so. That's why." Other families on the block might have begun to experiment with a new permissiveness, but whatever the child-rearing philosophy, personal finances, like sex, were rarely discussed in front of children. The groundwork was not laid for facing the realities of finance and old age together.

## Our Expectations

We were the first generation to be strongly influenced by television. If we did not have such a perfect family of our own, we certainly had plenty of media models that showed us what life should be. We believed that when we grew up, we would have spouses who adored us, clean, witty children, and a beautiful home. "Father Knows Best," "Ozzie and Harriet," and "The Donna Reed Show" painted very clear pictures. When we left home, we thought it was for good, and we expected our new families to last forever.

Playing against this idyllic backdrop was the fact that we were also the first generation to be raised with the knowledge that mankind had developed the possibility for total annihilation of the world. If we did not get what we wanted quickly, it might not be there to get. We developed a lust for instant gratification and were nicknamed the "me" generation. Our parents, who had lived through the Depression, wanted more for us than they had had for themselves, and we learned to expect it. Our homes would be bigger, our cars faster, our lives better.

The problem with fiction is often not what it says but what it omits. Where were Ozzie's and Harriet's parents? Did Donna Reed ever have a sick elder in her family? Did Father, who knew best, have a father who knew even better? If they did, we were never told. We had no sense that caring for our family would one day include caring for our parents. Nor were we prepared for the fact that our spouses might divorce us, or that a woman's role in life might not be as clear-cut as that of our favorite TV housewife. Should we stay in the home, as our mothers had? Should we insist on being the sole breadwinner, as our fathers had?

## The Adult Daughter

Adult life for our mothers generally had one blueprint: they grew up, got married, and had children—with a prescribed grand-parently role at the end. Since the Second World War, more changes have taken place in the lives of adult daughters than for any other member of the family. We were raised with roughly the same expectations as our mothers, but as we grew up the blue-print was discarded.

New choices—without a blueprint—were presented to us. Women suddenly had more options than ever before.

- College. Education began to change the picture for many. As more and more colleges solicited female students, and doors began to open in the workplace, marrying one's high school sweetheart and settling down was not an automatic decision. For many women, this signaled the beginning of an era in which women would marry later, gradually postponing the child-rearing years. It was our first big choice.

· Marriage. With the ability to support ourselves, marriage itself became a question of choice for many.

· Children. With the advent of more-reliable birth control methods, and a society that felt free to discuss the possibilities, when to have children within a marriage, or whether or not to have them, became another matter of choice.

· Staying at home. Pressure grew from all our options and staying at home was not automatic after having children. It became another choice, which often met with its share of conflict. If we worked, our parents wondered why we were not at home with the children. If we were at home, our peers wondered why we were not out realizing our potential. Our husbands liked the second paycheck *and* the dinner on the table. And we were busy thinking up good answers for the inevitable party question: "What do you do for a living?"

· Job vs. career. Deciding to be in the workplace was only the first decision. Many of us became bored with the dead-end jobs we first took and struggled with how much commitment we could make outside the home. Job-sharing as well as part-time work and free-lance employment were creative solutions used by some who wanted the meat of a full-time job without the hours. Others made the decision to go for a career. For some of these women, that decision meant returning to school for a specialty. Many others decided to take charge of their lives by starting a new business. (By the year 2000, it is estimated that 50 percent of all small businesses in the United States will be owned by women.)

Although there were many women before us who worked very hard so that alternatives would be available to us, we war babies and postwar baby-boomers were the first to be faced with such a complexity of choices to be made every step of our adult lives. There has been a richness of opportunities for change available to us as never before, most of it in very uncharted waters.

Seeing our abilities appreciated in the marketplace has given many of us a heightened esteem for women in general. A steady upward shift in our own sense of the value of women in today's society has taken place as our skills have gained recognition in the business and professional world. Those of us who, as young women, felt that our identity was enhanced by the men we knew have realized a gradual change in focus. Those same women who avoided "women's groups" as boring and shallow now find themselves seeking the conversation of other women at social gatherings. This female camaraderie has been one of the gifts of our new freedom, and it has created networking possibilities that are essential in coping with the downside of our choices.

The major downside of a woman's right to choose her own lifestyle is that few of her mother's domestic responsibilities have been lifted to make room for the new. Most of us still have the pressures of household chores, raising a family, contributing to the community, school, and so forth. And many of us have the added pressure of doing all this as single parents. Unlike our mothers, whose roles were clearly dictated by society and by religion, we have no clear role models to follow. We do not know when it is all right to say no! As we have seen, our backgrounds are basically traditional, and the emotional involvement with all the traditional family values with which we were raised is still with us. Our sense of responsibility is strong, and we feel guilty if we neglect any aspect of our lives. It is hard to say no to anything. Therefore, many adult daughters fall into the superwoman syndrome of trying to do it all.

## The Sandwich Generation

Suddenly, our conversations seem to take on a new twist. No longer when friends gather are we content to discuss our children, careers, spouses, divorces. . . . Now we are talking about our parents, too. We have entered the "sandwich generation."

All too soon we find ourselves sandwiched between the ever-increasing needs of our parents on one side, while continuing to face responsibilities to children, spouses, careers, community involvements, and personal goals on the other. Middle age has been described as "the fifteen minutes between the time that our children go to college and we start to care for our parents." For some, that statement is a luxury. Of the working women now in the forty-to-sixty age range, four out of ten are still caring for children, while one out of ten already has the additional responsibility of caring for an older parent, a responsibility that could last decades. Trying to meet the demands of two generations simultaneously is very stressful. It often means having to choose between two worlds, putting drops in our parents' eyes or wiping the tears from the eyes of our children.

It is even harder to cope when confronted with changing relationships for which we are not prepared. Coping with the changing family dynamics that occur when a needy parent enters the family circle is demanding enough. When divorce puts the responsibility of caregiving on the shoulders of one adult child, the stress is compounded. Not having the support of a spouse with whom to share the caregiving can leave us feeling the guilt of overburdening our children with adult responsibilities, real or imagined. The biggest loss to the caregiver, however, may be the total lack of social life.

Elizabeth can attest to that. She had been divorced for five years and was working full-time as a computer programmer. She shared custody of their three children with her former husband, Tim. On the evenings when Tim had the children, Elizabeth went to night school, where she was earning credits toward a master's degree. Her social life had been relegated to the weekends. It was a busy life; Elizabeth had well-defined goals and was willing to work for them. What she had not anticipated, however, was the death of her father and the rapid deterioration of her mother's health, which followed. For someone who had so carefully restructured her life after divorce, it came as an enormous shock to realize that she would be the mainstay now in helping her mother re-create her life as well.

One does not have to be divorced to lose the support of a spouse. This situation can occur within any marriage, particularly in a second marriage, in which the new spouse has not had the time to cultivate a relationship with an in-law who requires care. The adult child is often reluctant to ask for, and frequently does not receive, help from the new spouse. Caregiving within a second marriage can be further complicated by the demands of stepchildren, who have no relationship with the frail parent.

Connie's situation is a clear example of such complications. Divorced and forty-four, Connie moved with her children to California, where she eventually remarried. She was working on her Ph.D. in psychology when her mother, living on the East Coast, was diagnosed as having cancer. Although her brother lived closer, it was Connie, three thousand miles away, who assumed the responsibility for her mother's needs. Not wanting to burden her new husband financially, Connie returned to a full-time nursing position in order to cover her mother's medical expenses. She also flies east monthly to tend to her mother's needs.

Connie's new husband never knew her mother when she was well, and with his own financial obligations to his first wife and their children, Connie felt that it was out of line to accept any financial support for her mother.

Although Connie's case is quite individual, her complex family situation is representative of the sandwiching of hundreds of thousands of adult children in America.

## The Feminization of Caretaking

The sandwich generation has limitless variations on how we find ourselves squeezed and, as in Connie's case, the "we" is almost invariably female. The feminization of caretaking is nothing new. Women have always been the nurturing ones who were looked to whenever care was needed. Eighty percent of adult children caretakers are female, and our research has shown that even if aging parents have an only son, the caregiver is most likely to be the daughter-in-law.

What has changed is the picture of the women's role. Nearly half of all women between the ages of forty and sixty have jobs outside the home, and 72 percent of women in the baby-boom generation work full-time. Our instinct is still to care for those who cared for us, yet the pulls created by jobs, children, and family often leave us with feelings of guilt, resentment, frustration, and inadequacy as we shoulder this sometimes overwhelming load.

Another big change for women is the delay in having families. Even among married families with a full complement of support,

11

the caregiving role has a more disruptive effect on some than on others, depending often on the ages of the children. Among the baby-boom generation, many couples have postponed having children until their thirties, which increases the chances of simultaneous parent and child-care responsibilities. Currently, the highest incidence of dual care falls to those women between the ages of forty and forty-five.

We know that our parents have an extended life expectancy from that of their parents, who are already outliving their parents! What this means to us as adult children is that, for the first time in the history of America, we can expect to spend more time caring for our aging parents than for our children.

At the turn of the century, parents spent an average of nineteen years providing for their children and nine years looking after their parents. With increased longevity, it is now estimated that we shall spend seventeen years taking care of our children and eighteen years involved in the care of our parents.

Marlene exemplifies this possibility. She was forty-three when her third child entered her senior year of high school. With her husband's encouragement, Marlene finally accepted a major promotion with a public relations firm, one that would require a certain amount of travel. It was a very exciting time for Marlene, but it could have ended abruptly with the trauma of her mother's stroke.

Marlene became one of the millions of Americans providing care for an elder parent; she took her parent into her home to live. Marlene's mother has been living with her for ten years now and, with all of the children out on their own, Marlene is one of the new caregivers who will probably spend more time caring for her mother than she did for her children.

Happily, for Marlene and for her mother, she has been able to make use of a strong network of friends and of community resources to make life most productive for the whole family. Good counseling made her realize that she was not the only one who could help her mother. Her mother attends an adult day care center four days a week, where she gets physical therapy as well as companionship. Although Marlene was not able to accept the promotion that required travel, she has been able to continue at her job, knowing that her mother is in very good hands.

Another aspect to longevity is that we have adult children caring for parents who are caring for their parents. It is not unusual at caregiving seminars to have seventy-year-olds who are caring for parents in their nineties.

Paula, forty-two and an only child, is concerned about her parents, who are both in their seventies. Although they are in excellent health, it concerns Paula that they insist on driving the mountain roads to visit Paula's ninety-three-year-old grandmother, who is in a nursing home two hundred miles away.

As life-spans increase, many people such as Paula's grandmother will remain grandparents for thirty to forty years. In fact, we probably have as many great-grandparents today as there were grandparents at the turn of the century.

With the increased popularity of four-generation families, and the examples of so many of our parents who are living healthy, full lives well past the traditional age of retirement, one would think that we would all be taking steps to prepare for an additional twenty to thirty years of life after sixty. The fact is, however, that Americans rarely think about their own aging or that of their parents before a medical or financial emergency forces their attention on it.

*Aging Parents and You* hopes to focus attention on our caregiving roles in time for most of us to lay some useful groundwork.

## The Role of Caregiver

It was during the mellow part of an evening, after an elaborate Thanksgiving dinner, that my mother, Ros, first asked what the book I was working on was all about. I found myself stumbling for words. How could I tell this independent woman who had just helped prepare such a delicious dinner that I was writing a book about me and my contemporaries as we care for our aging parents? Had our family been in crisis, it would have been obvious that help was needed, but when there is no immediate problem, it is less clear. For me to write about being a long-distance caregiver could easily be thought of as presumptuous by parents who had taken very good care of themselves all their lives. Was it not my mother who, just a few months ago, was still giving me advice on how to proceed with my career? How, then, could I presume to call myself her caregiver?

The problem, I realize, is one of semantics. There are many ways in which we can express our caring. When our parents are neither sick nor very old, the partial or long-distance caregiving we offer may be a far cry from that of the full-time health professional or family member who becomes responsible for the complete physical care of the elder. For some, the caregiving may be as simple as making our parents aware of the services available in their community. In many cases, the only difference between the relationships that we have always had with our parents and our "caregiving" role is that now we make the effort to inform ourselves about the special opportunities and services available for elders in America today.

Could my parents get along without my help? With good use of community resources and neighborly help, they would probably do fine. But, as I explained to my mother, that would not stop me from giving care. As offered by informed adult children today, most caregiving is simply providing the support necessary to keep our parents independent and in control of their own lives for as long as possible.

This book is purposely *not* directed to our parents. Unless they are no longer capable of making decisions, it is not our right to tell our parents what they should or should not do. This book is addressed to our contemporaries—to the adult children—telling of ways in which we can integrate our parents into our lives while trying to make their aging the most fulfilling journey possible for them. We are talking to each other, sharing experiences and resources because we care.

The first skill we must all develop as caregivers is the ability to offer our informed help to our parents in such a way that it is welcomed as a comforting solution to a potential problem, rather than being interpreted as "taking over."

The roles of caregivers are as varied as the conditions of our parents, with health a much greater factor than age. The full-time caregiver is one of the unsung heroes of today! The nation's public policy toward its elders may need improvement, and society's attitude vis-à-vis its elders could stand some polishing, but we certainly can take pride in the way in which the majority of American families take care of their aging loved ones. The full-time caregivers among us deserve our full support and admiration. Unlike the mother of an infant, who gets much sympathy for her sleepless nights, and has the wonderful knowledge that the job gets more rewarding daily, the caretaker of an aging parent who spends sleepless nights has very few friends who have any idea what she is going through, physically or emotionally, and she knows only that it may never get any better.

There is much that can be said of these hardworking women who give of themselves in a lonely and often thankless vigil—but that is another book. What we want to focus on here are the new stresses in our complex, busy lives and the many ways in which we might reduce some of them.

## The *New* Traditional Family

Although the structure of the traditional or nuclear family still exists in many households, the way in which the family functions has changed dramatically. Among the major changes are fewer children; fewer extended-family members at hand; less clearly defined roles for husband and wife; and the influx of women into the workplace. One of the results of this new family structure is that the mainstay of the American family—the wife and mother—is no longer available in the same unlimited way to be the family caretaker. As child day care has developed into a major industry to fill the void on one side of the generation, adult day care is a burgeoning industry on the other side of the generation, offering one option to help with aging parents who need full-time attention (see page 201).

The role of the husband/father has also gone through real change in the new traditional family. He is more actively involved in family affairs. Although there hasn't been a dramatic shift in the major life choices of the adult sons, it cannot be denied that all that has affected their sisters and wives has affected them. Many adult sons who were raised by mothers who devoted themselves exclusively to their families have found themselves with wives who expect them to be much more self-sufficient. It has not been an easy adjustment; the divorce rates can attest to that. Often these husbands are torn between being proud of the intelligence and accomplishments of their wives and resenting all the time and energy being spent on things other than themselves. Many still live with the expectations of their childhood, wanting their wives' total dedication and support. But, in addition, they want informed, interesting partners. Like the adult daughters, they have no clear role models for handling the new role of husband and father in today's society.

Added to the sometimes disjointed makeup of family life are the new stresses facing the children of today. There is increased academic pressure—from the preschool interview to the SAT scores for college entrance—and the social pressures are enormous. Sexual freedoms exist as never before, and the fear of disease is growing with it. AIDS makes the wrong choice life-threatening, and the availability of drugs complicates life even further.

It is harder to establish a closely knit, interdependent family unit when the family spends so little time together. Being aware of and discussing the additional stresses faced by the family today should help us feel less isolated in our attempts to cope with the changes. This is clearly a time when the establishment of family values is paramount if the family is to survive as a unit.

The changing of roles in the traditional family does not have to be a negative happening. It can allow much greater flexibility in our life choices. Children are being exposed to more possibilities in the world, with less stereotyping and a greater sense of choice for themselves. More importantly, perhaps, many of them are responding positively to additional family responsibilities, which can once again make a real difference to the family. For instance, if dinner is not started on time according to the directions left by a working parent, it might be as vital to the failure of the family's evening meal as it was in days gone by when a child failed to bring in the wood to keep the fire going.

Assigning jobs that are important, and appreciating the results, lead to the double bonus of helping to develop a true sense of family in our children, while relieving some of the stress caused by feeling overburdened. Whenever children are allowed a say in family problem-solving, they are more inclined to want to be involved, and setting such a pattern early can pay large dividends if the family should, for example, face a health crisis with grandparents later on.

A great deal has been written about the American family, and it is our intention here to explore its changing nature only so far as we feel it relates to our relationships with our parents, and our children's relationships with their grandparents. A positive result of the very busy lives we lead is that our lack of time can allow a relationship to develop between child and nearby grandparent. It is unrealistic to expect our children's cooperation or even understanding of our caretaking roles with our parents unless a relationship has been developed between them over the years. With our busy schedules, there are new conflicts. If we have no time to attend our children's activities, it will be harder for them to understand how we have time for our parents. The more energy we put into nurturing a loving, intergenerational relationship between our parents and our children, the more understanding and support we shall receive from our children when the time comes to devote more time to the care of our parents.

## Divorce, Remarriage, and Single Lifestyles

For many Americans, the original family unit—mother, father and children—has become a thing of the past, thus complicating our ability to create strong family structures. Divorce and remarriage have brought about a surge in the number of multiple families, with children often identified as "mine, yours, and ours." A hot new talk-show topic seems to be about "learning to live with someone else's children."

The positive side may be that these new combinations create larger family networks. If an atmosphere has been developed that promotes cooperation, there is the possibility for real division of labor, thus eliminating an overwhelming load for any one person. This type of cooperation, however, only comes naturally on "The Brady Bunch" television show. For the rest of us, it takes many family conferences, learning to air our feelings and to understand our new family, before a spirit of cooperation can be fostered. Such exercises in communication may represent an

17

enormous amount of energy and time for an already over-crowded schedule, but they pay high dividends, particularly if the family should have to face a health crisis together, either for an immediate member or for an aging parent.

The negative is that "combination families" may weaken old family bonds, thereby lessening the sense of family obligation. Children who move with their mothers, for instance, to live with a new stepfather, may lose close contact with their paternal grand-parents. And single parents, who face all the stresses of adult daughters and sons without any of the traditional family support systems, have even fewer immediate resources to help them take on the responsibility for the care of their parents.

A large segment of the population remains single by choice. A growing number of Americans have never married, thirty-six million in the baby-boom generation alone, the vast majority of whom work full-time. To this segment of adult children, many of whom have made a conscious decision to lead a life with less traditional responsibilities, the sudden needs of one or both parents can catch them ill prepared to handle the new demands on their time.

Part of the dilemma for all of us results from a lack of any psychological preparation for facing the needs of aging parents. Just reading about our situations and trying to understand our parents' concerns (see chapter 2) are big steps in avoiding the panicky feelings that pop up when no forethought has been given to helping our aging parents.

## Our Financial Stress

There is considerable financial pressure faced by these families of today. It may be caused partially by the thirst of the "me" genera-tion for more material goods than our parents seemed to need, but raising children also brings new costs for the family to meet.

For those families with two working parents, the second pay-check is considerably diminished by the cost of child care and the price of an office wardrobe. Although most families have fewer children to support than their parents did, the rising cost of education is a big burden to many families, who are increasingly

18

worried about the quality of the public school system. With the knowledge that our children represent the first generation of Americans who cannot assume a better lifestyle than that of their parents, we face the added pressure of trying to find them the best education so that they will be among those who find success in our changing world. Tuition has skyrocketed, from private preschools through the university level.

Additional financial stress comes from many sectors, including the new "feminization of poverty" faced by the divorced woman left with large house payments, children to raise, and inadequate job skills to stay financially ahead. Other women seeking equality in the workplace face the pressures of greater financial risk by running their own businesses, a path, as we have noted, that is chosen by many women.

Without a tradition of discussing finances with our parents, many of us do not know what their financial situations are. Those of us who have given it any thought are concerned that our parents may not have the funds they need to maintain a healthy lifestyle as they age, and we do not know what we will be able to do about it. Without proper planning, some of us may find ourselves in the unfortunate position of having to choose between college for our children or a good nursing home for our parents.

There is little most of us can do about catastrophic health care costs, but the more informed we are about insurance options, the better able we shall be to advise our parents and to prepare for our own financial planning. Sharing with our parents some of the financial planning suggestions made in chapter 7 may be the first step to opening the subject for further discussion and to relieving some of our own financial stress.

## Keys to Reducing Our Stress

We have outlined who we are and the stresses we feel, sandwiched between our many obligations. The new superwoman myth can make today's woman feel inadequate if she needs help, but in this busy world, we do not get help unless we ask for it. Here are some suggestions for finding this much-needed assistance.

SUPPORT GROUPS

The easiest way to ask for help may be by joining a support group of people who share the same problems. As society addresses this growing phenomenon of women and men caught between the dependency of two generations, more and more support groups are being organized for adult children of aging parents. Churches, community centers, mental health associations, medical centers, and national organizations are lending their expertise by creating vehicles through which caregivers can vent their emotions and gain support.

Full-time caregivers often protest that they have no time for another commitment in their already crowded schedules. But they are precisely the ones who most need the support. The health of the caregiver is crucial to being able to provide care, and without the psychological help of peer support, the toll on the health of the full-time caregiver can be very heavy.

Support groups also can function as a valuable network for information and services available in a particular community. For very busy caregivers, the support groups can actually save them time by exchanging information and sharing experiences that have worked for others.

One of the problems with full-time caregiving is that we become too close to the situation to see it objectively. Support groups provide a sympathetic environment in which we can see our situation through the eyes of others. They give us a clearer understanding of the choices we have, and they help us cope as our roles with our parents continue to change.

Perhaps the most valuable role of the support group is that it can reduce the feelings of isolation experienced by many full-time caregivers. Even immediate family members do not always understand the enormous stress felt by the adult child responsible for a parent's full-time care. Some of us are lucky enough to have siblings with whom we can share our feelings. For others, close friends in similar situations step in to fill the void. Nonetheless, a support group of peers who are experiencing many of our same concerns can do wonders to eliminate our sense of isolation. (See page 163 for more information.)

TIME PLANNING

In a crowded schedule with many demands, we may find ourselves constantly promising to spend more time on a project, or with someone, only to have to cancel—with great apologies and renewed promises for another time. Time-planning can be a marvelous tool in reducing this kind of stress.

When my husband and I both found ourselves traveling more and struggling to clear our calendars for family matters, Howard called a family conference. He made a suggestion that has reduced the stress for all of us and put the emphasis where it should be. We all gather with our calendars at the beginning of the school year and we choose our weeks of vacation and our special holidays and/or long weekends for the year. It is important for all of us to know that the family comes first. The rest of the time can be scheduled for business, school, and so forth, without having to check with everyone else for conflicts. Periodic updates are necessary within the year to note special events as they occur, but the general pattern is set.

Variations on the theme are numerous. What is important is that the family schedules what works for them—in advance. For some, it might be a dinner out, alone with your spouse, one night a week; a weekend a month at a hotel; or a long walk together every Sunday afternoon.

When Marsha was newly divorced, moving to a new city and starting a new life, she felt concern that the closeness she had developed with her children, and which she valued so highly, might suffer. To make sure that did not happen, Marsha scheduled a 6:00 A.M. breakfast once a week with each of the three children, so that they might have time alone together. "When it is a high priority, it is easy to do; no one grumbled, because each child felt very special."

If we are in a caretaking role that precludes spending as much time with our children or our spouses as we would like, this kind of special attention is great for all of us. It relieves the guilt of not being together more, it makes our loved one feel special, and it makes him or her more sympathetic to our busy life.

21

ROLE REVERSAL (ROLE-SHARING)

Another good tool for relieving stress and making other family members sympathetic to our tasks is role reversal. Intellectually, we can understand the stress being experienced by other family members based on their responsibilities and commitments. It is the emotional involvement that is most stressful to us in managing our various tasks, however, and that is difficult for someone who is not participating to understand.

Knowing the frustrations of hiring good child care or of getting someone to help our parents, for instance, can be understood intellectually, but who can imagine the anxiety we cause for ourselves after the fact with a thousand "what ifs?" until we learn to trust our own judgment? Only someone who has been through the experience.

Certainly, the emergence of women in the workplace has created wives who are more sympathetic to husbands, tired after a long day at the office, who do not want to go out. The sharing of parenting and household tasks is the necessary next step for the husband if he is to know what it feels like to come home from such a day aware that the second half of one's work is still to be done at home. Sharing of parenting and household tasks is equally important for the wife who has been at home all day. We must allow other family members to assume some of our burdens—we must insist that they do—if we are to relieve ourselves of the stress and resentment of doing it all.

The key is to put others in charge, to give away the job, and that is hard to do for some women who find it difficult to give up their traditional roles. Asking for help with dishes, for example, is not the same as abdicating any responsibility for the dishes. If the family rule is that the person who makes the dinner does not have to clean up, then the cook should not even supervise the cleanup. The cook walks away from the table allowing the others the full responsibility for their task.

Such advice always sounds a lot easier in a book than in reality, but with the proper attitude, it can work, and role-sharing can make a big difference in caretaking situations—whether it be for the household, the children, or one's aging parents.

It is important to remember that communication is critical

to cooperation in any endeavor. We must take the time to let our family know what we are feeling and not assume that they will figure it out on their own. Allowing ourselves to become exhausted before screaming for help is not doing anyone a service. Sharing our roles with other family members before we are spent is really a gift to our families. It makes them contributing, valued members of a group, and it spares them the trauma caused when we become overstressed, resentful, or sick.

ACKNOWLEDGING OUR FEELINGS

Communicating our feelings is not possible until we have acknowledged them to ourselves, and that may not be easy. Support groups, siblings, and good friends may help us sort out just how we feel about ourselves, as adult children, in a variety of caregiving roles.

For some, whose parents are in crisis, the role is clearly that of caretaker, and the immediate concern is finding appropriate resources to help the situation. We may be feeling great insecurity in having to make so many quick decisions, fear over the possible loss of a parent, or even abandonment by family members who are not involved.

For others, whose parents are not in crisis, the concern is far less focused. It is more the nagging awareness of the passing years, the regret of time not spent together, the thought of life without our parents, and the fear that comes from the awareness of our own immortality made so poignant by the increasing frailness of our aging parents.

Whatever the role or situation we face, most of us suffer from some form of guilt. For some, it is the guilt of not wanting to spend more time with our aging parents. For others, it is the guilt produced when having to make choices, the guilt of choosing the needs of our children over those of our parents, the guilt of agonizing over the financial choices to be made—a family vacation or plane fare for a family visit to our parents, and the guilt produced by peer disapproval. There is the guilt of not getting along better with our parents, and the guilt of not having enough time for them in our daily lives, or it may simply be the guilt of being youthful and well, while those whom we love so dearly are becoming weaker.

No child has been reared without ambivalent feelings toward his or her parents. It is the nature of the struggle to become adult and independent ourselves. As we begin to reach our own middle age, some of our old feelings are resurfacing, and at the same time we have to deal with a new sense of who we are. The baby-boom generation, which boasted that it did not trust anyone over thirty, is turning forty! Acknowledging, and trying to understand, how we feel is essential to reducing the stress of caregiving.

And after we feel that we have a handle on who we are, we need to take a good look at who our parents are.

---

## Points to Remember

· Do not dwell on what you cannot change.

· Accept that you cannot do it all.

· Share the work; distance and lifestyles have lessened extended family support, so let friends and immediate family help.

· Develop good intergenerational relations to promote family support.

· Keep family communications open.

· Take steps to reduce stress through:
  —support groups
  —time planning
  —role sharing
  —acknowledging your feelings

---

*Chapter 2*

# Understanding Our Parents

THERE are no other houses within sight of my parents' home in the Poconos, so the tradition is to start honking the horn as soon as we pull out of the Woods Road and turn right at the fork. Sometimes, Mother will be out on the road already, anticipating our arrival. If not, our signal brings everyone outdoors for a big greeting.

On this particular visit, my father, Trot, had heard our honk and was awaiting us in the driveway. He took my arm when I got out of the car, almost in a conspiratorial way, and said that he had something to show me. We left the gleeful family hellos and headed across the lawn and toward the edge of the woods. We walked slowly, commenting on the special green of the new spring leaves, the blueness of the expansive country sky and the ever-changing tableau that nature painted for us there. I thought that Daddy was taking me to his studio, which was farther along, but he stopped unexpectedly and pointed to something on the ground.

"I have been nursing this one back to health," he told me, "and I think it's going to make it."

There, sticking out of the ground about eighteen inches, was a scrawny pine sapling. It was obvious that the ground around it had been cleared of the excess branches and leaves that make up the floor of the woods, so that it might have a better chance at survival.

I was overcome by emotion and knelt down, pretending to take a better look at the tree, so that I could regain my composure. How could my father, then ninety-four, really care about the future of this tiny pine tree, a tree he would never live to see grow tall?

It was then that I realized that I had not really thought about what made my father happy at his stage of life, and how much more there was to know about him. Undoubtedly, his continuing interest in the future was a big part of why he was so young in spirit.

It is startling to realize that what we think life must be like for our parents, and what they actually feel about their own lives, are two, often very different, perspectives. If I were to lose my parents, all my siblings, all my aunts, uncles, and first cousins, all my contemporaries, my classmates, my friends, and even a son, I cannot imagine that I would ever be capable of experiencing happiness again. Yet, for my father, that is precisely what had happened by this stage in his life—and he still was able to get great joy from the growth of a small pine tree.

Understanding that we are not our parents, that our script is not their script, is a big step to understanding them. We are at very different stages of life; but let us step back and take a peek at who our parents are.

## Their Background

Who are our parents? They are older people who have wisdom; they have life's experience under their belts. Many are first-generation Americans, whose parents—who often did not speak English—risked everything for the dream of a new life in America. Some were immigrants themselves.

Our parents were fiercely patriotic toward America, where hard work and education were rewarded with a good life. Honor and duty to one's country were openly expressed with enthusiastic flag-waving, and war would remain far away and glamorous. Even the horror of Pearl Harbor did not have today's media coverage, capable of bringing the destruction of war into the living room. They had a great respect for authority and were very influenced by convention—how things were done. They rarely questioned the morality of the government or of the social conventions with which they lived. (In this very short synopsis of our parents' background, it is important to note that those in the black and other minority communities were experiencing a very different reaction to the status quo—as were a growing number of women—and were setting the stage for great civil rights struggles.)

Many of our parents educated themselves; they built businesses and they cared for their families.

The traditional family was the strength of American society. There was a great sense of pride in "taking care of our own," as well as a sense of responsibility to the community, and appearances were very important in maintaining the image of the self-sufficient family unit. Cultural and racial barriers were maintained based on family tradition.

When our parents went into the workplace, they did not assume that their parents would be there to help them financially. They got the best job they could and usually stuck with it. Many of our fathers have gold watches representing forty years with the same company. These were one-career people, in a society that valued stability.

America lived through the Depression and our parents became great savers. "Waste not, want not" was a motto in many homes, and we all had to eat everything on the plate so that the poor babies in China would not starve. Financially conservative as well, many of our parents even lost trust in banks. They paid cash for their purchases, generally buying only what they could afford, and parties to "burn the mortgage" were quite popular.

Under this conservative work ethic the country gained financial stability and witnessed the growth of a very strong middle class. It also experienced enormous social change. For my father, born in 1890, this had been an age of adventure and wonderful explorations, as well as a period of great inventions—exemplified by electricity, the airplane, and the automobile. For most of our parents, not as old as my father, it was a period to enjoy the fruits of these innovations. The many uses of electricity for home appliances, the telephone, and the family car helped create leisure time for the American household, which allowed women the luxury to address social issues outside the home and to join the ranks of volunteers, previously filled primarily by the wealthy.

Our parents, who experienced Prohibition, the Depression, and at least one world war, have gone from riding in a Model T Ford to witnessing the flight of the Concorde. They were a literary generation that lived through the heyday of magazines filled with good short stories. Reading and listening to the radio allowed them avenues to develop their imagination, and they had the vision to put a man on the moon. They are a strong generation with a clear sense of work and play. They danced their way through the twenties, when the Charleston was all the rage, and lived to see the Beatles come and go. Our parents have seen enormous change in their lifetimes, and it has made them far more flexible than we probably imagine.

## Their Diversity

Possibly the most recurrent theme throughout this book is that it is impossible to lump our parents together with any single definition. They represent an enormous spread both in age and in health. We can generalize when discussing the experiences that most of them shared, but how old they are and the way in which they are aging defies categorizing.

Most of our parents fall into the age bracket of sixty-five to ninety-five, which, since it is beyond middle age, is generally referred to as old age—but that really tells us nothing. Thirty years at any other chronological phase would represent far more than one category. Consider the years from one to thirty, including infancy, childhood, adolescence, and young adulthood; or thirty to sixty—baby-boomers or yuppies, midlifers and the young old, all lumped together. As silly as that sounds, it is even more ridiculous to assume a likeness for those from sixty-five to ninety-five.

There is far more similarity among the six-year-olds in a first-grade class than there is among sixty-five-year-olds at a class reunion. In fact, there is more divergency among America's elders at any chronological age than among Americans of any other age. We all know seventy-year-olds who have far more in common psychologically and physically with those in their fifties than with their contemporaries; and there are other, less healthy, seventy-year-olds who are rapidly approaching the "frail old" designation, with more in common with those in their late eighties both physically and psychologically than with their contemporaries.

A more accurate judge of age than chronology is how a person perceives of himself or herself. As Mark Twain said, "Age is a thing of mind over matter; if you don't mind, it don't matter." The inner age, how we see ourselves, is what counts. That perception that our parents have of themselves, or of their state in life, may be something that we can affect.

First, we need to focus on the interests of our parents, instead of on their age. When brainstorming about activities for a parent who has time on his or her hands, for instance, a senior center may be a good idea for a father looking for a chess game, but working at a museum or joining a French-conversation group may be more appropriate for a mother whose interests lie in those directions.

Understanding our parents will certainly make a wonderful difference in helping them find what will make them happy.

Secondly, how our elders perceive themselves may be influenced by the myths and stereotypes prevalent in our society. Avoiding labeling based on age brackets, and focusing on the individual instead, may help rid us of some prejudicial myths regarding old age that are bound to affect our parents' self-image. (More will be said on this in chapter 3.)

## Myths and Stereotypes of the Elderly

"Old folks are crotchety." "They don't like to be around children." "They are only interested in the past." "They can't remember anything." "They won't listen to anyone." "They are always sick." "They don't like to go out." "They only talk about themselves." "They don't understand." "They just sit around and watch television." "They aren't creative anymore."

We all know people, well under fifty, who fill these descriptions, and they will probably be that way for the rest of their lives. In our later years, we tend to be the same people we have always been. The only major change is the health factor.

Barring a physical disability, or the sad event of a dementia such as Alzheimer's disease, we continue to grow and develop all of our lives. Contrary to popular opinion, human development never stops, nor does the learning process. The best gift we can give our children for an ongoing, fulfilling life is an active, intellectual curiosity, since the activities that give our parents pleasure now remain generally the same as before. If they were interested in life around them, in people, in finding answers, in listening, in working on projects, they will continue to find joy in these pursuits. If they were complainers, self-centered, boring, lacking in imagination . . . there is no reason to expect that aging will make them any more interesting.

In order not to perpetuate the myths of aging, it is important to see personality traits, and talents, as factors of the individual and not as by-products of aging.

On Marlo Thomas's wonderful *Free to Be You and Me* record for children, one of the poignant scenes emerges as the grandmother says to her granddaughter that she, too, will be old and sour one day. The granddaughter replies no, she will be different, because she is a different person.

SEX AFTER SEVENTY

One myth that our elders would like to put to rest is that sex is not for them. First, it is not true. Second, the loss of our parents' sexual image as part of this insidious ageism is damaging to their egos and often invades their privacy.

Joan explains the feelings well. She was widowed and in her late seventies when she remarried. Her husband was in his early eighties and had three children and many grandchildren from a previous marriage. In discussing the book, I asked Joan what advice she might give adult children to better understand their parents.

"Tell them that we love their attention," she said, "but that we would appreciate respect for our private life. Don't always give us the room with twin beds!"

This message is being heard on many fronts. The Broadway

comedy *Social Security* addressed itself to precisely this issue. The aging mother had become a complainer until a new, elder lover entered her life. She explains the metamorphosis to a daughter by simply stating, "I'm still a woman."

As our parents age, many of them progress out of the various stages of acquisition and into a period of experiencing the subtler joys of life. For those of our parents whose failing health may preclude a robust sex life, for instance, the pleasure derived from tenderness and physical closeness may actually be heightened.

Sensitivity to this subject is a way of showing respect for our parents, and it is a concern until they die. Nursing homes have not yet faced the issue squarely.

"They are allowed private time alone, with the door closed," we are often told, but the answer to the next question usually reveals that all rooms have high, single hospital beds. How an institution handles the issue of sex is a valid one to raise when exploring any life care residence.

HEALTH IMAGES

With chronology less important at this stage of life, it may be fair to say that health actually determines who our parents are, and what they think of themselves. The well old often do not even consider themselves part of the older generation, no matter what their age. Most surveys show that elder Americans on the whole see their health very positively, defying the myth that older people are usually sick and/or senile. Most doctors will tell you that recovery is dependent far more on good health than the age of the patient, and hospitals base treatment options in the same way—on health, not on age. To further dispel the myth of older people as sickly, even those elders with chronic conditions such as arthritis are capable of far more activity than generally thought, and their greatest desire is to stay active.

Another myth to be dispelled is that once one's health starts to fail, it goes downhill from there. The pleasant surprise is that seventy can be better than sixty-five; even ninety-six can be a better year than ninety-five! As in all stages of life, older people can develop conditions that are mildly disabling, and with proper treatment and general good health they may be totally free of the

31

problem when they are several years older. This is important to know so that we do not jump to unnecessary conclusions, or make unnecessary plans, when one of our parents faces an initial health crisis.

A corollary to physical health is the result of a recent report by the American Association of Retired Persons that states that the mental health of older persons is better than for any other age group. Our elders may possess a good mental attitude because they generally see themselves with an inner eye, based on how they feel.

I remember my Aunt Mary describing a disturbing incident that happened to her as she was disembarking from an ocean liner following a transatlantic trip. As she stepped onto the stairs going down to customs, a young man came behind her and took her arm. Her first reaction was that he was after her purse, but as she glanced sideways, she caught the reflection of the young man and herself in the mirror and realized that he was just helping an old lady down the stairs. To her dismay, the old lady was she!

NEW IMAGES OF AGING

Happily, there is an evolution of attitude that has already begun in this country that says that older is getting better. Women are far less reluctant to tell their correct age, because they are feeling good about themselves.

When our neighbor turned sixty this year, my husband, Howard, expressed surprise. "She doesn't look older than fifty-four," he said.

"I think she looks sixty," I replied. "At least she looks the way I intend to look at sixty."

What has happened with people living longer, healthier lives in this country is that we are experiencing a change in attitude, dispelling many of the former prejudices of what life is like for those in their sixties and seventies. Faced with an increasing number of excellent role models for growing older productively and happily, the stereotypes of what aging means are actually changing.

## The Adult Child–Parent Relationship

This book centers on the relationships that we, the adult children, have with our aging parents. These relationships are very individual and can even differ from sibling to sibling within the same family. What they generally have in common is lots of baggage. What I mean is that we have a long history of acting in a certain way with each other; whether we are pleasing our parents, loving them, fighting with them, or even ignoring them, the pattern for our behavior has been set for many years. Taking a fresh look at how we interact may give us the impetus to work at strengthening our relationships. With our busy lives, we can always find excuses not to have the time for it, but the rewards are generous:

- The stronger, more honest your relationship is with your parent(s), the better you will face crisis together.

- The stronger, more honest your relationship is, the greater influence you will be in helping to keep your parents independent.

- The stronger, more honest your relationship is, the less likely you are to spend time in self-recrimination after the death of a parent.

THE ROLE-REVERSAL MYTH

One of the misconceptions about caring for our parents is that the roles are reversed and we become the parents. The further implication, of course, is that our parents become childlike. If there is senility present, there may be childlike behavior, but that is a disease condition and not the normal result of aging. Even in the situation of the frail elder with a full-time adult-child caregiver, who must provide physical help such as feeding and changing of clothes, the parent does not become the child. It is an image that our parents resent and one that is not accurate. They are not being helped with or taught something because they do not know how to do it for themselves. Rather, they are being

33

helped with a function that, because of a disability, they can no longer do alone. Psychologically, there is a big difference. It is an indignity to have to give up performing one's own personal tasks; and being treated like a child compounds the insult.

The urge to parent is present in most of us. Often, however, it is less a result of our parents' not being able to do something for themselves as much as it is our not liking the way they do it. It is easy to do something for someone else if it is of our choosing. Helping our parents with a chore, done their way, may take more than a little patience. Understanding how important being in charge of their own lives is to our parents, as they find tasks harder and harder to do, should give us the patience needed to keep their dignity intact. On a visit to their home, for instance, asking permission to help with certain tasks helps eliminate the impression that we are taking over. Whether it is preparing the dinner, getting the mail, or simply answering the phone, asking can turn a possible intrusion into a gesture of caring.

OUR PARENTS' POINT OF VIEW

Although the personal differences among our parents are great, there is a certain commonality to their life experiences that has molded the way in which most of them face their own aging. The prevalent attitude of self-sufficiency in which they raised their families has kept them an independent generation, to whom remaining in charge of their own households is primary.

Their children are very important to them. They never stop caring, and they want their children to care about them—but not necessarily for them. Some parents of this generation worked so hard, in order that their children could have a better life than they, that they live vicariously through the successes of their children. They dread the idea of becoming a burden. "I never dreamt I'd be in this position." They may want to live near them, but not necessarily with them. Nor do they want to be taken for granted by their children. We have been told more than once that they love spending time with their grandchildren, but not as automatic baby-sitters.

Our parents' point of view is often quite different from ours. We seem to express most concern about their safety, but they are far more concerned about the quality of their lives, their dignity and their independence. There is no better example of this attitude than with Marsha's grandfather.

Max continued to take the bus daily, from his home to the nursing home, where he was a volunteer. Although proud of his continuing community involvement, his family was concerned about his safety. Their fears were realized when he was robbed at gunpoint, waiting at the bus stop. To their chagrin, Max still refuses to heed their advice and take a taxi. His independence includes being able to make decisions for himself, so he continues to take the bus. At ninety-four, his life is still his own.

Often the choices that our elders make are difficult for us to accept, but in our desire to care for them, we must not overlook their fundamental right to choose. It is clear that what we want for our parents is not always what they want for themselves.

When building a new house in Atlanta a few years ago, Howard and I included a guest floor in the plans. The idea was that Mother and Daddy could avoid the harsh winters of Pennsylvania by coming south for the season and living with us. For my parents, however, the joys of facing the Pennsylvania winters independently brought them more warmth than the sun of the South. They never stayed for more than a week.

Understanding our parents is an ongoing task as they, too, are in the process of understanding their changing selves. They are coping with bodies that are changing and family circumstances that are in flux.

Pride is often a major motivating element in the behavior of this generation, and that means resenting when others try to take over. "I'm not in my grave yet" is the defiant cry of more than one resentful elder whose abilities have been discounted. They are used to staying busy and "doing for myself."

They are not used to asking for help, and their tradition of conformity, of "not airing their dirty laundry in front of the neighbors," is still strong. What this translates into in terms of caregiving is that they will ask adult children for favors they often do not want others to know they need. Furthermore, their indoctrination with traditional family roles will allow our parents to ask a daughter to alter her work schedule when help is needed much quicker than they would a working son. These sexual prejudices, which are a result of their background, are often unconscious. In some families, headway has been made through honest dialogue; in some, it may never be.

In other ways, understanding our parents is not very different from understanding people in all walks of life. They do not want to admit to having nothing to do, so those tasks at hand are stretched to fill the time available. Going to the doctor or taking the dog for a walk can become the focus of a day's activity, or it can be incidental to a person involved in other, more demanding pursuits.

As with all of us, the thrill of life is having something to look forward to. Surprises are fun for children; the fun of anticipation is much greater for our parents—including the anticipation of our visits. When possible, let them know when you are coming, so that they can savor the visit even before it happens.

## Our Parents as Caregivers

One-third of all caregivers are over the age of sixty-five. Although some of these elders are caring for their parents or other family members or friends, most of those in this category are caring for spouses. What that means is that many of our parents are primary caregivers to our mothers or fathers, and it is important that we understand the ramifications of such a task.

The physical strain is enormous. They may be tempted to lift, support, or move the infirm spouse—and furniture or other heavy objects—involved in the care. There is often little uninterrupted sleep for the concerned caregiver who listens for noises from his or her mate during the night, keenly aware of the responsibility. Fatigue is exacerbated with the work and the stress of caregiving, and personal health needs are frequently ignored, creating a ripe situation for the caregiver to get sick.

The emotional strains are equally enormous. There is a great loneliness, and actual grief, that results from the loss of one's spouse's companionship as an equal. For some, the hardest part is not having anything to talk about: "Almost no shared memories are left." Such regrets are often quickly followed by: "Still, I would not want to be without him." This loneliness is often heightened by the fact that people tend to stay away when there is illness in a household—they stop visiting—and it is not easy for the well spouse to get out. Often friends who would come by are discouraged by the caregiver who is protective of the ill spouse. He or she may not want people there unless they are very old friends who understand the situation.

A common emotion for caregivers is guilt. There is guilt for many things, including feeling vaguely responsible for the illness, or for not doing something about it sooner, and for the inevitable thoughts of how much easier life would be without such a burden. There also is concern for the future, and for one's ability to handle all the details of running the household alone—without a partner's help. This is a time of constant paperwork. For our mothers, who were not raised to handle the business aspects of life, learning everything from handling the checkbook to dealing with the maze of Medicare can seem overwhelming.

There are many variables that will determine how well our parents can handle their caregiving chores. Having the temperament for caregiving, as well as previous experience in what to expect, may make the tasks less overwhelming. Reviewing informative literature on the nature of the illness with our parents can help relieve some of the stress of the unknown. (Chapter 3 has some good recommendations.) The kind of illness makes a big difference, as does the personality of the patient.

Allowing our caregiving parents to express their feelings can be very helpful, as well as arranging for their inclusion in caregivers' support groups, where there are possibilities for an even greater expression of feelings.

One thing that we should consider arranging for our caregiving parents is to have a social worker come in with a fresh pair of eyes to evaluate the situation and determine whether or not more help—or placement in a care facility—is recommended. Not all of our parents have the temperament to be caregivers, and it could be a disservice to our ailing parent to keep him or her at home if the care is not appropriate.

It is often very hard for our parents to let their spouses do things for themselves, especially if the caregiver thinks they are being done badly. Letting the patient do as much as he or she can or wants to, even if it is done less than perfectly, can take more patience than the spouse is capable of giving, particularly if the caregiver is full of denial and secretly believes that the spouse could do the task properly if he or she really wanted to.

Having the family take supportive roles, relieving the caregiver as often as possible, and providing respite care for the sick elder, will obviously aid the situation.

A further way to reduce our parents' stress would be to review completely the costs of the illness and the family finances. There is a crucial sense of control that is returned to the caregiver when he or she knows the facts. Chapter 7 can help you with that.

## Death of a Spouse

Many of the emotions experienced by the full-time caregiver of a sick or very old spouse are the same feelings experienced by our parents at the death of a spouse—grief, loneliness, guilt, fear, and anxiety for the future.

What we need to be aware of in understanding our parents is that our reaction to the death may be quite different from theirs, particularly if the dead parent has suffered through a long illness. We may be relieved that our caregiver parent is freed from the weight of such daily care. What we may not understand is that there can be enormous rewards in the process of caregiving that are missed when it ends. The courage and dedication required for intense caregiving may have made our parent a stronger person, proud of doing a demanding job well. And the caring may have created a new loving bond between our parents, which makes the death even harder to accept.

The survivor can experience a sense of failure for not having kept the mate alive, however unrealistic that may be, and a very real loss of purpose for his or her own life when it is over. This is the time when gradual involvement in other activities is essential to refocus a life that has centered so exclusively on illness. Chapter 4 is full of possibilities.

If your parent is not likely to follow your suggestions, you might talk with his or her doctor. This generation, which has a great respect for physicians, is more likely to try an activity recommended by a doctor than one suggested by an adult child, and it can help your parents save face. No one wants to admit to being lonely. If he or she can join a group activity on the premise that "my doctor insists that I do this," it is a wonderful excuse to become a part of something. One gentleman started an active involvement with the local YMCA because his doctor ordered him to walk with a group there for at least one mile a day.

It is hard for elders in this hardworking, responsible generation to say no when they are needed. That may be the key to getting a parent back in circulation. Evelyn overcame her prejudice against senior centers when, after the death of her husband, his social worker asked if she might spare a few hours a week to read to those with impaired vision at the center. The initial involvement of a few hours has mushroomed into several days a week, and it is a very mutually enjoyable relationship.

Encouraging honest discussion of the feelings we all experience at the time of a parent's death will help us come to terms with them. This is a time when our surviving parent must be urged to let other people reenter his or her life, especially if the illness has driven them away. Friends can be very important in the recovery process for our newly widowed parents. There are widow/widower support groups in many communities where friends can be made with those who truly understand (see chapter 6).

It may be surprising for some of us to realize that death can be a shock, even when it is expected. Our parents may even have discussed the impending death, but they can never be prepared for the way they will actually feel. When my father dies, I will undoubtedly hear phrases such as "He had such a full life" or "It's probably for the best" because of his advanced age, yet I know it will be shocking for me to imagine the world without him alive in it. How much greater the shock will be for my mother, who has lived with him for the last fifty years!

Surviving spouses of any age often feel anger at being left alone to cope with the details of living. There can be a definite sense of abandonment, no matter how unwillingly the patient died.

Although nothing will prepare us for the shock of death, those who have the skills for running the financial and domestic aspects of the household seem to feel less vulnerable than those whose

39

fear of the unknown can actually make them sick. Curiously, men die at a much higher rate than women do upon the death of a spouse. They find it difficult to deal with grief; perhaps they are less able to share their feelings with family and friends.

There is no "correct" way to grieve. One woman in Pennsylvania handled her grief beautifully on the surface for four months, and then it became overwhelming. For others, the fear of being alone is immediate and diminishes with time. The monthly anniversary of the death is difficult for many spouses for a long while. Keeping our parents busy during this time can help them get through it.

In addition to creating an enormous void in the lives of our parents, many of us forget that this loss can also signal the loss of one's sexuality. Understanding this may help us understand some of our parent's behavior.

In *The Wash,* a play by Philip Gotanda, we are introduced to a woman who, after the death of her husband, refused to drive herself to work anymore. Her children were concerned over her apparent lack of confidence and bought her a new car to entice her back to driving. Still, she insisted on riding the bus. In a moment of candor with a friend, a confidence she could never feel comfortable sharing with her children, she explained that she missed the smell of men so much, since the death of her husband, that she rode the bus each morning just to enjoy the mixture of after-shaves!

## Friendships

The importance of friends in the lives of our parents should not be underestimated. As much as we care, nothing can replace the therapeutic value of a dear friend and confidant for our widowed parents. They are the ones who truly understand what our parents are experiencing. We may love our parents more, but we do not have the insight contemporaries gain from sharing their experiences. Friends may be of any age, but those of their own generation have a strong influence on many of the decisions our parents make, and through them we can often gain a better understanding of what our parents may actually be feeling.

40

If our parents are living in the suburbs or more rural areas where there are fewer social services, friends and neighbors become even more important in their lives. The loss of friends can instill a real fear of isolation. Who will know if something goes wrong? The death of a dear friend often precipitates major decisions in the lives of our parents, which cause them great concern and possible depression. Are they now the last of their friends in the neighborhood? Should they consider moving? Can they afford to move, or not to move?

One of the unexpected joys of aging, however, is that there is great empathy among those of common experience, and friendships can be easier to form than at other stages of life. The mutual awareness of the value of friendship, as well as the awareness of the lack of time for formalities, brings people together faster. Of course, personalities vary considerably, and for those who always had trouble making friends, it is unrealistic to assume that suddenly they will become social. But the more involved they are with new activities, the more likely they are to avoid becoming isolated.

## Remarriage

It often comes as a shock to adult children when their surviving parent decides to remarry or to live with someone of the opposite sex, after the death of the spouse. It is particularly difficult for us if we do not know the new spouse. I remember my surprise at the true resentment an otherwise kind friend was feeling when her father remarried, following the lingering cancer death of her mother. She thought it was an insult to the memory of her mother and could not imagine what her father saw in this new woman. That is not an uncommon reaction. My friend wanted her father to be happy, to live again, but it never occurred to her that another woman would fill the void in her father's life—at the age of eighty-two. Men, incidentally, remarry more frequently than women, which may simply reflect the greater number of available older women.

Psychologists tell us that finding a new mate quickly can be a great compliment to the previous marriage, attesting to the fact

41

that the bereaved enjoyed the state of matrimony so much that he or she does not want to live alone. We are also told that connecting with a new mate can be a confirmation of life for the bereaved, with the bonus that married elders tend to live longer.

## Pets

Many of our parents have lessened their sense of isolation with the inclusion of a pet in their lives. These animals, sometimes even fish or birds, can provide a big buffer against loneliness. They give acceptance, love, and affection, as well as a sense of purpose to the lives of their owners. In addition to serving as companions, pets, particularly dogs, can serve as aids to their owners and as safety precautions against intruders. The bond that forms is often very strong, and we should not underestimate the beneficial effect a pet may have on a parent.

When Annie and Brad were sent to Hawaii with the navy, they looked forward to a visit from his mother. The first Christmas came and went without her visit and one excuse followed another. They thought it was a fear of flying that prevented her from coming, until a friend explained that his mother could not bear the thought of leaving her dog behind, and Hawaii had a four-month quarantine for any entering pets.

Studies have shown the enormous value of a pet, for the physical as well as the psychological health of a person living alone. The results are so dramatic and so well documented that the state of Maryland has passed legislation to disallow the exclusion of pets from a number of retirement homes. Charlotte and Henry would have liked that ruling.

The luxury condominium in which Charlotte and Henry lived passed a regulation stating that no new pets were to be allowed in the building. That was not a problem for them until their beloved dog, Rustie, died. A sense of humor is the best foil for many of the frustrations of life. Henry and Charlotte decided to keep Rustie's death a secret. They immediately replaced Rustie with a young pup of the same breed, carrying him in and out of the building so that no one would notice the difference until he grew to full size. Now they smile knowingly when their neighbors comment on what an energetic dog he is.

When we discussed the therapeutic value of pets for elders with a prominent West Coast geriatrician, he pointed out that he has an aversion to animals in the house, as do many of his patients. So pets are not a solution for everyone, especially if there are allergies present. Showing up with an unexpected puppy may cause more problems than happiness, but if the choice is appropriate, the joy can be great. When I pass my building manager's apartment and hear him talking to his chirping birds, I smile at the enormous pleasure such simple creatures can give.

## A Sense of Humor, the Best Shield

What a far cry many of our parents are from the image of "crotchety old folks." Those who have keen senses of humor are truly blessed. If a sense of humor has been developed throughout one's lifetime, it is certainly a wonderful asset to draw upon when facing the indignities of aging. It can turn a potentially embarrassing moment into a delightful episode.

Howard enjoys spending time with my parents and occasionally he can arrange a business trip that allows him time to visit them in the Poconos. On one such occasion, he took Ros and Trot out for a very special dinner; they dined for several hours. Howard was particularly pleased that my father, then ninety-six, was having such a good time. The service was excellent and so was the meal. When the waiter pulled back Trot's chair, however, and he stood up, it revealed the floor covered with his crumbs. There was an embarrassing moment of silence as Trot stared at the mess. The tension broke when he turned to the waiter and asked, "You don't suppose we could have a doggy bag, do you?"

Ros also uses humor to get through some of her lonely moments. In a letter to her granddaughter recently, Ros commented that she had few visitors and found that she sometimes carried on conversations with herself, or recited poetry in an attempt to keep her mind alert. "But I always talk in French," she wrote. "It takes more time that way."

Knowing, as we do, what a powerful tool for good health laughter can be, and with the great examples of Bob Hope and George Burns to show us the way, we should try to use humor more frequently to defuse the tensions that build when caring for our elders.

## Communicating with Our Parents

How we communicate our thoughts and feelings is pivotal to all human relationships, whether it is sitting by the bedside of a loved one just stroking his or her hand, or an outpouring on paper of our feelings for another. Our styles are our own; the important thing is to find the medium that works for us.

Beth had difficulty communicating with her father, but she loved him very much. Having children of her own made her realize what a terrific father he had been. Wanting her father to know how much she loved him, but feeling uncomfortable about discussing it with him, Beth made her father a tape recording of her favorite memories of him. It was a comfort to Beth knowing that her father had heard her tape when, two weeks later, she received the shocking news that her healthy father, at sixty-six, had died suddenly of a heart attack.

The use of a taped message made communicating her feelings possible for Beth. There are many more common ways in which one can communicate: verbal, tactile, written or body language, and we generally combine several techniques, consciously or unconsciously, when expressing ourselves. For Anna, a tactile solution was more natural.

Anna said that it was not until her father was in his eighties that she felt comfortable enough to communicate her love for him. Her father was a very formal man who always greeted her with a handshake. Their breakthrough in communication came as a result of a very simple overture. When Anna's father stretched out his hand to greet her, Anna bypassed this gesture and gave him a hug. What a long-awaited thrill when, on the fifth such meeting, Anna's father opened his arms to her first.

LISTENING SKILLS

Many adult children are frustrated in their attempts to talk with their parents because the groundwork has never been laid for honest communication or because neither party knows how to listen. With the crucial planning needed to insure a fulfilling and financially sound old age for our parents, we may have more to talk about than ever before—as adults. Learn to listen—what we first hear is rarely what is important. "Everything is fine, dear. Thanks for calling" may be an automatic response having nothing to do with the present situation, or "How are you?" may be followed by a litany of illnesses, doctors' appointments, and medications purchased, which have more to do with wanting attention than with any physical problem.

Although we generally think of our conversational abilities as the gauge of whether or not we are good communicators, we can improve our skills by talking less and listening more. If we do improve our listening skills, we may develop the additional ability to hear what is not being said. When our parents refuse a dinner invitation, for instance, we may find upon further questioning that the first excuse of not wanting to go out was the smoke screen for being afraid to drive home in the dark.

We need to learn to break our listening mold and really hear. An easy technique that can improve our listening skills, while allowing our parents to feel heard, is to repeat back to them, in our own words, what is being expressed to us. It forces us to listen rather than to prepare our next sentence. Once our parents are assured that we have really heard them, they are in a better frame of mind to listen to a possible solution.

"We'd love to have dinner with you, but we are just too tired to come at night."

"I know you feel too tired to come and have dinner at night, but I'd hate to have you miss this party for Pat. Is there any way we could make it easier for you?"

"Well, you know Dad doesn't like to drive at night."

"Yes, I remember that Dad doesn't like to drive at night. Frank is planning on picking you up. Is six or six-thirty best for you?"

Another important listening skill is to pace your speech at roughly the same tempo as that of the elder with whom you are talking. Their thinking pattern is in tune with their speaking pattern. If we proceed at a rapid pace, putting pressure on our parents for rapid responses, their confusion may increase while their self-confidence decreases. This is a good skill to know, because it means that without any detective work, just with good listening, we can know immediately the best pace for optimum communication success.

## FEARS AND SENSITIVITIES

Knowing our parents' fears may give us some good clues to improved communication. Things that did not seem so important earlier in their lives may take on an exaggerated importance now because they no longer feel so invincible. Some of the most common worries of our elders are fear of:

· Physical collapse

· Running out of money

· Lack of respect

· Being a burden to their children

· Being abandoned by their children

· Being in pain

· Being alone, unable to get help

· Being dependent

· Losing control

· Being a victim of crime

Certainly, some of our parents are free from most, or all, of these fears. The more frail they become, the more likely they are to feel vulnerable and to worry about these things. The solution repeatedly suggested by experts in handling such problems is to tackle them one at a time. All together, they may seem insurmountable, but taken individually, no one fear is overwhelming. Active listening and awareness are our allies.

Knowing our parents' concern about certain physical conditions, for instance, will give us the clues we need to understand some unexpected responses. When Sharon's mother refused her invitation to attend a very special awards dinner for her, she was hurt and disappointed—until she suspected what the real motive might be. With some prodding, her mother admitted that, because of her incontinence, she was afraid of being trapped in a room where she might embarrass both herself and her daughter. Once the real problem was communicated, the solution became possible—an aisle seat with easy access to the rest rooms and appropriate undergarments.

One man was furious at his parents' rejection of all his attempts to discuss finances, until his sister explained that they were embarrassed at how poorly they had handled their money, particularly in view of his success, and they did not want him to know. Understanding their sensitivities and knowing their fear of becoming financially dependent, he took a different approach, arranging for the local bank to discuss the many options available to refinance their house. Without the worry of preserving an inheritance, they could make use of their assets and not have to leave their home.

Sheila knew that her parents did not want to be a burden to their children, but she had failed to communicate to them how important it was to her to be included in their lives. She was shocked when a call came saying that her father had been admitted to the hospital. It was only when Sheila called the doctor that she discovered her father had been diagnosed with diabetes three months before. In spite of frequent phone conversations with both her parents, his illness had never been mentioned.

As our parents grow older, we may find that they hesitate to tell us the facts of the situation, sometimes to protect us and sometimes for fear of losing control.

Phyllis's father did not allow her sister, with whom he lived, to notify Phyllis of his impending operation. This attempt at protecting Phyllis, because she lived too far away to help, resulted in making her feel left out of the family, and hurt that she had not been included.

It was important to the understanding process for Sheila and Phyllis to communicate to their parents their desire to be a part of their parents' lives. Being protected from a crisis can create more stress than being included in the solution. Communication can greatly reduce stress, even when it does not affect change.

The greatest help in good communication is a desire to really understand. Understanding is an evolving process that varies with our individual abilities. As in most worthwhile endeavors, the more we practice, the better we get. Family matters are rarely simple and are universally interrelated. As John Muir, the American naturalist, once observed, "When we try to pick out anything by itself, we find it hitched to everything else in the universe."

There is no doubt that good communication skills, developed over the course of a family's lifetime together, will be a tremendous advantage in helping us care for our parents as they age. Coming to grips with our feelings, and listening to the feelings of our parents, are skills that can be learned at any age, and they are critical in creating the right attitude for effective caretaking. "Just as few couples were trained to be parents, few adult children have any training for caring for their parents. Give me someone who cares, someone with the right attitude," comments Gary W. Stinke, M.D., a noted California gerontologist, "and together we can create miracles."

## Points to Remember

- There is greater diversity among our parents' generation than in any other age.

- Understanding your parents' background is key to understanding their behavior.

- Health, not age, determines who one is and how one sees oneself.

- Age-related stereotyping is damaging to all of us.

- Your parents' gauge of happiness is different from yours.

- We are concerned about their safety; they are concerned about the quality of their lives.

- Communication skills can be developed at any age.

- The stresses of caring for a frail spouse are enormous.

- Death of a sick spouse may be considered a personal failure by a surviving parent. Widow/widower support groups can be helpful.

- Recognizing our parents' sexuality is important to their self-image.

- Humor is a valuable tool at any age.

*Chapter 3*

# Helping Our Parents to Look and Feel Their Best

THE picture of a healthy life for our parents is brighter than ever before. Today, Americans are living both healthier and longer lives. At the turn of the century, men lived an average life-span of forty-six years, while women could expect to live for forty-nine years. The average life-span for a woman born in 1985 is seventy-nine years, and seventy-two for a man. Not only are our parents living longer, but the quality and independence of their lives have continued to improve as well. What has made them so much healthier? Certainly, modern medical technology, more attention to nutrition and exercise, increased availability of life-saving drugs, and a more positive self-image have made major contributions.

## The Importance of Attitude to Good Health

We know now that many of the stereotypical declines of our elders are not biological imperatives, but the self-fulfilling prophecies of those who expect physical and mental deterioration as a natural part of old age. This means that our parents' self-image, the attitude they develop toward their own aging, is an important criterion for determining their own health. One very positive aspect of this realization is that they have more control over their own physical destinies than previously thought.

When Norman Cousins was editor of the *Saturday Review,* he was stricken with a severe paralytic illness. His doctors gave him only a one-in-five-hundred chance of survival. Encouraged by his doctor to make use of his own psychological resources to fight his disease, Cousins checked into a hotel room armed with reels of Marx brothers movies, "Candid Camera" episodes, and other humorous material. A strong believer in mind over matter, Norman Cousins laughed his way back to health, prompting at least one major metropolitan hospital to establish a "laugh room" for the therapeutic use of its patients.

THE POWER OF SUGGESTION

The curative power of suggestion is so widely accepted that it is used increasingly in partnership with traditional medicine to help the sick. The technique of visualization is a method that trains the patient to imagine the problem—a disease, a tumor, or pain—as something recognizable, which can then be directed out of the body. One young cancer patient, interviewed on the Phil Donahue show in 1981, imagined a brain tumor as a giant castle made of hamburger meat. Birds would swoop down and peck at the castle, flying off with little pieces of it until there was nothing left. The doctors may not believe that sea gulls ate his tumor, but the X rays show that it is gone.

The National Hospice Organization sometimes makes use of visual images and self-hypnosis techniques as a part of their program to alleviate the pain of dying patients.

The mind has powers of control over the body that no one fully understands. No surgeon wants to take a patient "under the knife" who has a bad attitude. State of mind, they will tell you, is too vital to the survival rate. Some say that faith creates miracles, others call it a positive attitude. What we all know is that believing something will happen is a big step toward making it happen. Translated to our parents' situations, this means that expecting to be healthy and productive at advanced ages is a contributing factor to being that way.

FOR FURTHER INFORMATION: *Love, Medicine and Miracles: Lessons Learned About Self-Healing from a Surgeon's Experience with Exceptional Patients.* Bernie S. Siegel, M.D. New York: Harper & Row, 1986.

And *Getting Well Again.* O. Carl Simonton and Stephanie Matthews-Simonton. New York: Bantam Books, 1978.

## THE POWER OF ENTHUSIASM

Enthusiasm for life, which keeps us involved in the process, is another important component in staying healthy. Those of our parents who have a compelling daily involvement are not only the lucky ones, they are likely to be the ones in the best health as well.

There have always been gifted elders to show us the unlimited heights attainable by those with an enthusiastic zest for life and the good health to follow through: Verdi, composing the operas *Otello* at the age of seventy-four and *Falstaff* at the age of eighty; Titian, the Renaissance master still painting into his eighties; Rubinstein thrilling audiences with his piano recital at the age of ninety; Golda Meir guiding Israel as prime minister until the age of seventy-six; Churchill sitting in the House of Commons throughout his eighties; Benjamin Franklin capping his long career of service by attending the Constitutional Convention at the age of eighty-one, as a delegate from Pennsylvania; and the great humanitarian Eleanor Roosevelt, writing until her death at the age of seventy-eight. These exemplary seniors could never be accused of creeping inertia. The attitude that they all had in common was an undeniable enthusiasm for life.

The more we hear of extraordinary elders, the more the self-image of all elders improves. Today, what aging woman is not thrilled by the voice of Lena Horne, who is still a show-stopper and more lovely than ever in her seventies? Or what man, for that matter? Politics aside, who is not impressed with the vitality and appearance of President Reagan in his seventies? What senior is not dazzled by the stamina of Lucille Ball, or touched by the continuing caring of Maggie Kuhn of the Gray Panthers? Kuhn's concerns not only touch elders; they touch all of us.

52

MAKING THE EXTRAORDINARY ORDINARY

It is a fact that our parents will live longer lives. The quality of those extra years is very much a factor of their attitude—how they expect to age and how well they remain involved with life. They do not have to be extraordinary to lead extraordinarily fulfilling lives. Being reminded of the achievements of others can give them the encouragement they need to write brilliant new scripts for the second half of their own lives.

No one told the "Kids in Cubs" that they were too old to play baseball. In fact, their rule is that you have to be at least seventy-five years old to join the team. This tradition has been going on for fifty-eight years now. George has not been with the team half that many years, but at the age of ninety-four he still fills the position of catcher with flair. Tom plays in spite of a complete hip replacement and Bill shows no signs of trouble after returning from double bypass heart surgery. "What else should I be doing with my days?" Some fans in the bleachers seem to have an idea. When Bill misses a ball, you can hear them scream, "Send him back to Brooklyn!"

Every time the news reports that an old woman fended off a would-be mugger with her handbag, it lifts the spirits of thousands of her contemporaries across the country.

The real excitement of such role models comes with the realization that these are not innately extraordinary people. They simply are people who have stayed fully involved with life. *This is an important key to good health.* From the child who may start a Montessori school program at the age of three, where the motto is "Work is play," to the octogenarian who is still planting trees, work involvement is an essential ingredient to good health. The vast array of opportunities in which seniors can participate is limited only by our own imagination. (Many successful involvements will be discussed in chapter 4.)

As caregivers, we can be very helpful in showing our parents the many ways in which they can stay in control of their own health, allowing them the freedom to do as they please. Not only are attitude and enthusiasm vital ingredients for good health, but so is a basic understanding of the common physical changes

53

associated with aging. This chapter will tell us what we need to know in helping our parents: to choose and communicate with their doctor; to review special medical problems of aging, including impaired vision, hearing, and dental care; and to examine the dangers of chemical dependencies. Finally, we will discuss the enormous benefits of good nutrition and regular exercise, and the value of an attractive appearance.

## Notes to the Caregiver: Deal with What Is!

It is clear from the many vivacious examples we have in the over-sixty-five population, and from the growing change in attitude vis-à-vis our expectations for a productive second half of life, that aging is not a disease. In fact, it may represent a period of life that offers greater freedom of expression and ability to explore life than any other. We know that the quality of aging is more a factor of health than it is of chronology. Some of our parents will live to advanced ages free from major physical problems, while, ironically, some of us may have to face the fears of cancer, heart attack, or other major health crises in our forties. Statistically, Marsha and I are more likely to suffer from any number of ailments thought of as the prerogative of the elderly than my parents, both of whom have outlived the "dangerous" ages.

DON'T BORROW TROUBLE!

The most significant lesson we could possibly learn as caregivers is to do the best we can about that which we can effect (such as the areas of "preventive maintenance"), and not to worry about that which we cannot control. The biggest waste of energy, for ourselves and for our parents, would be to agonize over diseases or conditions that have not even happened. The "What if Mom has a heart attack?" or "What if Dad develops Alzheimer's?" questions are not a part of creative planning. We could spend a great deal of time worrying about the wrong thing. We may be concerned over the possibilities of cancer, when varicose veins is the problem that surfaces. Instead of worrying about things that may never happen, the caretaker must deal with what is known and find out what can be done about that. The list of possible medical emergencies our parents might face is about the same length as a list we all might face, and the caretaker's motto has to be: "Deal with what is."

If, however, there is a strong family history of a particular disease or condition, then the following steps are in order:

· Become aware of the symptoms. Your parents' doctor should be able to help you; or you can get in touch with a branch of the national organization for that particular disease for further information. The doctor or local hospital can give you the name of the organization.

· Help your parents take the recommended precautionary measures. Diet is often the best defense in prevention of diseases such as diabetes, heart attack, stroke, hypertension, and osteoporosis. (Read the information on nutrition and diet starting on page 73.)

· Be sure that your parents' health is monitored by a caring physician. For diseases such as cancer, we all know that early detection is very important. There are simple self-examinations for breast cancer, and a list of the seven warning signals is available by calling your local American Cancer Society. Making sure that your parents' doctor is aware of the family history is always important.

· Do not try to limit your parents' activities because of your own fears of what might be, and try not to instill fear in them for problems that have not happened!

PREVENTIVE MAINTENANCE

This chapter deals with those conditions common to all of our parents (and us) as we age. A good mental outlook, proper care for our eyes, ears, teeth, awareness of the problems associated with tobacco, alcohol, and drug abuse, the impact of diet on our overall health, the benefits of exercise, and ongoing contact with a family doctor are areas of impact on all our families. Good "preventive maintenance" is something positive that we can do for our parents' future. This is where communication with our parents, as we share the results of our knowledge and caring, may greatly enhance the quality of their lives.


## Choosing a Doctor

Your parents may be in the care of a trusted, longtime family physician, with whom they have established good communication, and one who has kept abreast of the latest in medical research. If this is the case, you and your parents are in an enviable position. The only step that we, the children, might take in this case is to be sure that their doctor knows how to reach us in case of an emergency. For many of our parents, however, their family doctor may be near retirement, or our parents may have moved to a different state and are in need of a new physician. Helping our parents find a qualified doctor in whom everyone has confidence is an important step toward achieving peace of mind—specially for long-distance caretakers.

When interviewing a new doctor, the following questions should be addressed:

- What are your parents' particular medical needs? Does this doctor have experience in that field—neurology, geriatric medicine, rehabilitation, cardiology, oncology, etc.?

- Is the office convenient for your parents to reach? Is it in a congested area, making driving and parking difficult? Is it near public transportation? Is there wheelchair access? Is it a safe neighborhood? Is there a comfortable waiting area?

- In which hospitals is the physician allowed to admit patients? Is it one with which your parents are familiar?

- What is the procedure regarding "heroic measures" to save life?

- Does the doctor make your parents feel comfortable, treating them like adults? Is he or she impatient? Does he or she listen to what is being said?

- Does the doctor take time to explain why he or she recommends a certain treatment, procedure, or medication? Is the diagnosis explained in layperson's terms? Is the doctor willing to answer questions?

- Is there adequate follow-up and emergency care? Follow-up for possible side effects to medication?

- Does the doctor make house calls? Does he or she return phone calls? How long is the wait, generally? Does the doctor regularly overbook?

- Does the doctor do X rays and run tests in his office? If not, where would your parents have to go to get them done?

- What is the attitude of the office personnel and the nurses? Are they respectful, patient, helpful?

- Is the doctor willing to confer with the caregiver, should the need arise?

ASSIGNMENT

Serious financial misunderstandings can be avoided by finding out ahead of time what insurance assignments the physician accepts. Medicare? Medicaid? And who does the paperwork?

Assignment is a key point, because Medicare Part B assigns a certain dollar value to each "doctor's office" procedure. If the physician accepts assignment, it means that the total charge per visit is that which is allowed for those procedures by Medicare. The patient pays 20 percent and any remaining deductible. And the doctor's office does the paperwork. Because the physician's profit per patient is limited, he or she may have little extra time to spend with the patient.

If the doctor does *not* accept assignment, it means that Medicare still pays 80 percent of their established fee for the procedure, but the patient—or a supplemental insurance policy— must pay the difference between that set fee and the real fee, plus any unmet deductible. In this case, the patient usually has to do the paperwork. Ask. At higher fees, the doctor at least should have more time to chat! (See chapter 8 for more information on Medicare and Medicaid.)

If the doctor is being chosen for a particular surgical procedure, getting a second opinion is an integral part to the follow-up investigation. There is little that we buy without checking at least one other place for a price comparison. We, and our parents, are deserving of the same energy we would spend to buy a refrigerator. Shop around, ask for referrals from hospitals, nurses, friends, other doctors, senior centers. *Get a second opinion.*

## Communicating with the Doctor

Once a doctor is chosen, it is important to provide him or her with complete information about the patient and to establish the line of communication. The more the doctor knows about your parents, the better the chances for an informed diagnosis. Complete records should be transferred to the new physician before the initial examination. When making the first appointment, it is a good idea for your parents to request that the medical history form be sent to them at home so that it can be filled out before the visit, calmly and in good light, not hurriedly in the waiting room.

Whenever a visit is made to the doctor, your parents should bring the following (which you can help prepare):

- A clear list of symptoms.

- A list of questions phrased clearly and in order of importance. (If Medicare assignment limits the doctor's time, the most important questions should be the first covered.)

- A list of all medications being taken, including nonprescription drugs such as aspirin, laxatives, etc.

THE DOCTOR IS NOT GOD

For many elders, the doctor is still a godlike figure, and being assertive about their problems is difficult. It is important that our parents understand what they are told without being too accepting. They must question and know the reasons for their treatment, and, if something is not clear, they must ask the doctor to repeat in layperson's language what he has said. Accompanying your parents can be of great moral support as well as a signal to the doctor that the care of this patient is being monitored by his or her loved ones.

I like to tell the story of my very Victorian Aunt Mary, who, at the age of seventy-two, went to see a renowned, rather aloof eye specialist in New York City. She was not pleased with his patronizing approach. "So, Mary," he said, "you seem to have a little problem." "Yes, Billy," she replied. "Do you suppose you could be of help?" "Of course, Mrs. Moser," came the professional reply. "What are your symptoms?"

Calling the specialist by his first name, as he had done with her, without permission, was a small incident and not of any medical significance. What it did was to allow Aunt Mary, with one short sentence, to establish herself as an equal seeking the educated opinion of a specialist.

## Your Parents' Vision

It is a rare individual over the age of forty-five who has not already experienced a dramatic change in his or her vision. The lens of the eye, soft and flexible in our youth, gradually loses its ability to change shape and we have increasing difficulty focusing, generally on nearby objects. This perfectly normal process is called presbyopia. As the eye loses its elasticity, older people will experience difficulty seeing up-close objects clearly. Our changing vision becomes apparent to most of us in our early forties as we begin to hold newspapers at a greater distance in order to see the words clearly, or we find that squinting helps us to read.

Reading glasses or bifocals will help correct this visual blur. Relying on glasses, whether for distance or for reading, may give us our first notion of what it is like to depend on an aid for full performance. This should make us more sympathetic to a parent's vision handicap.

Fortunately, medical advances, such as improved contact lenses and new laser surgery techniques, are making it increasingly possible for your parents to enjoy good vision as they age. Your parents may postpone visiting a doctor because they feel that their failing eyesight is a natural product of old age, and that nothing can be done. That is not so. We need to encourage them not to procrastinate in seeing a doctor if they are experiencing any visual problems or pain or soreness of the eyes. And they should have a complete eye exam every two to three years. Many problems, detected early, can be arrested and even corrected, thereby avoiding severe or permanent vision loss.

COMMON EYE DISEASES ASSOCIATED WITH AGING

1. Glaucoma. This is a condition that develops when the fluid pressure within the eye becomes so great that the optic nerve is damaged. There are no early symptoms, so everyone over the age of thirty-five should be tested for glaucoma as a regular part of our routine eye exams. Early detection is very important in treating glaucoma successfully. Left untreated, it can cause permanent blindness. Eyedrops, oral medicines, new laser treatments, and, occasionally, surgery are methods used to treat this disease.

2. Cataracts. These are cloudy or opaque areas that develop in the transparent lens of the eye. Formation of a cataract prevents light from passing through the normally clear lens, thus affecting vision. Removal of cataracts by surgery is a common and relatively safe procedure. Since cataracts usually develop gradually and without pain, how much the cataract affects our parents' lives may be the determining factor in deciding whether or not to have surgery.

3. Disorders of the retina. The retina is a delicate membrane at the back of the eye made up of nerves, which receives images formed by the lens and passes them on to the brain by the optic nerve. Retinal disorders fall into three general categories: (a) senile macular degeneration—a condition in which the central retina zone stops functioning properly. Clear peripheral vision generally remains, while the central vision becomes blurred or distorted. Straight objects often appear wavy. Some cases can be treated successfully with laser surgery, but only if they are detected in the very early stages of the condition; (b) retinal detachment—when the inner and outer layers of the retina become separated. This separation can often be surgically re-

attached, with laser treatments experiencing increasing success; (c) diabetic retinopathy—a condition in which the small blood vessels no longer feed properly into the retina. Leaking blood vessels at the back of the eye indicate changes in the retina. If untreated, this condition can lead to detachment of the retina and blindness. Although not all diabetics have this condition, it is a complication of the disease that becomes more likely with the increased duration of the disease.

The idea of being blind fills most of us with a dreaded sense of dependency, yet we often abuse this most valuable of senses. It is imperative to see that our parents have regular eye checkups, even if they are not experiencing any difficulties, as well as periodic checks for high blood pressure and diabetes, both of which can affect the eyes.

As with other disabilities of the old old, we are finding that more eye disorders are appearing simply because people are living longer.

Mildred had her eyes tested for glaucoma at a recent eye checkup. She was concerned because her mother has this condition and it is hereditary. "How old was your mother when she developed glaucoma?" asked the doctor. "Ninety-two," responded Mildred—at which the doctor laughed. Had Mildred's mother died at the ripe old age of ninety-one, glaucoma would not even have been in the family medical history.

We must help our parents and ourselves to take the best care now because we may need our organs to function healthily for many more years of life than in previous generations.

Good lighting is always important, but it is even more essential for the elderly. Although there is no evidence that poor light actually damages the eye, it can certainly cause tired eyes. We can do our parents a favor by replacing dim light bulbs with higher wattage, favoring regular light bulbs over fluorescent bulbs, and arranging several well-lighted reading spots, with a light source coming over the left shoulder to avoid shadows. Keeping eyeglasses in the same place to avoid a constant search (same as with keys) is another practical tip.

Some conditions require daily eyedrops, the receiving of which can be most disagreeable when the open eye faces the descending dropper. Tilting the head back and pulling down the lower lid is the preferred method, but a trick used by ophthalmologists to calm an anxious patient is to have the recipient tilt his or her head back with closed eyes. Administer the drops in the inside corner of the eyes and then let him or her open the eyes. The medicine will gently roll into the eye—no trauma, and no dreading the next time.

INNOVATIVE RESPONSES TO IMPAIRED VISION

One community has found a unique way to help its elders who have difficulty seeing such things as the traffic signals. In Oakland, California, an audible pedestrian signal gives out a cuckoo chirping sound when the light is green so that residents of the Senior Housing Development know when to walk safely across the street to do their grocery shopping.

In a number of states, including Hawaii, many of the grocery stores have audible item checkout systems. When the product is passed over the scanner, it says the product category and the price: "Cereal, two dollars and ten cents." No need to strain eyes trying to check the register printout.

Poor eyesight is not inevitable with age; nor are distortions of color. The wonderful artist Georgia O'Keeffe, like other notables before her, continued to create impressive canvases of subtle color nuances in her eighties. As most people age, however, they begin to experience changes in perceptions of color and dimensions, a fact that is being taken into consideration in the construction of new retirement homes and geriatric hospitals. The lens of the eye, which filters light, is clear when we are young. As we age, the lens can become cloudy and take on a brownish tint. The result is that the perception of blue is diminished.

The Wesley Woods Geriatric Hospital in Atlanta, Georgia, is an example of a geriatric facility keenly aware of the importance of what the eye perceives. Varying colors on different planes and boundaries aid their patients in distinguishing distances and areas. The shine we expect to see in clean hospitals has been replaced with surfaces free from glare in order to avoid pain, eye fatigue, and even tears; and soft peach and pink tones have been introduced to promote a feeling of well-being.

Geriatric facilities have a vested interest in compensating for the poor vision of its residents, and with education and understanding, local communities will become increasingly interested. The chirping cuckoo of Oakland may have rival signals in towns across the country who want to keep their elder population independent.

An individual with an active imagination can create innovative aids that will continue to enrich our parents' lives. One of my favorite aids came to my attention last November, while lunching with an old high school friend and her mother. They were talking of a recent trip to Midway in the Pacific, where Jane's parents, both in their seventies, had done some great snorkeling. I knew that they both wore glasses and wondered how they could enjoy the scenes underwater. "That's easy," said Jane's mother, "we used prescription eye masks. They were the best gifts we ever received." (Undoubtedly, the same has been done with ski goggles.)

A less exotic, but equally appreciated, visual aid was received by an older woman who reviews dance performances for a city newspaper. Her deadlines are tight and she often scribbles notes in the theater. A pen with a tiny light attached has made her writing far more legible! (Personally, I want some chic aid to help me read the menus in darkened restaurants—I hope my children are reading this!)

Whether it is a magnifying glass to be worn around the neck, taped stories from the library to listen to at home, or a subscription to a large-print edition of a magazine or newspaper, sensitivity to our parents' visual limitations can inspire us to find the perfect aid.

FOR FURTHER INFORMATION: Call the American Academy of Ophthalmology in your area or write for: *Seeing Well as You Grow Older.* Inquiry Clerk, American Academy of Ophthalmology, P.O. Box 7424, San Francisco, CA 94120-7424. Enclose a legal-size, self-addressed, stamped envelope.

Or *The Aging Eye: Facts on Eye Care for Older Persons,* free from the National Society to Prevent Blindness, 79 Madison Avenue, New York, NY 10016. Send self-addressed, stamped envelope.

Or the American Association of Retired Persons offers audio

tapes of their magazine, *Modern Maturity,* as well as the free pamphlet *The Eyes Have It.* AARP Fulfillment, 1909 K Street, N.W., Washington, DC 20049.


## Loss of Hearing

Deafness in one or both ears was an affliction that affected three million of the twenty-six million Americans who were sixty-five years of age or older, when reported by the National Health Interview Survey, January–June, 1984. Various degrees of hearing impairment affect an even greater number. A 1985 survey by the National Center for Health Statistics reported that of the twenty-seven million Americans then sixty-five and over, almost eight million suffered some kind of hearing impairment. As our youth expose themselves to heightened levels of amplified sound at the rock concerts and discos of today, these statistics are sure to swell. Understanding the ramifications of such an affliction can do much toward helping our parents overcome its antisocial implications.

Deafness can be psychologically more damaging in some ways than being blind. No one looks deaf, so there is little immediate empathy for the condition, and the inability to understand a question can create an impression of stupidity. Even when one's hearing problem is known, it can produce irritation in those of little patience who are trying to communicate. From the point of view of the deaf person, it is a very isolating experience.

A greater awareness of the problems confronted by the deaf is gradually producing a more sympathetic public. Never before in the history of the Oscar presentations had a deaf actor received a nomination for an award. Yet, in 1987, Marlee Matlin won the coveted Oscar for best actress of the year for her stunning performance as the complex, beautiful, and very intelligent deaf heroine of *Children of a Lesser God.* Marlee Matlin cannot hear a single word.

*Children of a Lesser God* had been playing to full houses for years on Broadway before it became a film. Audiences were captivated with the idea of life without sound. Although this story has nothing to do with deafness of the elderly, renting the film for home video use may give special insight to those with a deaf parent. Deafness affects every aspect of daily living, from not being able to use a telephone, to not hearing a speeding car approach while crossing the street, to not being able to hear music for dancing.

## SYMPTOMS OF THE HEARING IMPAIRED

Being alert to symptoms of hearing loss in our parents and making sure that they receive prompt audiological and medical advice can do a lot to eliminate a source of great isolation in hearing-impaired elders. Some of the common symptoms are:

- Having the television or radio on high volume
- Asking us to repeat what we have said
- Accusing us of mumbling
- Not wanting to be around people
- Not answering the telephone
- Not answering the doorbell
- Speaking very softly
- Talking too loudly
- Not understanding what is being said
- An intolerance for loud sounds
- Becoming depressed
- Becoming suspicious of people

Our parents may have common complaints that could alert us to a hearing problem, such as:

- Hearing a hissing or ringing noise in the ear
- Finding words difficult to understand
- Not wanting to attend large gatherings
- Complaining that someone does not enunciate
- No longer enjoying television

65

Ignoring a hearing loss can result in more physical damage than the inability to hear. The ear is a delicate mechanism very involved with our entire sense of balance. Conditions such as Ménière's disease may start with vertigo and nausea, accompanied by noises in the ear and muffled or distorted hearing, abruptly affecting our parents' independence. Without hurting their pride, we should insist on prompt attention to protect this most valuable sense.

COMMON CAUSES OF HEARING IMPAIRMENT

- Environmental noises

- Genetic makeup

- Excessive ear wax

- Heart conditions

- Extra fluid

- Viral infections

- Certain drugs

- Mechanical changes in the ear due to aging

Understanding the causes of hearing impairment can make us more aware of changes in behavior, particularly if there is a possible cause, such as a new drug being administered, if our parent has just recovered from a virus, or if there is deafness in the family.

HOW TO TALK WITH THE HEARING IMPAIRED

The best ways that we can help a parent, or anyone, with impaired hearing involve common courtesies. We should face them when we are talking and avoid shouting from another room. We should enunciate clearly, without exaggerating. One very helpful communication tool is to lead into a new topic by first mentioning the subject matter. Before asking my father if Nicole had talked to him about her new acting role, for instance, I might say that I am excited about Nicole being in the school play. Knowing the subject matter is a great help in following the subsequent conversation, even if we do not understand all the words. Those of us who have ever struggled with a foreign language know what a valuable aid such a clue can be!

Vanity, pride, and denial can eliminate beautiful music from our parents' lives, but a thoughtful presentation can overcome even these hurdles. With the technological advances in hearing aids, it would be a shame to have product unawareness leave a loved one in a soundless world.

Amy was a beautiful woman who always prided herself on how she was groomed. When her children began to notice her difficulty in hearing, she said it was nonsense and did nothing. They arranged for a hearing exam at her next physical and the results showed a definite loss of hearing, totally rectifiable with a hearing aid. She would not consider wearing such an ugly protrusion.

Amy's children did some homework, and presented their mother with a pearl necklace in which battery amplification control was camouflaged and attached to a *tiny* ear button. What a success. Amy may be the only woman in Florida to wear pearls with a bathing suit!

AIDS FOR THE HEARING IMPAIRED

Although it was perfect for Amy to have her hearing controls camouflaged in a pearl necklace, my Uncle Andy would never have gone for that! Amy's gift was quite unusual, but fortunately there are a variety of ready styles from which to choose. Some elders prefer to have the aid mounted into their eyeglass frames, while others choose the small behind-the-ear models. Another possibility is a canal hearing aid, which actually fits in the ear canal.

As with Amy, many of our parents feel a certain stigma attached to wearing a hearing aid, and it may take some diplomacy to get them to try one. Before doing that, however, a complete ear examination is in order. Not all hearing loss can be rectified with an aid, and determining what kind of device is best for their condition is an important step.

If your parents do agree to a hearing aid, do not assume that their hearing will be restored to normal. For some, the improvement will be remarkable, but aids generally make sound louder, not clearer. That means that in environments with a great deal of background sound, such as a crowded restaurant, having all the sounds amplified could make it even harder to hear. (Some of the more sophisticated, recent models do have greater sound-blocking capabilities.) Again, certain courtesies, such as choosing a quiet corner and seating them with their back to a wall, can make hearing easier for our parents.

As our society begins to cope with the hearing problems of an escalating number of its citizens, manufacturers are offering more devices to help those afflicted with hearing loss. Special telephone equipment is available for lease through local telephone companies, and receivers that flash a light to signal an incoming call are also available commercially. Teletypewriters allow the deaf to receive messages over the telephone, and businesses are beginning to install them, as well as organizations that deal with the hearing impaired. Various parts of the country have how-to television programming on signing, the hand language of the deaf, and many television news programs have a simultaneous signer for the deaf in a small box on the screen as the news is presented. (Unless the elder has been deaf for some time, however, it is unlikely that he or she will understand signing.)

One option, available for a monthly fee, is television captioning—the appearance of the words across the bottom of the screen, similar to subtitles, as they are being spoken. Although this may be a strain on the eyes, with large-screen television sets, the captioning can provide in-home entertainment for our deaf, or hard-of-hearing, parents heretofore unavailable.

There is a surgical procedure called a cochlear implant that can stimulate hearing in some people who have become totally deaf. With this device, electrical impulses are used to stimulate the auditory nerve. The implant consists of a signal processor, a microphone, and a receiver, and an external transmitter. The positive news for seniors is twofold. Medicare covers the cost of most cochlear implants, and it is estimated that over fifty thousand Americans over the age of sixty-five may be helped by this procedure. It has limited application in the population at large, but if your parent is deaf, it may be worth the effort to explore the possibility of his or her being a candidate for a cochlear implant.

The Elderhostel University study program for those over sixty years of age is described in some detail in chapter 4 of this book. Gallaudet University in Washington, D.C., the world's only university for deaf students, offers two elderhostel programs for deaf seniors who sign. Participants, teachers, tour guides, and dorm staff all sign. Write: Elderhostel Coordinator, Special Populations Program, National Academy, Gallaudet University, 800 Florida Avenue, N.E., Washington, DC 20002.

FOR FURTHER INFORMATION about nationwide services and programs for the hearing impaired, resource lists, and fact sheets write: National Information Center on Deafness, Gallaudet University, 800 Florida Avenue, N.E., Washington, DC 20002.

Or *What Should I Do Now? Problems and Adaptations of the Deafened Adult.* Helen Sloss Luey and Myra Per-Lee. Washington, D.C.: Gallaudet College Press, 1983.

Or for a free pamphlet on hearing loss write: *Have You Heard?*, AARP Fulfillment, 1909 K Street, N.W., Washington, DC 20049.

## Dental Care

No chapter on our parents looking and feeling their best can be complete without a section on good dental care. Healthy mouths are crucial to looking well, and, since the condition of our mouths has a direct impact on what we eat, they also influence how well we feel. It is important that our parents not avoid foods that are essential to good nutrition because their mouths hurt.

The good news, according to the Administration on Aging, is that "losing your teeth is not an inevitable consequence of aging. It's caused by an insidious gum disease that can be prevented and successfully treated." The stereotype of the toothless old person could become passé, but it is going to take some effort. A report of the American Association of Retired Persons tells us that past studies have shown that 70 percent of older persons have not seen a dentist in five years. Those who already wear dentures

69

particularly feel that checkups are no longer necessary. A yearly checkup is important to our parents' overall health.

The same guidelines that apply to choosing a doctor are appropriate for finding a new dentist. Location, personality, facilities, staff, recommendations, and fees are all important; and be sure that you find out what arrangements the dentist has for handling emergencies that occur outside of office hours.

Dental needs have changed dramatically over the past decade. Although it is true that the loss of teeth is not inevitable with advanced age, it is also true that longevity has put new strains on our parents' teeth, and we need to take special care of them to help them stay strong and last longer. As our parents age, it is more important than ever that they remain actively under a dentist's care. Some of the special concerns of elder dental patients are:

- Periodontal (gum) disease. The dental community is not sure why some people develop periodontal disease, while others seem more able to resist. General good health, a balanced diet, and good oral hygiene certainly are deterrents to developing the disease. One common thread for periodontal disease seems to be poor diet. For instance, a diet full of refined carbohydrates, as favored by many older Americans because they are less expensive than protein, feeds bacteria, which in turn feed periodontal disease.

- Sore spots. The altered physiology of the aging patient, due to diet and disease, has a negative effect on the health of the soft tissue in the mouth (oral mucosa), which makes it more prone to sore spots. They can become chronic if not recognized and treated.

- Poorly fitted dentures. If dentures are not properly fitted, they can cause sore spots. Even dentures that initially are well fitted can change due to alterations in the bone profile, possibly as a result of a calcium deficiency, thus creating a negative cycle. Ill-fitting dentures wear poorly, causing even more rapid loss of bone, which can result in irreversible bone damage. Sore spots and loss of bone caused by improperly fitting dentures can be noted and corrected by a qualified dentist, who is trained to monitor soft tissue and the condition of the bone.

- Cervical erosion. Due to increased recession of the mucosa (soft gum tissue) more root surface of the tooth is exposed as we age. This root surface is not as strong as the enamel and is more susceptible to breaking and to surface decay.

- Poor oral hygiene. An inability to care for one's teeth, which may be due to physical problems or lack of mental acuity, can allow fungal infections to develop. Third-party monitoring by an active caregiver, and thorough annual checkups, can help prevent such conditions. In difficult cases, more frequent professional cleanings are recommended.

Three guidelines emerge as the way to good dental care:

1. A balanced diet with plenty of calcium and protein
2. Good oral hygiene, which should include thorough flossing and brushing with a fluoride dentifrice (toothpaste or gel) at least once a day, and
3. Annual checkups with a qualified dentist, even for denture wearers

Good news for our parents: Dentists with large geriatric practices tell us that there is a positive side effect to aging for the older dental patient. The nerves become less prominent and, therefore, there is less discomfort for the patient.

DENTAL HEALTH AIDS

Difficulty in brushing because of arthritis or other conditions can be overcome with the use of special toothbrushes created with wide handles or with new grips to attach the toothbrush to the hand. These products are available through medical supply stores or their catalogues. Ask your dentist. A suction cup stand for cleaning dentures with one hand is also available. These stocking stuffers could make life much easier for our parents.

A manual toothbrush and dental floss are the mainstays of good dental hygiene. The American Dental Association generally recommends that manual toothbrushes be of a shape that can reach all the teeth, and have soft bristles with rounded ends or polished bristles to be least damaging to the gum. Toothbrushes should be replaced every three or four months. Dental floss, the second essential for good dental care, can be waxed or unwaxed, whichever our parents prefer.

Powered toothbrushes and water sprays are available in many designs and their effectiveness is best assessed on an individual basis. If a powered implement makes one brush longer, for instance, it can be a real help. Water devices may be useful in some cases, but if used incorrectly can damage the mouth tissue, and they are not a substitute for flossing. The dentist can tell you whether or not these products could be helpful to your parents.

Many of our children have no cavities well into their teenage years because of the fluoride that has been in their drinking water since birth, and fluoride continues to protect our teeth against decay. It is even thought to have regenerative properties. The latest recommendations indicate that daily application of fluoride is the best for our teeth. According to the American Dental Association, fluoridation of public water can reduce dental decay by 50 to 65 percent. The reduction of decay is even more significant when an effective fluoride toothpaste is used.

Although most commercial mouthwashes are cosmetic in nature, some fluoride mouth rinses, when used in conjunction with brushing and flossing, can create another defense against decay. The dentist can recommend such products.

COST FOR DENTAL CARE

Discussing fees with the dentist in advance is normal procedure, and often a dentist will allow extended payments for costly work. If your parents are not able to pay for dental work, contact the local dental society for information on what dental assistance programs are available in the community. Often public health clinics and dental school clinics offer their services for minimal fees.

Dental insurance is an option, available primarily through group plans, offered either by an employer or through the union. Approximately ninety million Americans take part in dental insurance plans, but the payments often do not cover the dentist's fees. The dentist's office generally is quite willing to send in an evaluation form to our parents' insurance carrier, asking what will and will not be covered by them, before a procedure is performed.

FOR FURTHER INFORMATION: Geriatric dentistry is a growing specialty. For a list of members, check your parents' area phone book or write to: The American Society for Geriatric Dentistry, 1121 West Michigan Street, Indianapolis, IN 46202.

For general questions about dentistry and dental health write or call: Bureau of Communications, American Dental Association, 211 East Chicago Avenue, Chicago, IL 60611; (312) 440-2806.

## Nutrition and Diet

If it is true that "we are what we eat," then as we age our looks and general health will reflect our lifetime eating habits—good and bad. When we are younger, our bodies seem to cope with nutritional abuse, but as we age, this abuse begins to take its toll. Although it is difficult to change the eating habits of a lifetime, an improper diet can lead to serious health problems such as lack of energy, malnutrition, and general bad health. If our parents have developed poor eating habits, it is well worth the effort to help them change. The older they are, the more good nutrition becomes a vital barrier against overall frailty and the threats of stroke and heart disease. A well-balanced diet can also help control high blood pressure and prevent diabetes.

CHANGING METABOLIC RESPONSES

According to the National Institute on Aging, most people gain weight more easily as they age. "Because of changes in the body and decreasing physical activity, older people usually need fewer calories. The requirement for nutrients such as proteins, carbohydrates, vitamins, and minerals, however, is not very different from that of younger adults." With age comes a slower metabolism and the body tends to lose lean mass. Our parents may begin to gain weight without eating any more than usual. What this means is that the quality of the foods eaten is more important

73

than ever. It is a time to eliminate high-calorie foods that are not part of the basic food groups and that offer few nutrients, such as butter, salad dressings, candy, alcohol, pastries, jams, and honey. In fact, it is a time to help our parents restrict all foods that are high in salt, sugar, fat, and cholesterol, as well as to encourage them to exercise to maintain good health and weight control. Since older people generally need less food, their diet must be well balanced and consist of foods high in nutritional content.

### THE FOUR BASIC FOOD GROUPS

From the time we study health in the first grade, we know about the four basic food groups. They are repeated here to jog our memories and to use as reference in helping our parents plan meals and snacks. Looking at these groups with the changing physical needs of our parents in mind will help us guide them to healthier eating habits. How our parents adjust their diet to these guidelines will depend on their age, their special dietary needs, and their level of activity.

- Fruits and vegetables. Rich in vitamins and fiber; eat one leafy green vegetable and one citrus fruit daily. Daily recommendation: four servings—one serving equals one medium-sized fruit, or eight ounces of juice, or one-half cup of cooked vegetable.

- Meat, fish, and eggs. Rich in protein; to build and maintain muscle tissue, which can decline with age. Be sure to cut the fat off the meat and skin the chicken. Daily recommendation: two servings—one serving equals three ounces of meat, fish, or poultry, or two eggs, or one cup of beans.

- Breads and cereals. Fiber, a natural laxative; buy whole-grain or bran breads, muffins, and cereals for good body fuel and mental alertness. Daily recommendations: four servings—one serving equals one slice bread, one cup cereal, one-half cup rice or pasta.

- Dairy products. Rich in calcium; stick with low-fat yogurts, cheeses, and milk. Daily recommendations: two servings—one serving equals eight ounces milk, two ounces hard cheese, one cup yogurt.

A HEALTHIER DIET

The lack or overabundance of certain elements in our parents' diets can cause serious health problems. Our gentle prompting at an early, healthy stage can postpone, or even eliminate, certain hazardous conditions. (As always, check with your parents' doctor for his or her approval on any dietary changes.)

1. Calcium. Adding sources of easily absorbed calcium to your mother's diet, for instance, may help prevent the deterioration caused by osteoporosis (something we should be doing for ourselves). Calcium is also important for strong teeth, and vital in maintaining good muscle and nerve function. It plays a role in the clotting of the blood. Since the absorption of calcium into the body slows with age, our parents may require greater amounts of high-calcium foods than before. In addition to dairy products, some high-calcium foods include tofu, canned salmon, green leafy vegetables, oysters, and shrimp.

2. Salt. Introducing our parents to low-sodium foods, such as fish, skinless chicken, rice, lean meats, plain nuts, and noodles, or good salt substitutes, such as herbs, garlic, pepper, and lemon, reduces their chances of high blood pressure (hypertension). Heart attack and stroke have both been linked to high blood pressure. It is important to realize that hypertension can exist without symptoms; therefore, it is imperative that our parents have regular checkups.

3. Sugar. Sugar is high in calories and low in nutrition, filling our parents with "empty calories." In order to provide the greatest nutrition in the foods they eat, we should try creative dessert substitutes that are sugar-free. Low-sugar products can also eliminate the emotional fluctuations brought on by too much sugar.

4. Cholesterol. We are more aware today than ever of the effects of high-cholesterol diets as they contribute to heart disease. As a result, manufacturers are wooing us with products low in cholesterol. The healthiest low-cholesterol diet, however, is still one low in animal fats. A low-cholesterol diet would include such foods as fruits and fruit juices, skinless fowl and fish, tofu, rice, or cereal, and fresh or frozen leafy green vegetables. If our parents are in the high-risk categories for heart disease because they are overweight, do not exercise, are heavy smokers, or have high blood

pressure, any opportunity to show them ways to eliminate cholesterol should be seized.

5. Fiber. The American diet is sorely lacking in daily fiber,
which is particularly significant as our parents age and constipa-
tion becomes more of a problem. As a natural laxative, fiber,
when taken with plenty of water, increases regularity and softens
the stool. In addition to the whole-grain and bran cereals and
breads, as mentioned in the food groups, foods rich in natural
fiber include fresh fruits and vegetables, beans, nuts, and peas,
and such dried fruits as prunes, figs, and apricots. For some of
our parents, bowel movements and irregularity is a topic of great
concern. Often their anxiety causes them much more anguish
than the condition warrants. Sensible dietary changes may be all
that is needed to give them peace of mind.

6. Vitamins and minerals. The necessary vitamins, A, C, D, and
B complex, and minerals are abundant in all four food groups
and are essential to good health. A balanced diet will insure a
proper daily supply. Too much of any one vitamin can be harm-
ful, and your parents' doctor should be consulted to determine if
supplements are needed. Vitamins and minerals are more easily
absorbed when taken naturally. Unless your parents have a
known vitamin or mineral deficiency, trying to coax them to take
vitamin pills, which can be very large and hard to swallow, may be
totally unnecessary.

7. Water. We mentioned water as valuable with fiber, but water
is an essential part of every diet. Without adding calories, water
promotes good digestion and cleanses out the urinary tract. Our
parents should be encouraged to drink several glasses of water a
day.

HELPING OUR PARENTS EAT WISELY

As anyone who has ever been on a diet knows, giving up the foods
we have learned to love can be difficult, especially since we all are
continually being wooed by the advertising medium with the
message that love is equated with sweets. Perhaps some clever
intervention on our part can make it easier for our parents to eat
"right."

Avoid the temptation of sending a box of chocolates on Father's

Day; make it a basket of fruit instead. We should experiment with healthy treats and low-calorie drinks until we find those that our parents enjoy and make sure they are always available. One friend keeps her mother supplied with dried apricots, a small luxury that the mother will not afford for herself, but a treat that she loves. There is nothing easier or better to prepare than fresh vegetables and fruits. We could help our parents establish the tradition of a fruit bowl, maybe in the center of the dining room table, making the fruit constantly available. We might prepare healthy snacks, such as carrot sticks, and leave them in water in the refrigerator. Cherry tomatoes can provide a tasty mouthful.

If your parents have a problem chewing or digesting raw vegetables, there are many other possibilities, such as steamed vegetables cut into snack bites and stored in the refrigerator, or prepared nutritious drinks left in the freezer. One such drink: blend low-fat yogurt and any fruit, pour it into an ice-cube tray and freeze it. Just drop the cubes into the blender again when ready to drink and it will come out like a soft milk shake. (Do not freeze pineapple, just add to second blending.) There are endless combinations for tasty, nourishing drinks in which ingredients such as wheat germ and tofu can easily be camouflaged. Do some experimenting.

Other healthy snacks might include: melon balls, low-fat cheese cubes, peeled cucumber scooped out and stuffed with cottage cheese and sliced, a bagful of bran muffins in the freezer to pop into the microwave at will, a selection of low-fat yogurt, or a selection of dried fruits, including raisins and nuts if chewing is not a problem.

Keeping in mind your parents' individual dietary requirements will guide you to appropriate selections for them. A few days' supply of snacks prepared by us is a terrific gift to leave our parents after a visit.

As our parents age, they often lose interest in eating. This loss of interest can be caused by a number of problems:

· Stomach and intestinal disorders

· Tooth or denture problems

· Loneliness

- Loss of family members

- Low income

- Physical disability (making it difficult to shop and to prepare food)

- Lack of exercise

- Medications, or

- Loss of the sense of taste and smell

We should try to identify the reasons for any disinterest in food and initiate the necessary corrective measures. Making sure that our parents eat properly daily is the best safeguard against malnutrition and related health problems.

LABOR-SAVING TIPS

Our parents have different eating habits and the problems they represent are varied. For some, we worry about malnutrition; for others, the dangers of extra weight. In all cases, poor eating habits are usually responsible. We should help them rethink how they prepare food, knowing that as they age, the tendency will be to eliminate any complicated preparations. Preparing food for one or two can be boring, and fast-food solutions are often tempting—if not nutritious. Some simple equipment for one-dish dinners such as woks, pressure cookers, and casseroles can make preparing a well-balanced meal more attractive. Food processors are being manufactured today in scaled-down versions appropriate for the preparation of one or two servings. Many cookbooks are available with meals specifically created for various methods of preparing appetizing dishes.

The success of one labor-saving device was demonstrated by an experiment organized by the On Lok Senior Health Services in San Francisco when funds made it possible to have microwaves installed in the homes of the aging who had great difficulty preparing meals at night. Skeptics felt that these frail elderly, most of whom were in their eighties and with poor eyesight, would never be able to adapt to a new form of cooking. The hot plates many of them were using were real fire hazards, however, and something had to be done. By following careful instructions that were taped to the microwave in large print, these elders quickly learned how to make dinners. Now many of the caretaker children who do not live close enough to come by daily prepare a week's worth of dinners for their parents and leave them in the freezer with clear labels. Their parents proudly use the microwave oven to make meals for themselves.

JOYS OF EATING

There is evidence that high levels of social contact and support have a positive impact on health and mortality, and they certainly can raise our parents' spirits. According to figures compiled by the Administration on Aging in 1987, well over 150 million meals were served in group settings to over three million older persons. About 350,000 volunteers, approximately 82 percent of whom were sixty years of age or older, offered their services to operate nutrition programs. Helping to involve our parents in such programs, as volunteers, serves the dual purpose of keeping them in social contact where their services are needed and of exposing them to good nutrition. The local social service agency or Area Agency on Aging can tell you if their neighborhood provides free or low-cost meals for older people at a community center, church, synagogue, or school and how to become involved. Transportation is often provided to and from a nutrition site. Going with a parent for the first time can help break the ice for him or her.

There are other ways we can help make mealtime more enjoyable, which is particularly important if your parent lives alone. Help organize a "potluck" club, where everyone brings a prepared dish. Encourage your parent to invite a friend to lunch once or twice a week, or begin a restaurant-testing club. Fewer time restraints on our parents may allow more-flexible mealtimes. Several small meals may be more appealing to them than the traditional three meals a day, and some restaurants have special menus for seniors that are in effect from four to six in the evening. (A good idea to start in your parents' community.)

GROCERY SHOPPING

Good shopping tips can insure better foods in our parents' kitchens. Shopping with a friend can be more fun and it allows them to share large packages. If alone, however, our parents should not hesitate to ask the butcher to repackage poultry in smaller amounts. Many stores have grocery delivery, which can be a great aid in bad weather, or when elders are not feeling well. Planning meals before going to the store prevents extra trips, and getting the ingredients for a new recipe on each shopping trip can be fun.

FOR FURTHER INFORMATION: Most of the health and exercise books recommended on page 91 include chapters on geriatric nutrition. Additionally, the following free booklets are available on the specific nutritional needs of older Americans: *Diet and the Elderly; Diet, Nutrition, and Cancer Prevention: Good News; Meat and Poultry Labels Wrap It Up;* and *Please Pass That Woman Some More Calcium and Iron.*

They can be obtained by writing to: Consumer Information Center, P.O. Box 100, Pueblo, CO 81002.

## Chemical Dependency

To insure that our parents look and feel their best, we need to inform ourselves about the hazards of chemical dependencies for our elders. In this age of war on drugs for our teenagers, it may be surprising to learn that the elderly are a major new area of concern.

With the miracle prescription drugs that have freed us from pain and have given us longer lives have come some insidious dependencies. The numbers speak for themselves. The National Institute on Drug Abuse tells us that ten years ago, less than half of the medicines now in use were on the market. And Americans over sixty-five consume about 25 percent of all medications taken in this country. The statistics on addiction of older Americans are not complete, but we know that our parents are being inundated by drugs at a time when their body chemistry is reacting differently, and when they are likely to need medications for multiple reasons.

Drugs affect each individual differently. Older people react differently to drugs than younger or even middle-aged people. Physical size and personal medical histories also have an effect. According to the National Institute on Aging, certain physiological changes that occur with aging affect the way our bodies respond to drugs. The amount of fat tissue in the body is on the rise, while the percentage of water and muscle is generally decreasing. Combined with the slowing down of the functioning of the liver and kidneys—two organs responsible for breaking down and removing most drugs from the body—the length of time that drugs stay in the body and the amount absorbed by body tissues are affected accordingly.

As a result of increased physical sensitivity to drugs, and the use of more drugs, our parents are vulnerable to developing a chemical dependency. Mood-altering drugs such as tranquilizers, sleeping pills, and pain relievers may be prescribed as helpful for short-term use, but long-term use can lead to dependency. Reviewing old prescriptions with them and monitoring how often drugs are being taken can make our parents aware of a potential problem before it becomes dangerous. Open discussion with the physician may help a parent recognize the problem.

Eliminating a drug dependency should be done gradually, under medical supervision. Some dependencies may require stays in hospitals or private clinics, while other, less serious problems, can be resolved at home with doctor and family support. Few communities are without individual, group, or family counseling in these matters. Being aware of the potential for chemical dependency for our parents and alert to their periods of heightened vulnerability (see discussion of alcohol on page 84) will do much to assure our parents' independence from drug abuse.

GUIDELINES FOR SAFE DRUG USE

- Make sure directions on the medicine container are legible and that our parents understand them; ask the pharmacist to use large type on the label to be sure.

81

· Ask for containers that are easy to open if this is a problem. Childproof tops can be a real obstacle to arthritic fingers. (Just make sure the medications are kept out of the reach of children.)

· All old medicines should be thrown away. Many drugs have a limited shelf life, changing their effectiveness over time, and having old medicines around can pose a possible hazard.

· The exact amount prescribed should be taken. (If a little is good, more is not better!)

· Encourage your parents to call their doctor if there are any unexpected side effects.

· We can all react differently to the same drug; prescriptions should never be shared.

· Help your parents prepare a complete medical history for the doctor so that he or she is aware of all medications being taken and any past negative reactions to drugs

· Devising an easy system for your parents to keep a daily record of all medications being taken can avoid much confusion and possible overdosing.

There are weekly pill containers available through medical supply houses, or their catalogues, but homemade solutions abound. One popular idea is to use an egg carton, with pills placed in marked grooves to represent hourly or daily dosages. Others prefer an oversized weekly calendar, which gets checked off as medication is taken. Just remember to make sure that any special directions accompany the pills.

GENERIC DRUGS

With the cost of medication constantly on the rise, drugs have become a real pocketbook issue for older Americans. One source of relief is the existence of generic drugs. These are drugs with essentially the same ingredients as the brand-name drugs, but without the name. In some states, the law requires pharmacists to fill a prescription with the less-expensive generic unless otherwise specified by the doctor. Your parents should check with the pharmacist before having a prescription filled. Perhaps you could help by calling a number of pharmacies in town for price comparisons. There can be quite a discrepancy in cost to the consumer, on any drug, from one drugstore to another.

FOOD AND DRUG INTERACTION

Most of us are aware of the fact that there is a direct relationship between the way food and drugs interact within the body. Whenever there is food present in the stomach and intestines, the speed with which a particular drug goes to work within the body is directly affected. It is important, therefore, that our parents follow the directions for ingestion very carefully (with milk, after a meal, before eating, etc.).

Just as certain foods affect the way drugs react in the body, some drugs affect the way the body uses food. According to the Food and Drug Administration, there are many ways in which drugs inhibit good nutrition. They can cause the excretion of particular nutrients and impair the absorption of others. Drugs can also alter the ability of the body to convert the necessary vitamins and minerals into usable forms. Although this depletion occurs gradually, for those of our parents who may be consuming drugs over a long period of time, these interactions may lead to serious deficiencies. As caretakers, we should help our parents do periodic reviews of the medications they are taking to see if they are still necessary and to assess any long-term negative effects.

In this overmedicated environment, one well-respected geriatric specialist, when speaking to groups of physicians, recommends that no at-home patient be taking more than three different medications. "New patients come to the office with as many as nine different prescription and nonprescription drugs they are taking. I automatically throw away half of them."

It is important to remember that "drugs" include over-the-counter medicines. Many of these nonprescription drugs contain strong agents, and when large quantities are taken, they can equal a dose that would normally be available only by prescription.

Our parents must avoid the mixing of any drug and alcohol unless they have been assured by the doctor or pharmacist that there are no adverse side effects.

Caffeine is not often thought of in discussions on drugs, but it is a stimulant that many of our parents have as a regular part of their diets. It is present in many foods, including coffee, tea, chocolate, and some soft drinks. Caffeine has an effect on the brain, which can cause insomnia, and on the heart. As with other drugs, our parents' reaction to caffeine may become exaggerated as they age. Some of our parents may be monitoring themselves by eliminating all coffee after noon. With a general awareness of the negative effects of caffeine for all of us, there are many new caffeine-free products on the market, which we might introduce to our parents—including chocolate substitutes. Moderation is the key.

FOR FURTHER INFORMATION: *AARP Pharmacy Service Prescription Drug Handbook.* American Association of Retired Persons, 1909 K Street, N.W., Washington, DC 20049; 1,000 pages; hardcover, $25 (#0-673-24887-9): paperback, $13.95 (#0-673-24842-9). A clear, easy-to-understand, and thoroughly comprehensive guide to safe drug use over fifty.

Or Elder-Ed, P.O. Box 416, Kensington, MD 20740 and ask for their free booklet, *Using Your Medicines Wisely; A Guide for the Elderly.*

ALCOHOL MISUSE

The misuse of alcohol among the older generation is an issue of greater concern than most of us realize. The longevity of our parents is bringing to light problems with alcohol, many of which heretofore went unnoticed. The chronic drinker generally died younger, and those who were retired were often socially isolated and, therefore, able to hide their problem from society. With fewer people living extended lives, there was a tolerance among many families, who had the attitude that drinking might be the only pleasure of a relative who had little time left anyway.

Now that the older generation is expected to live a full, contributing life well after the age of retirement, the medical profession is recognizing the problem of drinking among the aging as a serious one that needs our attention. According to the National Institute on Aging, the older problem drinker falls into one of two categories: (a) the longtime chronic drinker, who has managed to survive into old age in spite of his or her alcohol abuse, and (b) the elder person who drank little during his or her early life, but who has been driven by circumstances to start heavy drinking. The times of greatest concern for our parents seem to be those surrounding major changes in their lives: retirement and lowered income, loneliness—particularly following the death of a loved one—and adjustment to a health problem. The habit may even have been encouraged by us, initially, as we tried to help our parents through a tough time.

Recognize the outward signs of alcohol dependency:

- Reduced appetite
- Chugging drinks
- Angry denial of the problem
- Drinking more frequently in private
- Unexplained bruises (from unreported injuries)
- Needing more alcohol for the same effect
- Getting drunk
- A preoccupation with alcohol, and planning its use
- Setting limits on its use (setting time guidelines for the first drink of the day)
- Irritable or unreasonable behavior when not drinking
- Medical problems caused by alcohol
- Insomnia
- Forgetfulness
- Reduced attention
- Confusion

(These final three symptoms are also signs of senility, and it is important to determine the problem in order to avoid improper diagnosis. Protecting a parent's privacy by not telling the doctor of excessive drinking, for instance, may lead to an incorrect evaluation.)

Know the effects of alcohol on the body:

- Impairs brain activity
- Hinders good judgment
- Decreases physical coordination and increases reaction time, making our parents more vulnerable to accidents
- Affects mental alertness

Chronic drinking can result in major damage to:

- The brain and central nervous system
- Kidneys
- Heart
- Stomach
- Liver

Knowing the physiological changes in the elderly that keep drugs such as alcohol in the body longer makes it easier to understand why the same gin martini that used to relax your parent at cocktail hour may now make him or her quite tipsy. You can help minimize the effects of alcohol on your parents by making sure that they are drinking on a full stomach. Sipping a drink will also minimize the effect of the alcohol, while giving the elder a chance to stop if a negative effect is noticed. Remember, if your parents are on any medications, they must be particularly careful about drinking. Alcohol can dangerously alter the effects of drugs, often causing rapid intoxication.

A real danger for a parent who drinks too much, besides the obvious possibility of falls from lack of balance, is that the alcohol may be an appetite suppressant. It is certainly easier to continue drinking if one does not feel hungry than to get up and prepare food. It becomes an easy path to malnutrition. Further complications occur when alcohol dulls pain, thus eliminating the body's natural warning signal for heart attack and other problems.

FOR FURTHER INFORMATION: If you suspect that one of your parents has an alcohol or drug problem, you can get advice through the local Alcoholics Anonymous or write to the national chapter at: Alcoholics Anonymous (AA), P.O. Box 459, Grand Central Station, New York, NY 10163. Ask for their free pamphlet *Time to Start Living,* on acoholism and elders.

Or National Institute on Drug Abuse, 5600 Fishers Lane, Rockville, MD 20857.

For a free copy of the large-type reprint of *Food and Drug Interactions,* send a postcard to FDA, HFE-88, at the same Maryland address.

THE DANGERS OF SMOKING

The dangers of smoking have been fully revealed during our parents' lifetime. Not only are all cigarette ads banned from television, but the surgeon general's dire warnings are in print for us to see on each packet of cigarettes we buy. In addition, there are increased risks of fire as our parents age and face the possibility of falling asleep with a cigarette. Many who would never consider smoking in bed now fall asleep in the comfortable stuffed armchair in the living room. The dangers of smoking include other family members in yet another way: the damage of secondary smoke inhalation is becoming known, and children are particularly sensitive to its effects. Understanding the way in which a smoker can negatively affect the whole family might help a parent "kick the habit," especially if you spend much time together.

What smoking does to the body:

- Irritates, inflames air passages and lungs
- Produces excess mucus
- Causes chronic cough and, in severe cases, chronic bronchitis
- Leads to long-term lung damage and emphysema, which prevents normal breathing
- Increases risk of heart attack, especially in combination with high blood pressure or high cholesterol
- Causes cancer of the lungs, mouth, larynx, and esophagus, and plays a role in cancer of the pancreas, kidney, and bladder
- Causes higher risk of influenza and pneumonia

Why, then, do our parents continue to smoke? The addiction to nicotine and the habits of a lifetime are hard to break, and the misconception persists that after a person has smoked for thirty years, it is too late to stop.

The National Institute on Aging claims that it is never too late to stop smoking. "When a person stops smoking, the benefits to the heart and circulatory system begin right away. The risks of heart attack, stroke, and other circulatory diseases drop. Circulation of blood to the hands and feet improves. . . . The risk of smoking-related cancer begins to decline and within a decade the risk is reduced to that of a nonsmoker." According to the United States Department of Health and Human Services, some studies have found that older people who take part in stop-smoking programs have higher success rates than younger people.

As an ex-smoker, I can say from experience that one of the hardest parts of giving up smoking is being in the company of those who still smoke, particularly in the beginning. What better gift to our parents and ourselves than for us to stop smoking with them, eliminating all old smoking habits.

For some people, a good scare from the doctor, pinpointing the damage being done by smoking, is sufficient to stop on their own. For others, the nicotine addiction is too strong to quit without help. Nicotine chewing gum is available by doctor's prescription to help those dependent on nicotine. It is not recommended for patients with certain heart problems, and denture wearers may find it hard to chew.

If the dependency is more social than chemical, however, regular gum may provide the oral satisfaction needed, and there are many flavors in gums especially manufactured for denture wearers. Some quitters find that carrot sticks help, and others chew on pencils! What our parents need to avoid is a massive caloric intake to substitute for smoking. Weight gain is the most prevalent complaint of those who have stopped smoking. Intervention on our part with suggestions for noncaloric substitutes can help avoid this negative side effect. This also may be the perfect time to entice our mothers or fathers into starting a regular exercise program. Changing daily habits makes quitting easier, and exercise will help stave off added pounds.

Sometimes a parent may say he or she wants to stop smoking

but finds it impossible to do so. You can find out if there is an unconscious desire not to stop through a smoker's self-test, which can be obtained, free, from: Office on Smoking and Health, 5600 Fishers Lane, Park Building, Room 110, Rockville, MD 20857.

FOR FURTHER INFORMATION: Many organizations now have programs to help us stop; some of the most convenient may be your local heart, lung, or cancer societies. If there is no local program, you can write to the national offices: American Heart Association, 7320 Greenville Avenue, Dallas, TX 75231; or American Lung Association, 1740 Broadway, P.O. Box 596, New York, NY 10019; or American Cancer Society, 4 West 35th Street, New York, NY 10001, (800) 4-CANCER.
Or contact:

· Your local hospital or health maintenance organization

· The company medical or health services department, if your parents are still working

· Telephone book listings under "Smokers' Information and Treatment Centers"

Or write to: S. James, Consumer Information Center—C, P.O. Box 100, Pueblo, CO 81002, for free booklet *Clearing the Air: A Guide to Quitting Smoking.*

## Exercise

No discussion of overall health is complete without a word about exercise. According to Robert N. Butler, M.D., former director of the National Institute on Aging, "If exercise could be packaged into a pill, it would be the single most widely prescribed, and beneficial, medicine in the Nation." We adult children are aware of the benefits of exercise for ourselves, but we may still think that advanced physical deterioration is an inevitable result of aging. According to the President's Council on Physical Fitness and Sports, much of the physical frailty attributed to aging is actually the result of muscular disuse and poor diet. With a regular

89

exercise program and good nutrition, many physical problems can be halted, or even reversed. The council goes on to say that good exercise and proper eating habits actually can stimulate the formation of new bone tissue and improve cardiovascular endurance, muscle strength, and flexibility.

The amount and intensity of exercise for our parents depend greatly on what their lifestyles have been, and any exercise program should be tailored to fit their own level of ability and special needs.

Pam, an active cyclist and all-round athlete at thirty-five, was very disappointed in her mother, a retired schoolteacher. "She is just letting herself go," bemoaned Pam. "I gave her a membership in the Y for swimming and she won't even do that." When questioned further, it turns out that Pam's mother was never an active swimmer or an athlete of any kind. It was unreasonable to expect her to start such a program at sixty-six. But she was always a good walker, and now meets regularly with a neighborhood group for morning walks. It is not Pam's idea of exercise, but it is most appropriate for her mother.

If our parents have always been active, they will probably know what they are capable of doing. New fitness programs should be checked by their doctor; certain heavy new exercises can be more dangerous than helpful. Those who have kept in shape can participate in a wide range of activities—from walking and slow jogging to ballroom and square dancing to senior aerobics, yoga, and other exercise programs, to swimming, cycling, and a variety of team and individual sports.

I gave Ros an English bike for her seventy-sixth birthday, and my sisters and I surprised her on her eightieth birthday with a membership in an indoor tennis club. It allowed Mother to play on a team through the snowy winters. At her age, she worried that a winter's inactivity could seriously affect her game. Although extremely inappropriate for some, these activities were what Ros loved to do. They brought her the great pleasure of continuing involvement.

Biking is an activity enjoyed by many Americans over sixty-five, and the popularity of the all-terrain bike has made it safer and easier to enjoy.

What kind of exercise is done is as much a matter of interest as it is ability. The Senior Olympics have shown the world the variety of extraordinary physical feats possible at very advanced ages.

FOR FURTHER INFORMATION: The booklet *Pep Up Your Life—A Fitness Book for Seniors* is a joint venture of the Travelers Insurance Company, the President's Council on Physical Fitness and Sports, and the American Association of Retired Persons and can be obtained free by writing: AARP, 1909 K Street, N.W., Washington, DC 20049.

Or *Fitness for Life*. Theodore Berland. An AARP Book ($12.95). At your local bookstore or write: AARP Books, Scott, Foresman and Company, 400 South Edward Street, Mt. Prospect, IL 60056. (Add $1.75 for shipping and handling.)

Or *Fitness after 50*. Elaine LaLanne. Lexington, Mass.: Stephen Greene Press, 1986. A complete fitness program with Richard Benyo—also includes nutritious recipes.

Or the exercise sections of most bookstores yield colorful selections of books on exercise specifically aimed at seniors.


## Appearance

The concept of beauty in age is a matter of conditioning. As the baby-boom generation grows older, it is logical that their looks will continue to set the popular standard for what is "in," which means that it may eventually become chic to have gray hair. A female newscaster will not be considered mature enough if she does not show at least a streak of gray. For the moment, this concept of elder beauty still needs a lot of fostering. There are, however, some wonderful new ads on television that depict beautiful, aging Americans. California Blue Cross features an adult daughter worrying about her elder parents. Why? Because they are about to go off on a bike tour of Europe! All goes well, we are told. Next year, China.

The trend is beginning, and it is up to those of us with aging parents to help promote this correct image of the well old as vigorous and healthy with a very special beauty. We must protest any media images that are based on stereotypes and encourage new programming that depicts elders as total, sexual people with more variety of experience and personality than their younger counterparts. One's feelings are so closely related to one's exposure.

Judy, forty-five and the mother of two high school boys, worries because her children have so little contact with older people. For two weeks each summer, they go back to see her parents in West Virginia. Although they always seem to have a wonderful time, she is disappointed when they return with the observation that all the people in the town had gray hair. Judy realizes that she lives in a generationally segregated society. Her boys are not exposed to older Americans in their daily lives. This, she feels, is a real lack in their childhood and she wonders if they will have the warm, loving feelings for their elders when they are adults that she has—a result of being raised in a small town where she knew everyone's grandparents as well as their parents.

Good media images will help fill the void, and we can enrich both our children's and our parents' lives through more intergenerational contact.

HELPING OUR PARENTS LOOK THEIR BEST

How our parents look remains as vital a link to how they feel at eighty as it did when they were forty. The difference may be that a lack of energy at eighty makes the thought of shopping or reviewing wardrobes an exhausting task. The idea of having to try on clothes in a store dressing room is enough to dissuade all but the most ardent of shoppers. "And who is going to see me, anyway?" The cycle creates itself. If our parents know that they look spiffy, they are more likely to ask a friend to lunch, or to volunteer in a social setting.

Many adult daughters have had a hand in selecting their mothers' wardrobes for years; it was we who made sure that our fathers had ties wide or narrow enough to be in fashion.

Here are some tips to make fashion easier.

- Choose complete outfits. This may be the best way to avoid awkward mix-and-match, especially if your parents' eyesight is inadequate for color distinction and their energy is low. Complete outfits that take no further thought are sure bets for a well-dressed mother.

· Choose easy-care fabrics. Ironing has passed out of many of our lives and we should make sure that our mothers are no longer subjected to that task either. There are wonderful, new low-care fabrics that look super without putting our parents in the shiny polyester pantsuit brigade. Colorful jogging suits are particularly well suited for elderly men and women. The elastic waistband makes the pants easy to put on and spills are not a big problem. The whole outfit can be thrown in the washer. They are warm, attractive, and very comfortable.

· Choose comfortable shoes. With the variety of comfortable shoes marketed today, there is no reason for our mothers to be stuck in "old lady shoes," or to suffer in out-of-date high heels. Velcro attachments on many sports shoes replace difficult laces.

· Have a makeup update. As with many generations, our mothers' makeup may be locked in a past time zone. With the less-is-better philosophy of today, a makeover could produce a happy new attitude. This can be a touchy area, though, so here we suggest a change only if we feel some parental dissatisfaction. If our mothers are happy with bright red lipstick, so should we be.

Perhaps the finishing touches on how to help our parents look their best are aids that can make dressing and undressing easier for them. There are implements that they can use to facilitate dressing when there is no one available to "get that zipper." A long-reach zipper pull, which you hook into the zipper before putting on the dress, saves the day. For those with restricted finger movement, a button aid that slips through the buttonhole to grasp the button, much as a needle threader grasps the thread, pulls the button back through the hole. Bras that attach in the back are no easy matter, unless they are attached in the front before being turned around; and now you can buy bras with the attachment right in the front. There are implements into which you slip your foot, while sitting or standing, with which your parents can pull off their shoes without bending down. And, of course, there are long-handled shoehorns to help get the shoes on in the first place.

Recognizing a particular hardship your parent may have, and then keeping an eye out for a solution, can be a great help. The best place to start may be a store that rents and sells medical equipment. If they do not stock such items, they often have an array of catalogues on hand that can be of help.

PLASTIC SURGERY

Throughout history, there has been a human quest to remain young. Plastic surgery, which holds the promise of taking ten to fifteen years off one's looks, is the twentieth-century answer to this quest. It has become more popular as the techniques for performing this restorative surgery have become more sophisticated.

Although good diet and exercise are far more important tools to truly remaining young, there is something to be said for the psychological advantages of liking how you look. To the widow in her sixties, who hopes to find another husband but lacks confidence in herself, a face-lift may be a spirit lifter that gives her the gumption to reenter the social scene.

Still, it is not for everyone. The cost is prohibitive for many, generally considered to be less than a car but about the same price as a cruise, and insurance rarely covers any of the procedures.

There are several considerations to be faced before deciding to proceed with plastic surgery, in addition to the cost.

- Is the patient in good health? Most plastic surgeons will not consider operating on anyone in poor health, and generally EKGs are run and blood counts taken just to be sure. Health relates to the individual and is not dictated by age. One plastic surgeon with whom we talked had operated successfully on two women in their eighties within the past year.

- Is the family supportive? It is very difficult to get through the recovery period for an older woman if her husband is opposed to the surgery. (If a widow's husband had been strongly opposed to it, she may still have to deal with a certain amount of guilt.)

- Is the patient prepared for the recovery period? An older patient may be debilitated for two to three weeks following surgery. The wounds must heal, and the swelling needs time to subside. It is not as problematic as other surgery as it only deals with the skin, fat, and little muscles, but the use of any anesthetic requires time for the body to recuperate. The surgery *can* be done under local anesthetic with intravenous sedation, but many surgeons prefer a light general anesthetic. It eliminates concern for patient movement during crucial moments.

· Does the patient have reasonable expectations of what the results will be? A face-lift can remove wrinkles and tighten the skin, but it will not make you young again, and it does not stop the aging process.

· Is the patient prepared for the stares of friends, and the questions? This may be where adult children living out of town could be co-conspirators, allowing their mother, after a month's stay, to return home to friends who simply notice that she looks great.

Since there are a number of surgical options, and a great variety of skill among surgeons, it is important to get several opinions and referrals from former patients if possible.


BEAUTY CARE PRODUCTS

Another benefit to the expanding number of Americans over sixty-five is the abundance of new products directed at this lucrative market. From special shampoos for gray hair to stationary foot massage products, there are manufacturers anxious to supply our parents with anything it takes to keep them attractive and happy. The most successful products are those that are marketed with a "mature" woman as the model, but with little or no reference to the fact that the product is specifically for the older consumer. Tricks such as shifting to a dry lipstick to reduce the seepage of color from the lips can be tried, but cosmetic considerations are based generally on the same criteria as always: coloring, skin type, taste, cost, etc.. The cosmetics counters of most stores are staffed with trained personnel willing to take the time necessary to explore their products and find what combination works for you or your mother. Remember that they often represent only one manufacturer. You may want to shop around.

## Points to Remember

· Good attitude promotes good health.

· Aging is more a factor of health than of chronology.

· Our parents are living longer lives. Preventive medicine is critical to helping them live healthier lives.

· Choose a doctor carefully.

· Always get a second opinion for important medical procedures.

· Become fully informed about a parent's medical condition or disease. Knowing what to expect can facilitate successful pre-planning.

· Be sensitive to your parents' changing vision.

· Recognize the symptoms of hearing impairment and learn how to be heard.

· Insist that your parents continue regular dental checkups, even with dentures.

· Explore ways to make meals pleasurable experiences for your parents.

· Follow the guidelines for safe drug use. Throw out all medicines not currently in use.

· Recognize the signs of alcohol dependency.

· Try to switch your parents to caffeine-free products.

· Encourage your parents to stop smoking. The benefits to the body start immediately—at any age.

· Understand that seniors are capable of great amounts of exercise. To be healthy, exercise must be appropriate to the individual.

· Looking great makes us feel great—at any age!

*Chapter 4*

# The Busier the Better: Second Careers, Volunteering, Traveling, and Staying Involved

"No matter where you live in this nation and no matter what your level of income might be, you can always find things to do that are productive, helpful to others, challenging, interesting and to some degree adventurous.

"The second half can be the best half. It can also prove that when you think you are making a sacrifice for the benefit of others, that can turn out to be the greatest advantage and most enjoyable experience of your own life."

President Jimmy Carter
*Washington Post,* June 2, 1987

THE well old in America today have fabulous opportunities to stay involved with life. The state of retirement has taken on new meaning. When "the experienced" combine their richness of experience with an ability for creative thinking, the results can be dramatic.

Elsewhere in this book we have referred to "the elderly," "seniors," "the old old," the "well old," and other euphemisms for our aging parents. We know that many people over sixty-five resent any reference that tends to lump them with others in a chronological sameness. Even terms such as "retirees" and "golden agers" are strongly disliked by some. It is true that the diversity is so great among the over-sixty-five population that there is no such thing as accurate age-related grouping. Since this chapter is about the great variety of involvements enjoyed by a group of mentally and often physically active people, we shall simply refer to them as our parents.

From an adult child's point of view, there is very little care-giving needed for these active, experienced parents. The ideal is for us to use these years to enjoy our parents, to mend weak relationships, and to weave a stronger fabric as the basis for understanding and clear communication, skills that make future planning so much easier.

## Helping Our Parents Get Involved

If our parents have the vitality to seek out and partake in life's experiences on their own, our involvement at this stage may be only one of (1) information giving, (2) encouragement, and (3) financial planning (see chapter 7).

For those of us whose parents are shy about trying new ventures, are hard to motivate, have a diminished self-image, or have a particular handicap, there are many ways that we can help.

- Become fully informed. Finding out what is available in the community is an important step to involving a parent. This chapter will give you many ideas and tell you how to find out more. Do some investigating on your own. If an activity, travel opportunity, or business venture sounds good, get some feedback from those involved before convincing a reluctant parent to venture forth. Go yourself, if possible; see how new people are greeted.

- Know their interests. The key to success is to match our parents with their interests. It would be much easier to convince a parent who loves cardplaying and hates to cook to join a community bridge group rather than starting a potluck lunch club!

- Identify the obstacles. We can spend much energy trying to convince our parents of something they already believe. Finding out their particular objection to an idea is crucial to overcoming it. Is their reluctance to participate a factor of shyness, fear of failure, disinterest, lack of adequate finances, transportation problems, or something else? Try to develop good listening skills as described in chapter 2 to discover the true objection.

· Motivate. Once we know the problem, we are in a better position to solve it. We should use this understanding of our parents, and patience, to encourage their participation, without pushing too hard. Leaving material for them to look at on their own, or talking of several involvements so that the choice is theirs, are possible approaches. Many parents like to think that what they do is their idea, so give them time to make it their own. Arranging an invitation from an active peer may also motivate a procrastinating parent.

· Solicit help. Remember that friends and neighbors of our parents may know more about their interests than we do. We can use their input to help choose an appropriate activity and to help us motivate our parents' participation. Their pastor or rabbi may be a good ally; or a word from their doctor on the need to stay active could be what is needed.

· Follow-through. To work hard for an initial commitment only to have an immediate failure can be disheartening, and if the first experience is bad, it will be harder than ever to convince your parents to try again. If there is a contact person, make him or her aware of your parents' situation and ask that there be someone to welcome them to the group, etc. If there is no such person, then try to arrange for a friend to accompany them or go yourself, if possible. Remember that any time and energy we put into helping our parents to remain active is directly rewarded by keeping them independent and healthy for as long as possible.

## Second Careers

Our parents come from very different work histories. Some of our parents have jobs from which one does not naturally retire. Working as an artist, an author, an editor, a farmer, a real estate broker, a lawyer, a doctor, or any self-employed position allows them the privilege of working for as long as they wish. Others are forced to retire or are subtly ushered out of work environments at a time when they feel they have much more to contribute and they need the income. Second careers can offer our parents an opportunity to continue to earn a full-time living while focusing in a new direction, or supplemental income if they are receiving

Social Security. Since the latest surveys depict Americans as having three different careers before they retire, even those not forced to retire may well consider the adventures and advantages second careers offer.

### TURNING A HOBBY INTO A BUSINESS

One obvious direction our parents may take is to develop a for-profit business from an avocation. Grandma Moses, who started painting at seventy-six, turned her primitive art into a lucrative business, achieving fame for the first time in her late seventies.

Pamela is not nationally recognized, but the patrons of Galdy's restaurant in Scranton rave about her lemon meringue pies, which she bakes at home daily and sells to the restaurant exclusively.

We have watched many of our parents turn their at-home talents into marketable professional skills. Giving piano or other musical-instrument lessons can be an easy service to provide with no additional overhead. This creates the possibility for intergenerational contact, while earning extra money. Opening a cooking school may offer the same opportunities. A love of cabinetmaking can open the way to many salable items: bookshelves, wooden cradles, planter boxes, dollhouses.

Our parents may have the talent for the hobby, but not the business skills necessary to make the transition from pleasure to profit. We can help by providing guidance for:

- Financing
- Bookkeeping
- Publicity
- Advertising
- Sales

These kinds of details can seem overwhelming at first, but for someone with the proper background, they pose less of a problem than producing the product. The local small business administration should be the first place to go for guidance. Some communities have special organizations to help with "cottage industries" (products produced in the home).

### REMAINING IN THE SAME FIELD—WITH A DIFFERENT FOCUS

Often the idealism with which one enters an occupational field must take second place to the realities of the job. Retirement can provide the opportunity to return to one's first love.

Paul had a passion for drawing buildings, and when he graduated from architecture school, he entered a large firm prepared to do that which he loved. His flair for accurate specifications led him to much work in that area and he never seemed to get back to the purity of design that attracted him to the field in the first place. Upon retirement, however, he felt free to redirect his career and is now designing homes for selected clients. And someone else does the specifications!

Occasionally, doctors and nurses who have spent their careers in a specialty have reported with great enthusiasm the joys they now get from a small general practice where they can take the time to know and to treat the whole patient.

To make a living in photography, Tayna had to do mostly portraits. After selling her shop, she has headed for the hills of Idaho to indulge, with her seasoned eye, in her love of nature photography.

### TURNING HOME INTO A BUSINESS

It is not unusual for our parents, at the age of sixty-five, to own their own homes. This situation can give them the freedom to turn that home into a business. Bed-and-breakfasts are becoming increasingly popular in America, and an empty-nest home can be a perfect setting for such a business, zoning permitting. Rural areas are often exempt from specific zoning regulations. Even if a variance is required, it is not difficult to obtain with the cooperation of the neighbors. A low-key operation should raise few objections.

Bob and Stella Jordan, who live in a resort area in the New York Adirondacks, got into business by renting a room to their neighbor's children, who were visiting from Europe. Now that they are both retired, they have turned their home into a boardinghouse catering to European visitors, who generally stay from three to six months. The Jordans find the international atmosphere stimulating, and the additional money allows them travel opportunities of their own.

With the proper licensing, a home can also serve as a social service business. Respite care for the elderly, child day care, and adult day care are the most common examples of services needed.

BUSINESS DONE FROM THE HOME

Just as women with small children are finding jobs that can be done from the home, so can our parents. Telemarketing, mailings, telecommunications (survey work), and work on home computer terminals are some of the possibilities.

There are two basic approaches to this kind of job. One is to respond to an employer who is looking for someone to fulfill a need. Look in the want ads in the paper, or investigate possibilities with employment agencies in your area.

The second approach is to create a job that has not existed before. In this scenario, you evaluate your parents' skills, discussing what they enjoy the most, and then help them translate that ability into a way to make money. If your parent has accounting skills, for instance, he or she could approach small businesses not large enough to hire their own accountants, but too large to handle the work themselves—maybe a series of "cottage industries" in the area—and keep the books at home.

EMPLOYMENT OPPORTUNITIES AIMED AT THE OLDER WORKER

The squeeze that service businesses are feeling between expansion possibilities and lack of available young workers has made the older worker a valued target for full-time or part-time employment (see chapter 11). The following are a few prime examples.

- Fast-food restaurants are suffering from lack of employees, particularly in suburban areas where there is a dearth of unemployed youth.

102

· Newspaper delivery is a prime service in which the older worker is being wooed. According to an article in the *New York Times* of March 22, 1987, "Letting Grandpa Deliver the News," approximately 72 percent of this country's newspapers now use adult independent contractors, and some of these contractors are actually senior centers. The money is useful and the work is therapeutic.

· Retail sales is another area of opportunity. Many stores that cater to a more-mature market have found that their customers prefer to have sales personnel close to their own age, a phenomenon that will continue to provide employment as the population ages.

## Life Stages, Continuing Education, and Retraining

There have been numerous studies done in this age of introspection to tell us what stage we are in and what we can expect to experience as we continue through life's cycles: studies about the empty-nest syndrome, midlife crisis, the passages from young adulthood through retirement, the constant readjustments within marriage, divorce, and widowhood. Now the second half of our lives is under intense scrutiny.

Americans tend to experience different stages of satisfaction, which correlate directly with our shifting desires to possess, according to David B. Wolfe in his article "Age-Less Market" for *American Demographics,* a monthly journal of demographic research written primarily for the business community. People forty or younger get satisfaction from owning products, especially for the first time, such as the first car, the first stereo, and the first home, states Wolfe. He goes on to explain that the focus is shifted toward services or catered experiences as they grow older, between forty and sixty. "Travel, restaurants, art, and major sports events assume a larger role in the quest for satisfaction." It is during this stage that we are inclined to pay for jobs that we no longer like to do: gardening, housekeeping, painting.

Wolfe describes the "being experiences" that determine the choices made by those in the sixty-to-eighty age bracket. "Intangible things grow in importance, like getting in touch with oneself, enjoying the sunset, taking a walk in the woods, or having a

103

friendly conversation." One of the joys of getting older has been the traditional concept of becoming wiser. Learning, questioning, understanding our world and the people in it are certainly "being experiences."

## BACK TO SCHOOL

Perhaps this theory explains why the idea of continuing education is so appealing to many of our parents. We have all seen the newspaper articles that highlight graduation ceremonies that feature grandmother and granddaughter graduates in the same university class. The numbers of these "grandmothers" and "grandfathers" seeking further learning in a formal setting have grown to such an extent that colleges and universities are beginning to look to the over-sixty generations to fill the classroom seats left vacant by the decreasing enrollment as a result of the exiting of the baby-boomers from college campuses.

According to a survey conducted by the National Center for Education Statistics (NCES) in 1981, entitled "Participation in Adult Education," there were 768,000 Americans age sixty-five and older, or 3.1 percent of all older Americans, enrolled in some form of higher education. A 1985 report of the Special Committee on Aging of the U.S. Senate went on to tell of more dramatic news. The number of persons sixty-five and older participating in adult education has almost tripled, growing at the average rate of 30 percent for every three years. Today, those figures are well over a million.

It is interesting to note that while older people certainly have the ability to learn, the desire to learn seems to be directly related to their previous educational experience. The NCES report in 1981 showed that the level of participation in adult education rose at each higher educational level from 2.2 percent of the total population with less than an eighth-grade education to 31 percent with five years of college or more. Later studies have confirmed this correlation between years of schooling completed and enrollment in adult education.

If your parents have not had much formal education, then it is unlikely that they would take advantage of these adult education opportunities without some prompting. Showing them the variety of programs available requiring little or no formal educational background (not even a high school diploma) for many of the course offerings may be the impetus needed to open exciting new doors for them. There are high school equivalency courses for parents who have not finished high school, and special courses for those to whom English is a second language. Many parents may have thought that it was too late, but communities across America are realizing that it is never too late to learn.

In Florida's Sarasota County, adult education programs are actually considered a minor industry. *American Demographics* quotes the county's adult education director as saying that of the ten thousand registered students per semester within their 375 community education classes, half are students fifty years old and older.

Charles Longino, director of the University of Miami's Center for Social Research in Aging, states that "one out of four elderly interstate migrants chooses Florida," which helps explain why Florida has a disproportionate number of older citizens, and why it is considered an indicator of what trends are likely to spread to other states with growing older populations.

Our parents came from a generation that respected education and most of our parents have instilled in us the value of education. They are aware that nothing brings us closer to the experience of life than continual learning. Now, with time available to them, they can couple their full complement of learning derived from life's experiences with more classroom exposure offered by adult education. This combination of experience and intellectual curiosity makes them the quintessential student.

Those of us who are footing the bills for college students today often salivate over the university course catalogues, while our children are more curious about the system of Greek sororities and fraternities, roommates, and what goes on during weekends. We often wish we could have the opportunity to go back and take the subjects we want to take, but it is not our turn. For many of our parents, however, it is their turn, and they are doing it. They are in the classroom for the thrill of knowledge, not for the grades or the degree. They are more likely to speak up in class and desire dialogue to be part of the learning process. In community colleges, in particular, they are often an integral part of the class, contributing as much knowledge as they glean.

Enrollment is open to qualified students at public and private colleges and universities across the country, regardless of age. These same institutions often offer noncredit programs specifically designed for the older learner. Community colleges, community centers, and even some high schools are seeking to lure the returning student to take part in special programs.

INTERGENERATIONAL SCHOOL PROGRAMS

Intergenerational school programs were introduced in the early 1970s in an effort to counter the trend toward an increasingly age-segregated society where few natural opportunities existed for meaningful contact between older adults and youth, according to the U.S. Senate Special Committee on Aging. Today, there are more than one hundred intergenerational school programs nationwide. Over 250,000 volunteers participate in these programs in grades kindergarten through twelve. New programs continue to appear throughout the country.

One successful intermingling of high school students and sixty-year-olds happened in New York State. "Age Barriers Fall," by Jean B. Rose in *Aging Magazine,* tells of a program she teaches in upstate New York that developed out of a recognition of the fact that soaring divorce rates, decline of the extended family, and the growing popularity of senior housing were contributing factors in distancing the old from the young. She invited her creative writing program at the senior center to take part in her high school writing class. The seniors came to school for the lecture session and assignment at the beginning of the week, and returned at the end of the week to read their works with the teenagers and to take an active part in the discussion groups. "The natural affection and ability of the two age groups to communicate emerge quickly when they are brought together for a common purpose or task," observes Rose.

The success of the writing experiment led to other learning

experiences, the most successful of which were discussions following field trips. These made use of the knowledge of the elders who had lived through the period in question—for instance, a photographic exhibit of Jews in Poland prior to World War II led to heated discussions of war and its consequences, calling on those who had firsthand experience in the war to add insightful comments.

"Outlooks change as people at two different stages of life share and discover common fears and concerns," comments Jean Rose. In a society where the senior citizen population increases by sixteen hundred individuals each day, such lines of communication are imperative.

Although the federal intergenerational programs are less geared to formal learning for older Americans than they are to intergenerational contact through volunteerism, it cannot be denied that they are learning experiences. The outgrowth of having the sixty-plusers in the school is to integrate them into the classroom, as Jean Rose did.

The Department of Health and Human Services has expanded the federal role in promoting intergenerational school programs by a joint initiative of two of its divisions—the Administration on Aging and the Administration for Children, Youth, and Families. This federal effort consists of four major components: (1) establishing an information bank of intergenerational programs across the country; (2) disseminating this information to organizations interested in establishing such programs; (3) working with professional organizations to stimulate interest; and (4) funding intergenerational demonstration projects.

Your local Area Agency on Aging may be able to provide information on intergenerational school projects in your area, but it is not always that easy. You may find yourself being transferred from one department to another, so if your parents have an interest in this program, you would be doing them a big favor to get the information for them. In the White Pages of the phone book under city government offices, you may be lucky enough to find a listing for a "Commission on the Aging," under which will be listed "Senior Information Referral." They may put you in touch with your city's volunteer center, who should point you in the right direction. The program has a lot of merit, so do not give up too soon.

In some communities, you will have better luck contacting your local school board or neighborhood schools, where the information may be available. In some states, such as California, the State Department of Education has taken the lead in these intergenerational programs.

ELDERHOSTEL

Elderhostel is an educational program for older adults, sixty and over, and their companions or spouses, who want to continue to expand their horizons and develop new interests and enthusiasms. Inspired by the youth hostels of Europe, Elderhostel is based on the conviction that retirement and later life represent an opportunity to enjoy new experiences. The programs take place at over nine hundred colleges, universities, and other learning institutions in the United States, Canada, and over thirty other foreign countries. In 1986, more than 112,000 adult students took part in an Elderhostel program.

The courses are taught by the regular faculty of the college or university for a week or more, during which time the students live on campus in dormitory rooms. The classes are taught year-round and vary from such basics as English literature, language, and art to the less usual—computers, astronomy, philosophy, and religion. Up to three noncredit courses can be taken at a time, and no particular level of formal education is presupposed on the part of the student.

The cost of just over $200 per week in America includes registration, tuition, room and board, use of campus facilities, and a variety of extracurricular activities often related to the history or culture of the host area. Financial aid is available under a "Hostelship" program. For complete information, write to: Elderhostel, 80 Boylston Street, Suite 400, Boston, MA 02116; (617) 426-7788. Elderhostel publishes its regular catalogue three times a year: fall/winter, winter/spring, and summer. Between each catalogue, they send out a newsletter, *Between Classes,* which includes an updated course list.

> GIFT IDEA: Has your mother ever harbored the secret desire to study at Oxford in England, or has your father dreamed of courses at the University of Miami? What a wonderful gift idea: get together with your siblings and give your parents their dream for the next holiday!

There is also an International Elderhostel program, which generally lasts for three weeks, with each week spent on a different university campus. Air fare and all land travel is included in the quoted cost. Study of the area is an integral part of the program. This idea seems to dovetail well with the concept discussed in the upcoming section on travel. Our parents are interested in "experiencing" and not just collecting.

Just as we mentioned that colleges and universities have their own adult education programs, some of them also have their own senior study abroad programs. Contact your state university for further information.

LIBRARY SERVICES FOR OLDER AMERICANS

The authorization for library services that extends through 1989 was established through the Library Services and Construction Act of 1984. At that time, special spending was authorized to provide for the following services for the elderly:

1. Training librarians to work with older Americans
2. Conducting special library programs for the elderly, especially those who are handicapped
3. Purchasing special materials for the elderly
4. Paying salaries of elderly persons who work in libraries as assistants in elderly library services programs
5. Providing in-home visits by librarians
6. Establishing outreach programs to alert the elderly about available services, and
7. Furnishing transportation services to the library

109

Complete services do not exist in all communities, and budget cutbacks may eventually curtail the program, but it would be worth a call to see what your parents' community library offers.


RETRAINING

Job retraining is increasingly important in a society that is rapidly changing its way of doing business. Technological advances, and the introduction of computers into almost every industry, have forced many Americans to learn new skills if they are to remain employable in their fields. The rising number of company mergers is leaving many able workers jobless at an age when it is difficult for them to reenter the field. For others, the possibility of long life affords them, with proper retraining, the opportunity to have multiple careers within a lifetime. Many older women seek the help of job-reentry programs after divorce, the death of a spouse, or when their children leave home.

There are local organizations throughout the country that focus on different skills. Options for Women Over 40, for instance, concentrates on redirecting the skills acquired from years of caring for others, through job counseling, to applications in the job market. The local senior services number should direct you to retraining programs in your parents' area, and the Area Agency on Aging can tell you how to find out about the federal programs.

In addition to vocational retaining opportunities available for seniors through the Older Americans Vocational Education Act, the Job Training Partnership Act (JTPA) has allocated funding for the older worker, fifty-five and over. Some of these monies are distributed through PIC (the Private Industry Council) for the economically disadvantaged older worker. Contracts are written with small and large businesses of all kinds that are willing to train workers on the job. Generally half of the trainee's pay is subsidized by the government for a predetermined period of time, based on the complexities of the job, with the business agreeing to continue employment after the training period expires. If your parents fall into this category, you may want to contact their local PIC office for more information.

There are a number of exemplary programs offered in different parts of the country that have created opportunities for both retraining and also counseling for reentry into the job market. The government programs generally are aimed at the economically disadvantaged; others focus on all older workers.

An example of one successful retraining program is the Gerontology Program at the University of Massachusetts. Designed to harness the enormous ability of those over sixty, while creating new careers or volunteer commitments, the program has been developed to prepare these adult students to serve the community as professionals in the field of gerontology. These are elders helping elders. Their empathy toward the issues of the aging population contributes enormously to the success of the program.

This studies program began in 1979 with funding from the Administration on Aging. Although the program is not limited to those over sixty, most of the students are that age, and the average age is sixty-seven. The elder students receive subsidies to cover tuition for this two-term state certificate program in gerontology.

What makes the course interesting is the diversity of the students' backgrounds. Some already have graduate degrees and others have never been to college. This diversity is used to the advantage of the program.

Although the University of Massachusetts's program is limited to sixty students per term, the impact on the state has been dramatic. They have attracted the attention of the media for many of their special interest issues, and the course work has directly influenced legislative changes at the state level, as a result of their in-depth research studies.

Many major universities are developing institutes on aging or gerontology centers. Although we are not aware of other programs as extensive as that at the University of Massachusetts as far as retraining is concerned, much is happening in this field, and a call to a nearby college or university to find out what they are doing would be in order.

AFTER RETRAINING—JOB HUNTING

Looking for a job can be discouraging under the best of circumstances. When a parent has been phased out of a position, or has not worked for many years, it can be particularly difficult. We

111

should be able to help our parents by doing some of the tedious fact-finding—what placement programs exist in their area, and which organizations cater to the older worker—and by offering continuous morale boosting.

Operation ABLE (Ability Based on Long Experience), in Chicago, is a leader in serving as a nonprofit placement agency for the older worker. It promotes the advantages of hiring older workers, counsels the applicants in developing interview skills, and is capable of linking the right ability with the right job. There are ABLE offices across the nation, with variations on the name. California ABLE in San Francisco has a hotline to place older workers in jobs by networking with a number of other concerned organizations in the Bay Area.

FOR FURTHER INFORMATION: *Out the Organization: Gaining the Competitive Edge,* by Madeleine and Robert Swain (MasterMedia, 1988), labeled "the job-hunting book for professionals whose careers are no longer satisfying or safe," this book gives much information to help the older worker who finds himself or herself facing new career paths due to retirement, reorganization, retraining, or just plain dissatisfaction.

## Volunteering

For many of our parents, volunteering is the most rewarding of all endeavors. Dr. Ethel Percy Andrus, founder of the American Association of Retired Persons (AARP) in 1958, had as her motto "To serve, not to be served." Those who are aware of the contributions of this vital segment of our population do not think in terms of what can be done for them, but how society can best use the productive capacity inherent in their experience and energy.

The number of volunteers in America is estimated at over ninety million, and the profile of those who are contributing their time is changing dramatically. Women have traditionally been the backbone of volunteerism in this nation. They were the ones who made the bulk of the civic contributions in the family, because they were the ones with flexible time. The mass exit of women from the home into the work force left a void in the volunteer ranks that is being filled today by the retired and partly retired segment of our population, with men the surprise volunteers of the eighties.

The reasons for volunteering are as varied as the volunteers themselves. For some recently retired, it is the fulfillment of a dream to have time to dedicate to a cause they love. For others, it may simply fill a gap, or it may be a way to continue with a professional talent by redirecting it. Recipients are in the best position to understand the value of the volunteer, and often are inspired to become volunteers themselves. The common thread that entices most of our parents to volunteer is the innate understanding that retirement by no means precludes active involvement in life.

If our parents bemoan the loss of involvement, whether it be from job retirement, the empty-nest home, or the loss of a spouse, volunteering may bring new richness to their lives. The following overview of volunteering possibilities should provide us with plenty of suggestions for our parents.

TRADITIONAL POSSIBILITIES FOR VOLUNTEERING

Religious organizations have always run their programs with the help of their congregants. With their expansion into social service programs, including most of the programs designed for elders described in chapter 6, there is a growing need for volunteers. If, however, our parents would prefer intergenerational involvement, church and synagogue youth programs abound, and are run with help from volunteers.

The community at large presents the same opportunities for involvement through local United Way chapters, YMCAs and YWCAs, community centers, Girl Scouts, Boy Scouts, and so forth. Another avenue to explore is the neighborhood school, library, and hospital. Often an experience with a particular disease is the impetus to donate time to its national organization. The American Cancer Society, the American Heart Association, and dozens of others have representation in almost every community and can always use help.

The arts and cultural life of a community is as rich as the interests of its citizens. It is often volunteer energy that inspires local museums, theaters, dance groups, and symphonies to stretch beyond their norm to create new experiences for the community.

## POLITICAL INVOLVEMENT

The world of politics is a natural for volunteers. No political campaign could be run without them. Nor could any of the advocacy groups, such as the Gray Panthers, Owl, AARP, etc. (see chapter 11), exist without their active participation. Political campaigns and civic organizations—such as the League of Women Voters, the National Women's Political Caucus, and the National Organization for Women, among many others—offer ample opportunity to remain active in the political process, even between elections. Participation is possible on all levels, from a grass-roots write-in campaign on an issue of personal importance, done from the living room, to running for office. See chapter 11 for more on legislative action for seniors.

If our parents are interested political volunteers, they can work to create a senior legislature in their state if none exists (see page 253), or join a consumer action group that responds to their special interests. Or, like Claude Pepper (Democrat, Florida), they may decide to run for the U.S. Congress.

## FEDERAL PROGRAMS

ACTION, a national volunteer agency, is the umbrella organization for a number of programs instituted by the federal government that are run through the efforts of volunteers. The distinguishing characteristic that separates these programs from other similar community programs is that they are directed toward the low-income volunteer. As a result, funding is allocated to provide a small stipend that generally covers transportation, hot meals, and volunteering expenses. These volunteers are also eligible for an annual medical checkup, and they are covered by accident and liability insurance. The best reward for these seniors, however, is the job itself.

The Foster Grandparent Program, one of most popular of ACTION's senior programs, involves 19,000 volunteers, men and women sixty and over, and about 66,500 children throughout the United States. This unique coupling of children in need with caring adults has had heartwarming results. These special volunteers serve troubled youngsters in medical and child care facilities, in detention centers and halfway homes, in schools and treatment centers and in therapeutic programs, often when there is no one else to give them hope, to love them, and to be their friend.

The Senior Companion Program, another facet of ACTION, is discussed in chapter 6 as a community service link. It is a marvelous example of the elderly helping each other, particularly in situations in which there is little or no family participation for the recipient. For someone who wants to feel needed, this is an answer.

RSVP (Retired Senior Volunteer Program). This ACTION program was specifically formulated to engage older Americans in community service once they leave the work force. RSVP volunteers serve in locally run, cost-effective programs such as neighborhood watch, in-home care, hot lines, and youth programs.

For further information about any ACTION program, write to: ACTION, The National Volunteer Agency, Washington, DC 20525, or check your local phone book.

The Service Core of Retired Executives (SCORE) is a national organization of retired business and professional people who offer the benefit of their experience, without charge, to small business owners who seek their advice. Under the auspices of the U.S. Small Business Administration, this volunteer service allows retired executives who wish to maintain contact with their fields of expertise an opportunity to do so after retirement. Begun in 1964 with the founding of sixty-eight chapters in as many cities, SCORE has mushroomed into an organization that boasts more than 13,000 volunteers providing counseling in over 600 communities nationwide. Making the local SCORE office aware of your parents' talents, with a resultant call from SCORE for help, could propel your parents into a rewarding volunteering position. It's worth a try. Get information through the local Small Business Administration office, or call toll-free (800) 368-5855.

Other programs are being developed to prevent our parents' valuable human resources from being wasted. A landmark decision in the Florida Supreme Court (the Emeritus Attorney Amendment, 1986) was made to give attorneys who have retired to Florida and are not members of that state's bar a limited right to practice law provided their services are free. The Administration on Aging took advantage of this ruling by funding two projects in Florida for which they recruited and trained retired lawyers to serve the needs of the low-income elderly. As the Florida experience proves successful, we can expect to see more states enacting similar laws enabling our experienced parents to share the wealth of their knowledge.

SOME UNIQUE OR PERSONALIZED VOLUNTEERING INVOLVEMENTS

Some of the most successful volunteers are those who have created a way to use their talents for the benefit of others without fitting into a predetermined volunteer slot. MaryBeth was a great-grandmother, and if there was anything she did well, it was rocking babies! Her granddaughter, a nurse in the maternity ward, suggested to her supervisor that MaryBeth be asked to help out with a premature baby who needed loving attention. The success of that first contact has been repeated by MaryBeth many times, and by other volunteers in hospitals across the country to the great advantage of hundreds of babies.

If you play a musical instrument well and are under twenty-two or over fifty-five, you, too, could join the Intergenerational Orchestra of Omaha. This volunteer symphony lends itself to the fine tuning of intergenerational friendships as it performs its concerts in homes for the elderly, churches, and community gatherings. Perhaps our musical parents could be instrumental in starting such a collaboration in their own town.

When Max placed his wife in a nursing home in Los Angeles after forty years of marriage, it was natural for him to assume that he would continue to be with her every day. During the visits, he also made friends with the staff and other patients. Soon, when he served Clara her morning coffee, he was serving all of the patients on the floor. It became a tradition, so when Clara died five years later, it was not surprising that Max continued to visit the nursing home every day. He developed exercise programs for the residents and read to those who had limited mobility. At the age of ninety-two, Max received the California State Volunteer Citizen of the Year Award.

Lorraine never had the time to garden as much as she liked until she and her husband retired. Together they surprised even themselves with the beauty of their flowers. At the urging of friends they have opened their garden and share what they have learned with visiting clubs, who view it as a living classroom.

Many parents who were raised with a second language can make a valuable contribution by giving foreign language instruction or translations in schools, museums, and hospitals. Marie's mother, Emmanuelle, had no friends when she came to live with her daughter in America, but that changed as soon as she volunteered to translate at the International Visitors' Center. Now it is Emmanuelle who introduces her daughter to new friends.

Helen had no trouble deciding how she might like to become involved with a volunteer activity. She simply continued with her first love, designing and making theatrical costumes. After being told by her doctor to keep active or she would become bedridden with arthritis, she traded her retirement for volunteerism. She and a staff of ten women in Florida spend over eight hours a day at the theater when working on a show. Helen says she retired when she was eighty, but they asked her to stay on until she could be replaced. That was eight years ago. "I hope to retire before I'm ninety," she says. "But I don't know, the way I'm going."

Although volunteer situations usually assume good health and mobility, great aid can been given others from the confines of one's home. Latchkey grandparents, for instance, are a strong, caring link for young children returning from school to an empty home. They provide a voice on the phone that is loving and interested in what the child did that day. They give the youngster a chance to boast, complain, and mainly connect with a surrogate grandparent who has the time to listen, unlike the working parent, who wants to know that the child is home safely but who cannot take the time to talk at length. Daily phone contact can also be of great comfort to elderly shut-ins.

If the community does not have such programs, they can be instituted on an individual basis.

FOR FURTHER INFORMATION: *Beyond Success.* John Raynolds and Eleanor Raynolds, C.B.E. (MasterMedia, 1988) offers a detailed presentation of satisfying volunteer options for everyone.

## Traveling with Confidence

The travel industry is booming in America today. At this writing, the latest statistics compiled by the United States Travel Data Center are for the last quarter of 1986, and we know that the industry is continually making travel more easily accessible to all people. Here are some interesting statistics:

Number of air trips by individuals—58.5 million

Percentage taken by persons sixty-five and older—9 percent (17 percent in second quarter)

Percentage taken by persons fifty-five and older—19 percent

Number of pleasure trips by individuals—220.9 million

Percentage taken by persons sixty-five and older—12 percent

Percentage taken by persons fifty-five and older—23 percent

Obviously, many of us have parents who are seasoned travelers. They know the prime time to travel and the best sights to see. What they may not know are all the travel benefits that their age has brought them. Today, travel remains an appealing option for our parents in light of the ease and comfort offered by the industry.

The over-sixty-five traveler in America today is one of the most sought-after customers in the travel industry. Contrary to those who might assume that our parents would be a difficult group to please, the travel industry knows better. Our parents are more sophisticated than most younger travelers, with a good understanding of what is involved in taking a trip and a clear sense of what benefits they expect to gain from their voyage. The reasons for travel vary at differing stages of life. Our parents are less likely to be shopping for paintings and assorted objets d'art than they are to be looking for experiences that will enrich their lives by bringing them closer to an understanding of the cultures that they are visiting. Often such understanding comes from programs that combine study abroad with sightseeing tours (see section on continuing education, pages 104 to 109).

During their lifetimes, they have seen distances shrink as technological advances have made the world smaller, tickets cheaper, and travel available to everyone. Now that the children have grown and the dog is dead, they have the money to travel and the time to go! And to the delight of travel agents, they have flexibility. This means that they are prime candidates for all specials, even those with stipulations on weekday or weekend travel. They are also considered by the industry to be a very sociable segment of society and lend themselves to prime group travel. This growing segment of consumers is being wooed by all aspects of the travel business.

DISCOUNT TRAVEL FOR SENIORS

It will not be news to many that airlines offer discounts to seniors. They may be surprised, however, at the diversity of programs and the very real savings. Club memberships with names ranging from "Golden Travelers" to "Silver Wings Plus" are established to lure the over-sixty-fiver (sometimes younger) to their airline counter. Most airlines will give an additional senior discount on all tickets, even those already discounted. These reduced fares must be requested, and the buyer should shop for the best available.

The benefits offered include:

- Flat fee discounts

- Membership privileges

- Frequent flyer bonus miles

- Coupon books, and

- Annual passes for a one-time fee

Airline membership clubs often offer combined discounts for rental cars, lodging, and even theater tickets. These corollary benefits may be extended to those under sixty-five. Seniors

119

should also know that a younger companion can travel with them for the same discount under certain conditions—a great opportunity for our parents to show their grandchildren America. These benefits are not limited to domestic carriers. I was tickled to see a television advertisement recently in San Francisco by Highland Express Airways that announced the cost of a round-trip ticket to England or Scotland entitled the purchaser to take a senior citizen free of charge. It is unlikely to be in effect at the time of publication, but look for others; it is definitely a trend.

The airlines are not alone in offering carrier discounts. Bus lines, trains, rental cars, and cruise lines are equally anxious to attract this growing market. Cruise berths and other reservations unsold at the last minute can be purchased by those whose flexible schedules allow them to take advantage. Ask your travel agent about "last-minute travelers' sales" or standby cruise fares, which can save up to 50 percent of the regular fare; these are often listed in the Silver Pages (a special telephone book similar to the Yellow Pages, but focused on seniors—call your phone company for further information), or advertised in the newspaper.

The lodging industry also is wooing seniors with reduced rates, and some options that are available to all of us may be of special interest to our parents, who have more flexible schedules. One such option is to exchange homes with people in foreign countries—or other cities in America. (Having our parents stay in a home of their own when they come for the holidays may be just what they would love to give them independence and a break from the chaos—and not a bad idea to consider if you and your family are going to visit them.) There are two ways this is generally done.

- One is by joining a club for an annual fee and receiving a list of members and their homes. The details are worked out between parties.
- The second type of organization arranges the entire exchange for a fee.

Your travel agent should be able to recommend companies that do this.

A second option, very popular in the lodging industry now, is the purchasing of time shares in vacation homes. You can buy a week, two weeks, a month, depending on the development, and these shares can usually be exchanged for comparable lodgings in other resorts around the world. Remember that someone has to want your share in order to exchange, so if you buy something in a beautiful but only regionally known spot, it will be harder to trade than a share in Puerto Vallarta, for example.

FOR FURTHER INFORMATION: Your travel agent will know the details, or you can call (800) 555-1212, "Information," for the toll-free number of hotel chains and carrier lines. Most airlines have an 800 line just for senior information.

TRAVEL AGENTS AND SERVICES FOR SENIORS

There are a bewildering number of prices and conditions offered today's prime consumer. A travel agent can be a buffer, at no cost to the traveler, against having to ferret out the best deal for your travel needs. With over twenty-three thousand travel agencies in the United States, a growing number are specializing in the senior trade, particularly in urban areas. Our parents should take advantage of those agencies that have accumulated experience with travel for seniors. The use of computers has made it easier to get quick ticket information, but the myriad prices and schedules make it harder for the individual traveler to understand.

Ticketing is only part of the job of a good agent. He or she can advise on passports, visas, inoculations, and customs requirements, as well as describe the weather, health considerations, shopping, and so forth. Agencies often offer special travel club memberships for those over fifty that include newsletters, monthly lectures, and videos or slides of successful trips. Some even offer complimentary bingo with free trips as prizes! The club memberships do have a small annual fee.

New special services are being offered all the time in the competitive marketing of senior travel. Although a travel agent is still the best source of information, you should check to see which in your area has had the most experience catering to seniors. The advantages for your parents include:

- Group travel opportunities with special services offered through church, senior centers, alumni associations, and clubs, to mention a few. Group travel eliminates most handling of baggage and arranging for interim transportation and tipping, and it usually provides for the exchange of currency as different countries are entered. Group tours that cater to seniors generally leave later in the morning, make more frequent stops, and serve evening meals at an earlier hour.

- Dietary considerations. Special dietary requirements are honored throughout a trip schedule, but they must be made known to the travel agent if you are using one, or to your carrier and hotels, well ahead of time.

- Provisions for the handicapped. If a parent is confined to a wheel-chair or has a sight or hearing impairment, the world of travel is still open to him or her. The greater the lead time, the easier the trip will be. Although the travel industry has made provisions for the handicapped, their ability to accommodate specific needs improves with early bookings for such things as seats with more leg room, room for guide dogs, rental cars with hand controls, recreational vehicles with wheelchair lifts or ramps, and so forth. Any travel agency can make all of the arrangements necessary to determine which hotels, air and land carriers, cruise lines, restaurants and tours are most appropriate, and to make sure they are prepared for our parents' individual needs. Over three hundred travel agencies in America belong to the Society for the Advancement of Travel for the Handicapped, 26 Court Street, Brooklyn, NY 11242. For a list of its agency members and the booklet *The United States Welcomes Handicapped Visitors,* send a self-addressed envelope with 39 cents postage. Upon request, they will provide specific information for hearing or visual impairment and wheel-chair confinement. Additionally, they provide information on camping and outdoor recreation, audio-loop systems that amplify sound, and Braille programs for access to the arts.

- Roommate matching services. The parent who is alone can take advantage of the roommate matching services that most tours provide. This allows him or her to profit from double occupancy rates while offering companionship. If one of your parents is reluctant to leave the other behind, respite care can provide the peace of mind necessary to enjoy the trip (see chapter 9).

TRAVEL INSURANCE

Insurance policies are available for almost any eventuality in traveling, and with the penalties for canceling on most special-fare trips today, they may be a good idea for your parents. Fines for cancellation of charter trips are particularly high. Many airlines do not charge the cancellation fee, however, if a letter from a physician states an unavoidable medical reason. Insurance can cover lost baggage, medical emergencies, and even poor weather conditions. In Great Britain, a thirty-one-day medical insurance plan can be bought at any large post office for $15 for $84,000 worth of medical coverage in the National Health Service regardless of age.

It is significant to note that Medicare does not cover treatment abroad and most foreign hospitals require cash payments, which may or may not be reimbursed by our parents' private insurance company.

Most bank cards and traveler's checks offer insurance coverage for travelers, as well as a twenty-four-hour hot line for English-speaking doctor referral information. Costs range from $18 to $75 per week. Some will actually advance funds up to $5,000 for hospital admissions. In the unlikely event of the death of a member while abroad, certain coverage includes the expense of flying the body home. There are a number of private insurance companies in the same price range, including Access America International, which is a twenty-four-hour help and insurance protection plan for medical, legal, or travel help. (Call 800-851-2800 for further information.)

HEALTH TIPS FOR THE TRAVELER

We adult children can suffer great anxiety when our parents travel, particularly if they have physical problems. The cure is not to curtail the traveling but to help our parents take all precautions to avoid unnecessary complications.

- Choose the trip carefully. An obvious precaution is to plan a trip that takes into consideration any physical limitations. The high altitude and thin air of Mexico City, for instance, would not be a prime vacation spot for someone with respiratory problems or for a recovering heart patient. It is important, therefore, that our parents make known to their travel agent any health problems they have, so that he or she can plan a safe trip.

· Wear medical bracelets. These are available in most large drugstores and should be worn when a condition warrants it.

· Make medical conditions known. Any medicines, allergies, blood type, and pertinent medical information should be given to the tour guide, ship's doctor, etc., for emergencies.

· Extra refills of prescription medicines should be taken along, and a spare pair of eyeglasses can save a lot of grief.

· Our parents should tell their doctor of their plans, and he or she may even suggest a modified diet to avoid problems.

· Inoculations can take several days for recuperation and, if a number are needed, it is a good idea to suggest that your parents take them weeks before the trip starts.

· Maintain eating, drinking habits. Our parents should avoid the temptation to overeat and overdrink, particularly on a cruise. New foods should be taken in moderation and quantities should parallel their normal eating habits. Book first seating on a cruise, for example, if they are used to an early dinner. And they should be forewarned of the effects of tropical drinks in the sun!

· Ask about local eating places, particularly if the ship is calling at many ports during a cruise. The purser should be able to recommend places for your parents and to tell them if the water and ice cubes are safe. They should be especially careful of outdoor settings where there may be flies and insufficient refrigeration.

· When planning a cruise, ask your travel agent to find out what ports have docks and where your parents may have to go ashore by launch, and plan accordingly.

· Maintain sleep habits. Even for those of us not our parents' ages, maintaining our normal sleep pattern can give us the energy to partake of the many opportunities of the day.

· Again for cruises, choose a large ship if there is a special medical consideration. It will probably have a fuller medical facility and, more importantly, room for a helicopter to land in the case of an emergency evacuation.

124

· In helping our parents prepare for a trip, we should pay attention to comfortable clothes and, above all, comfortable footwear. Many walking surfaces abroad can be uneven, and twisting an ankle can spoil a trip. Shoes should be easy to walk in, with fancy heels saved for evenings inside.

FOR FURTHER INFORMATION: The International Association for Medical Assistance to Travelers, 417 Center Street, Lewiston, NY 14092; (716) 754-4883. A nonprofit organization, funded exclusively by donations. Allow six to eight weeks for response.

## Entertainment

As a cap to the concept that the busier our parents are, the better they are, we cannot close without addressing the possibilities for their sheer entertainment. Having stressed the diversity among our parents, it would be presumptuous of us to assume that any activity would appeal to all of them. Happily, the choices are unlimited. Whatever entertained them in earlier years—dancing, skiing, golf, travel, walking, painting, going to the theater, shopping, reading a book, watching the sun set—will undoubtedly be of continuing pleasure, health permitting.

The new twist is that many of these entertainments are discounted to attract the elder market. Did you know, for instance, that a ski lift ticket at Squaw Valley is only $5 a day if you are over sixty-five? (It used to be free if you were over seventy.) Theaters and movie houses offer senior discount tickets and city transportation systems accommodate seniors as well. The famed cable cars in San Francisco will take passengers over sixty-five up and down its scenic hills for only 15 cents, with a free Municipal Transportation ID card (and 75 cents instead of $2 without a card).

Speaking of scenic pleasures, many cities have senior walking groups, which meet at different starting points and are free to anyone who wants to join the walk of the day. The newspaper often lists the walking tours, and shopping malls sometimes have their own. The local senior center may even have a walk organized. This could be a good way to get parents interested in the activities of the senior center, an institution that heretofore might

125

have conjured up misconceptions of nothing but paste-and-paper exercises.

For the more ambitious, there are hiking groups, from leisurely to strenuous, organized in suburban or rural areas, which have a large number of retired people who have the time and the desire to enjoy nature in the middle of the week. The Parks and Recreation Department knows of most groups in a given area and may organize some outings of their own.

SUMMER CAMP

The idea of going to camp as adults has become so popular that tennis camps, computer camps, and other special interest organizations have sprung up across the country. Even Club Med, which used to be thought of as a singles resort spot, is now referred to more often as having the atmosphere of a family camp. Not to be excluded from the fun, those fifty-five and older will find that camps for them are on the rise.

According to Andrew L. Yarrow's *New York Times* article dated March 9, 1987, "The Elderly Enjoy the Respite of Summer Camps," some ten thousand older people each summer attend the Vacation and Senior Centers Association's (VASCA) seventeen camps dotted throughout the Northeast in New York, New Jersey, Connecticut, and Pennsylvania. Born of an inspiration to give attendees of New York City's centers for the elderly an opportunity to spend two weeks in the fresh country air, VASCA was created for the aging, most of whom were living on fixed incomes with little or no family support. Today, anyone over fifty-five may attend, with accommodations ranging from $80 to $250 per week, including meals and transportation. There are still scholarships available, however, for those in financial need. In fact, 60 percent of the campers are on scholarship.

The campers range in age from fifty-five to one hundred. Seventy-two percent of the campers are women, and couples make up about 25 percent. Because the majority of people come to the camps alone, there is a strong emphasis on companionship activities for those who want to participate. You will find the usual camp recreational facilities for activities such as tennis, swimming, and boating in beautiful rustic surroundings.

126

The special attraction of the camps just for seniors is the informality, security, recreation, and companionship offered. Generally, the camps require that the vacationers be in good health and able to care for themselves. There are a few camps, however, that are geared to the blind, severely disabled elders, and those with mental impairments (the cost is slightly higher at these specialized camps).

In addition to the regular activities, the recreation differs slightly from one camp site to another, depending on facilities, age of participants, and interests of campers, and might include lectures, folk dancing, concerts, or just sitting and talking. The evenings are filled with films, talent shows, barbecues, and so forth. There are trips to bowling alleys, summer theater, and nearby points of interest.

Rooms, though not very spacious, generally accommodate two people with shared bathrooms. Although the rooms are rustic, they are very comfortable, as the number of returning vacationers can readily attest.

This is really a very special camp experience for our parents and not to be mistaken for a childlike tented experience.

FOR MORE INFORMATION: Vacation and Senior Centers Association, 275 Seventh Avenue, New York, NY 10001; (212) 645-6590.

As a result of the growing interest in vacation centers for the elderly, religious institutions, social service agencies, and other organizations are sponsoring camps for the elderly in many states.

The Salvation Army runs about fifty-five camps throughout the United States for seniors. These rural programs run from a week to ten days, and some campsites are open throughout the year. The cost is roughly $100 and includes all meals and transportation. For information, contact the local Salvation Army or write to the national headquarters: The Salvation Army, 799 Bloomfield Avenue, Verona, NJ 07044; (201) 239-0606.

WEEKENDS IN THE CITY

Many of our parents no longer feel comfortable with the weekday traffic of the big cities, or with the headaches inherent in finding a parking place. What might appeal to them, however, are the

127

weekend packages that so many urban hotels are offering, some of which include discounted theater tickets, Sunday champagne breakfast with the newspaper in bed, and other enticements to lure them in from the suburbs. Not a bad respite for a caregiver, either.

---

## Points to Remember

· Continued involvement with life can extend our parents' independence for many years.

· Explore employment opportunities with your parents, including:
  —turning a hobby into a business
  —altering the focus of a given field of work
  —turning a home into a business
  —finding work that can be done from the home
  —seeking opportunities aimed at older workers

· Review back-to-school possibilities, such as:
  —adult university courses
  —Elderhostel
  —intergenerational programs
  —retraining

· Guide parents toward volunteering, turning free time into quality experiences. Some options:
  —traditional charities
  —federal programs
  —political involvement
  —intergenerational possibilities
  —creative new involvements

· Learn about senior travel opportunities, which may offer:
  —age-related discounts
  —special services provided by travel agents
  —health guidelines for worry-free travel

· Propose unique adult camp opportunities.

---

*Chapter 5*

# Home Sweet Home: Independent Living for Our Parents

"As a daughter, daughter-in-law and one who hopes to live a long and productive life myself, I long to find these options (which allow for meaningful, dignified and independent lives) available everywhere for everyone. Family, friends and neighbors are the core of my personal support network and that is the way it should be.

"But for those times when extra help is needed for those among us who do not have family, it is essential to have a coherent, organized system of appropriate public and private resources that can help in time of crisis or need. I work with the State Units on Aging and the Area Agencies throughout this country in hopes that someday this dream will be a reality for all of us."

*Carol Fraser Fisk*
*U.S. Commissioner on Aging*

## How Do America's Elderly Live?

According to *Advancedata* of the National Center for Health Statistics, about eight million of our elderly—age sixty-five and over—live alone. That is about one-third of the 26.3 million Americans over sixty-five who were living outside of nursing homes or institutions in 1984. Eighty percent of those living alone were women; those alone tended to be older, widowed women. Most of these elderly had lived in the same place for many years. "Only twenty-four percent had moved into their current house, apartment or mobile home within the previous five years." The irony, of course, is that the greater their age, the more likely they are to be alone. *Advancedata* warns that these elderly are likely to be left without a support system as their spouses, siblings, and even their children die. Many of the elderly living alone had no children (29 percent). Those who did, however, had frequent contact with them. "They lived near their children, saw them frequently, and talked with them frequently on the telephone." Half of this group, roughly four million, felt that a child could be there in a matter of minutes if help were needed.

When quizzed on their health, 70 percent of the people living alone rated their health as good or better, on a five point scale of poor to excellent. Whether they are healthy because they are living independently, or they are able to live alone because they are healthy, is open to discussion. Most researchers feel that a direct correlation exists between a perception of good health by those with a good social support system and the healthy elderly.

An interesting note was reported by this survey: "Mail is apparently not used now as the means for older people staying in touch with children." This is an obvious area in which adult children can encourage their own children to mail postcards, drawings, and weekly notes to have something in the box when our mother or father makes that daily stroll to see what the postman has delivered. The telephone has made it much easier to stay in touch, but the joy of receiving mail is actually enhanced by the resulting decline in frequency.

One of the joys of independence is having choices. Our parents today can exercise their independence by deciding how and where they live. Although many bemoan the loss of "the good old days," when large core families of three generations often lived together in harmony, the truth is that such a romanticized image is largely myth, and the expectations of the elderly today are very different. Many of our parents would hate the idea of giving up their freedom to come live with us, even if we had the spacious homes and extended family necessary to facilitate those three-generational homesteads. Our parents are healthier much longer and they have very definite ideas as to how they want to spend their retirement years. As long as they are among the well old, the variety of possibilities is quite exciting. Here we will examine some of the most popular choices, and then talk about the services and aids available to keep our parents independent, even as they grow more frail. (Nursing homes and housing for the sick old will be discussed in chapter 10.)

## Housing Options for Independent Living

There are many emotional ties that bind our parents to their own homes, and there are practical reasons for remaining there. Knowing the territory and feeling a sense of belonging are bonuses for our parents as they age. They are surrounded by the things that they love and neighbors whom they know. Church or synagogue is nearby, also shopping centers, doctors, and dentists.

Many of our parents have paid off the mortgage and unless property taxes are outrageous, they have very small monthly expenses. A mortgage-free private home is likely to be the least expensive housing available. If cash becomes a problem, there are a number of innovative home equity conversion plans that allow the elder homeowner access to the equity that has built up in the house. A U.S. Senate report that estimates that $600 billion is held in home equity by American homeowners over the age of sixty-five is enough to cause the financial world to develop some rather creative plans to share in that money. Although we must always be aware of possibilities of fraud, there are some interesting programs worth exploring that create monthly income for specific expenses or for the lifetime of the elder. This permits our parents to remain in their own homes while making use of the benefits of their years of saving. Ask your bank's mortgage banking department for information regarding home equity conversion loans. (See chapter 7 for more specific home equity conversion possibilities.)

If, however, the home is large and help is hard to find; if the age of the house means it requires constant repairs; if the garden is a chore to keep; if the neighborhood has deteriorated; if good neighbors have moved away or died—then perhaps it is time to look at some alternatives. The pleasure of living out of town may be giving way to a desire to be closer to services, or the climate may have become too harsh.

Sometimes the problem with a particular neighborhood or living situation is more ours than our parents'. Concerns should

131

be discussed with the whole family, and if our parents intend to remain in their home, then there are a number of improvements, discussed in this section, that can make life more comfortable as the elderly owner-occupants age.

Note that if our parents decide to move to a smaller house or to one in a better location, they should be aware of all the costs involved in the purchasing of a home; closing costs, mortgage loan points, down payment, insurance, property tax, monthly mortgage payments, utilities, and special assessments. If they live in a state that gives a property tax concession to owners who are sixty-five and over, the financial burden will be somewhat lessened. Additionally, the federal government allows homeowners over the age of fifty-five a one-time opportunity to exclude the capital gains tax on up to $100,000 in profit on the sale of their home. (If either spouse has ever taken this exclusion, however, neither can ever take it again. In other words, if your father sold his house after your mother died and took advantage of this exemption, then remarried a woman who had never taken the exemption, the new spouse would lose her right to this benefit as long as she remained married to your father.)

If your parents are moving to another community, it might be worthwhile for them to rent first in order to determine what section of town is best suited to their needs and to verify that the community is compatible for them before making the financial commitment of purchasing a home or condo.

APARTMENTS AND CONDOMINIUMS

Apartment living has many advantages for the elderly. The space is self-contained with very little home maintenance, and most apartment buildings have some security system. Neighbors are close by in case of emergency, and building managers or landlords are generally available to help with repair problems. In many cases, elevators eliminate the inconvenience of climbing stairs, and bathrooms are likely to be easier to get to on a one-floor layout.

In an apartment, our parents should be free from the tedium of calling the plumber when a pipe is broken, and certainly they should never worry again about mowing the lawn, assuming, of course, that the building is well managed. A good landlord is as important as a good apartment and can be assessed not only through his or her personality, but by judging the appearance of the building and in talking with other tenants—all of which should be done before any lease is signed.

The true joy of apartment living is that for the price of monthly rent, our parents should only have to turn the key in the door when they decide to take a trip.

Condominiums share many of the advantages of apartments. They both come in a variety of sizes, shapes, and locations, allowing our parents to choose the lifestyle that best suits them. Raising flowers or having a vegetable garden, for instance, is not precluded by renting or living in a condo, while total freedom from such chores is available at the other end of the extreme. Condos have the added advantage of tax benefits similar to those enjoyed by homeowners. Condominium owners actually hold title to their living unit and pay tax on it. The other areas of the building or complex are owned in common with all the other unit owners.

Besides a difference in ownership, there is a second difference between apartments and condominiums. Condos require a monthly maintenance fee based on the size, location, and floor plan of each unit. These funds are for expenses associated with common areas and for management salaries. Special assessments can be made for unusual expenses such as painting the building, or putting on a new roof, or removing asbestos, or for reserve funds. The business of running the condominium building or complex usually is carried out by a board of directors elected by the condo owners; the board may in turn choose to have a professional management company take over most of the tasks. This kind of potential involvement with an elected board and implied aesthetic control of the building and grounds may be very attractive to some people. To others, the lack of room for individual expression may pose a problem.

Since many apartment buildings are facing condo conversion, if our parents are apartment dwellers, they may be forced to deal with the decision such conversion brings. Be sure that they understand the obligations of condo ownership, and that it is clear what repairs are to be carried out in the building by the developer

133

before conversion. In these situations, tenant organizations are often created to seek and share information. They can be a big help in getting exemptions from the developer for older tenants who may not want to buy. The reputation of the building is an important factor in developing a successful marketing program, thus providing substantially more clout to these tenant associations than their individual members would otherwise have.

Laws regarding the status of residents in the case of condo conversions vary from state to state, and some municipalities have passed ordinances that make it illegal to oust an older, renting tenant who does not want to buy. Clearly, this is an area in which we and our parents should have good legal advice.

There may be more freedom from maintenance with apartments and with condominiums than with a private home, but there are also restrictions that should be investigated in advance.

Here are some questions to ask in anticipation of such a move.

1. Would a move to an apartment or condo mean having to give up a favorite pet?
2. What are the terms of the apartment lease, and is it automatically renewable?
3. Are there restrictions on rent increases? Many cities have rent controls in effect that can be of help to our parents.
4. What is the monthly maintenance fee for the condominium? Our parents should read the condominium homeowners' agreement carefully beforehand and have a good sense of the intentions of the other owners.
5. Are they likely to vote in building expenses that might not be of interest to your parents? a swimming pool? an exercise room? These could be advantages to some and disadvantages to others.
6. What percentage of the other owners are investors, people who bought their units to rent and make a profit? Too many absentee owners could produce a less-caring attitude concerning the general maintenance of their units.

    Leaving a home for an apartment or a condominium may not have prepared our parents for some other potential problems. Noises from building machinery and even from the elevator should be assessed from their unit, and they should visit when neighbors are home, particularly upstairs neighbors, to see how much sound is heard. If possible, it would be good to spend a night in the building before making a binding decision.

7. What are the restrictions on noise in the evening? on parties?
8. What are the visitor limitations? Are grandchildren welcome? Are they welcome in the pool?

Checking to see if the elevator doors are broad enough to accommodate a wheelchair, as well as the doors to and within the unit, is a good precaution for future possibilities. (That is something to think about in your own home or apartment so that your parents can always visit unencumbered.)

COOPERATIVES

Cooperative housing can be very similar to condominium living, because it, too, involves living in a building or complex owned and shared by many. The big difference is that co-op owners have shares in the total project as opposed to ownership in a particular unit, although their share entitles them to live in a particular unit. This can create a greater sense of "being in it together" with more control for the tenants themselves. The number of co-ops appear to be growing in America, perhaps because they can create community spirit with a greater sense of tenant involvement and perhaps because they are flexible in their use of reserve funds collected through monthly occupancy charges. Some uses include bulk purchasing of food, sharing of services, and development of common area amenities. Property taxes can be lower in co-ops because the assessment is made on the total project and is not the sum of many individual assessments. Cooperative projects formed in an intergenerational context, with elder services available, may be very attractive for your parents. Such facilities lend themselves to federal and local subsidy programs, often not available to other forms of housing.

MOBILE HOMES

Trailers or the more permanent mobile manufactured homes attract many seniors because they most resemble the traditional private home—with much less maintenance. They are a far cry

135

from the narrow, small trailers of our youth. The factory-built homes of today can have as many as three bedrooms, with porches added to the outside and peaked roofs for more ceiling height. With over 475 different manufacturers, the choice of floor plan, color, and materials is extremely varied. To maximize the use of space within the home, many manufactured homes are sold with all the appliances and much of the furniture built in. This popular form of housing is attractive to many seniors. According to the American Association of Retired Persons (see booklet information, page 139), "mobile manufactured homes now account for one out of every three homes sold in the United States," and Florida and California abound in mobile home parks filled with senior citizens. These parks can provide newcomers with a ready source of potential friends.

Living in a mobile home can be more economical than in a private home or a condo, mainly because it costs so much less. From a tax point of view, mobile homes are considered personal property and not real estate. The differences in cost come with ownership of the land. Lots are usually sold separately, or rented from planned communities with a great variance in both the monthly rental and the number of services provided. There are many questions to be asked regarding the financing of mobile homes; and the reputations of the manufacturer as well as that of the community your parents may be considering are key to a successful purchase.

HOME SHARING

Home sharing is one of the creative ways that elders are coping with the finances of homeownership and a desire to return to an extended family style of living while staying independent. By 1986, at least thirty-eight states offered some form of shared housing services with over four hundred programs in effect. Home sharing exists when two or more unrelated people live together. Each resident has his or her private space and there are common areas, such as kitchen and living room, which are shared. Possibly the greatest advantage to this arrangement is the potential for intergenerational living, a concept embraced by Maggie Kuhn, eighty-two, founder of the Gray Panthers. She shares her home in Philadelphia with three housemates, all under forty, who split the chores of running the house. They provide Ms. Kuhn with companionship, and a modest rent from each housemate helps defray costs.

The financial advantages are obvious, and if our parents are reaching the years when certain tasks are no longer welcome— driving, cooking, cleaning—they could be exchanged for all or part of the rent. If our parents are receiving Supplemental Security Income, they may jeopardize some or all of such proceeds with house sharing. The local legal services office should be able to explain any restrictions. Local zoning may not allow some house sharing combinations, but when the advantages of continued property maintenance and upgrading of the neighborhood are presented at zoning hearings, they often generate much community support.

This concept may be worth the effort. The security of knowing that someone would notify us in case of emergency is a bonus for us, the adult children.

Home sharing has become so popular that there are nonprofit agencies now in many communities that will match elders with younger people. The National Shared Housing Resource Center, Inc. (NSHRC), provides resource development, technical assistance, and up-to-date shared housing information to regional and state-wide coalitions. If your parents are interested in this kind of program, the NSHRC can put you in touch with the agencies nearest to them that can be of help. For further information contact NSHRC at 6344 Greene Street, Philadelphia, PA 19144; (215) 848-1220. They also have a manual that is a planning guide for match-up programs. The Area Agency on Aging should know what is available in your parents' community.

CONGREGATE HOUSING

Congregate housing has developed as an answer to elders who feel the need for more communal support while maintaining the privacy of independent living. It usually takes place in large apartment buildings where residents have separate apartments with their own kitchens, but with access to a communal dining room where mealtime can be shared with other tenants.

This alternative lifestyle provides the additional security of some professional supervision and a wide range of resident services. Although it precludes intergenerational living, families are welcome to visit. There are usually many planned activities that involve both exercise and companionship. For the well old who like being around their contemporaries, it is a good option.

In an era when there is not enough senior housing to go around in many parts of the country, we may be seeing more congregate housing developments in the near future. Developers like to build them because they can squeeze more units to the acre, typically forty to sixty units, and there seems to be less community resistance to housing permits for senior communities even in areas concerned with no-growth measures.

Many major national companies are entering the field of senior housing. The Marriott Corporation has seven senior projects planned in California, Virginia, Pennsylvania, and Maryland, with three times that many projected over the course of the next five years. Other hotel chains, including Hilton and Hyatt, are exploring the field, and Avon, the beauty-product conglomerate, is developing Retirement Inns of America.

This activity in the field should insure future retirees greater options for housing choices.

LIFE CARE COMMUNITIES

Life care communities are becoming increasingly popular as they come to resemble country club living. Many of our parents with ample resources are choosing this carefree lifestyle for their remaining years. The financial commitment is usually substantial and often nonrefundable, but the particulars are as varied as the types of retirement homes. Some deal exclusively with the well old, and in time of medical crisis, an alternative solution must be found. Others, as the "life care" name implies, offer a multitude of choices within the community, from totally independent living to totally dependent living. The community may offer houses, town houses, apartments—and hospital care—all within the same complex.

The best advice for life care living is to be sure that our parents understand the commitment and that they not make the decision in a time of crisis, such as immediately after the death of a spouse. One of these communities may be exactly what our parents need, but they represent large investments, and that means high-pressure sales tactics. Some facilities have long waiting lists, and our parents may feel the need to "jump at the opportunity" to get in. Such a major financial obligation is best undertaken after thorough family discussion and a complete understanding of the commitment. With such a booming housing opportunity, many firms are entering the field. Some have less experience than others, and a few life care facilities have folded due to poor fiscal management. Having a family lawyer or accountant review the financial statements may be a wise precaution.

FOR ADDITIONAL INFORMATION: *Housing Options for Older Americans,* AARP Fulfillment, P.O. Box 2400, Long Beach, CA 90801; or *The Continuing Care Retirement Community: A Guidebook for Consumers,* American Association of Homes for the Aging, 1129 20th Street, N.W., Suite 400, Washington, DC 20036. (Include a self-addressed envelope with correct postage to Washington for their free brochure and $2 for the more complete handbook.)

## Facilitating the Move

Any housing situation that our parents choose that involves a move is likely to offer less living space than they had. The upkeep will be much easier, but many of our parents' possessions may need to be sold, divided among the children, or given away. The division of estates can create friction within families, and being aware of this potential has caused the invention of creative ways to avoid trouble. If it is our parents' choice to have the possessions that they cannot take with them divided among the children, the lottery system seems to be one of the fairest methods of division. Numbers based on the number of siblings are drawn from a hat. Number one has first choice of anything offered and so forth. Some children will opt for sentimental value while others prefer the monetary value. Nothing will be equal, but the choice will be theirs.

If there is anything that is true of America, it is that we are a mobile society. We have had experience moving, and if our parents have not been a part of this trend during their lives, at least there is much expertise from which to draw. There are guidebooks galore to help them every step of the way. Here are some tips to get started:

- Some of the best advice comes from the moving companies themselves. Look in the Yellow Pages under "Moving" and then call two or three of the major national firms and ask for their literature on making a safe move.

- Do the same thing with real estate companies if your parents are planning to sell their home. Even if they intend to sell it themselves, there is much they can learn from a professional approach, and reputable agencies do not mind sharing the information. Their hope, of course, is that if you decide to choose any agency, it will be theirs. There is no commitment—even if they give a thorough appraisal of the market value of your parents' home, a service that your parents should request.

- Help with a checklist of things to do before they leave: send change-of-address notices, discontinue services, close accounts, gather records, transfer insurance.

- Make a calendar with your parents, itemizing what needs to be done by which date. What may seem overwhelming at first can be chipped down to size if done over a long-enough period of time. Remember that packing only three boxes a day becomes ninety boxes at the end of a month!

- Help your parents with information to decide whether or not they intend to do their own packing. Major moving companies have detailed information on the differences in price and on how to pack, including: type of boxes to use, paper, what items go together, labeling, weight mix, etc., and, if nothing is broken, self-packing does save money. Money permitting, however, the experienced advice is to let the moving company do it. They have techniques that are sound and an enviable record of safety. Breakage is much more likely to occur with the handling of bulky furniture items than it is with the very fragile objects that concern us. An additional benefit to professional packing would be your parents' use of their home, intact, until a day or so before the move.

140

- Make sure that you are dealing with a reputable moving company; ask friends and real estate people whom they recommend. Local packers may vary in reliability, which makes local recommendations most valuable.

- Ask for a guaranteed price and not an estimate before your parents sign the contract.

- Insure the items being moved. If you have packed yourself, you may not be able to insure those items. Double-check.

- Find out if the pickup and delivery dates are guaranteed or just estimates. This varies considerably from company to company and the cost of waiting in a hotel or motel with three meals a day for a week or ten days can increase the cost of the move significantly.

- Make special arrangements for pets. Movers cannot take them. There are special containers your parents can buy from the airlines or pet shops for shipping by air or rail. Try to put pets on direct flights to avoid stress. Their vet may recommend a tranquilizer.

- Defrost and dry freezer and refrigerator the day before the move.

- Throw out all combustibles. They cannot be shipped. Candles melt in the heat of the van and should not be shipped either, and plants and bulbs are regulated by state and federal agencies. Your parents need to check with their mover as to how that might affect them. If they cannot take their plants, it could be a lovely housewarming to have some fresh greenery awaiting their arrival!

## Home Aids to Independence

Whether our parents choose to remain in the family home or to live in a more contained situation such as an apartment or condominium, there may come a time when their lifestyle becomes more difficult due to sensory loss or increased frailty. Today, there are hundreds of new products available designed specifically to aid the elderly in remaining independent, thus preserving their self-esteem. It is interesting to note that many of our parents are not particularly curious about these breakthroughs, preferring to remain with more familiar ways to operate their daily lives. Thus, they are often not the ones to shop for or discover these products. When properly introduced, however, new products can make day-to-day tasks much easier and often safer for our parents to perform—for example, cooking with a microwave oven.

Technology has made many breakthroughs that make the environment more friendly, and many more are envisioned. What a breakthrough it will be when our parents with hearing aids can enter a noisy restaurant and have their conversations amplified while the background noises are filtered out, a big improvement over the standard models of today that are based simply on amplification, making hearing in crowded places almost impossible.

With the needs of the elderly becoming of market value to many businesses, there is also a repositioning of existing products for their needs. Light switches with broad plates, designer items when they emerged a few years ago, for instance, are perfect for arthritic fingers. They can be switched on and off with the pressure of a forearm.

As the dollars warrant it, more and more products are being offered. According to Helen Harris & Associates, a market-research firm in Westport, Connecticut, as reported in the *New York Times* September 1, 1986, article "New Products for the Elderly," the market for home health care items reached $2.5 billion in 1986, with the elderly consuming by far the largest proportion.

Caretaking puts a great deal of pressure on the entire family. Our hope is that the products introduced here will be instrumental in reducing the stresses for us, the caregivers, and produce greater ease and comfort for our parents. A well-chosen product can make a major difference in the quality of a person's life.

The first step is to observe our parents' daily lives and make note of the areas that seem the most burdensome for them, whether it be getting around town or writing a letter. Secondly, we should familiarize ourselves with the products and services available in our parents' community that might be of help. Once we begin to think in a creative, problem-solving way, many other products may come to mind that were not designed specifically for the elderly but that could work beautifully in their particular situations. For instance, many of us used intercoms to hear the crying of our newborns. Now that same product could be the ideal way to avoid constant climbing of stairs when a parent is caring for an invalid spouse.

What is greeted with enthusiasm by some parents may be viewed suspiciously by others. This will be a time of trial and error for the caretaker, with an emphasis on communication. It is a time for much diplomacy. Our parents' home is no longer our home, and though we may feel the responsibility for our parents' well-being, we should avoid the appearance of "taking over." It will be difficult to handle the protests of a parent who does not want to try something new, when we know that it could be of great benefit to him or her. Perhaps an initial negative response can be overcome when the suggestion is made by someone else—a grandchild, neighbor, good friend, or doctor. Often the first step in using an aid is the most difficult, and if we can introduce products that really make life easier for our parents—clever can openers, for instance—they may be more receptive when the time comes for more personal aids, such as a cane or a walker.

HELP IN THE KITCHEN

The kitchen is a good place to start. Much thought has gone into the redesigning of everything from the position of the cabinets to the grasp on a soup spoon for those with disabilities. An overall evaluation should keep safety and convenience as the primary guidelines.

- Building cabinets low for easy access is a major renovation for an elder's kitchen, but make sure that no drawers or cabinet doors stick (a simple task with a wax bar or soap that any cook would appreciate).

- Raise the table by adding blocks of wood or risers to the legs to make wheelchair access possible.

- In order to avoid the lifting of awkward and sometimes heavy kitchen appliances, a socket strip can be installed at the back of the counter and appliances can be kept in place ready for use.

· More extensive renovation may allow you to install springboard shelves inside lower cabinets that enable anyone to lift even heavy appliances onto the countertop.

· Can your mother and father reach all that they need in the kitchen, or anywhere else in the house, without standing on footstools or bending down? "Reachers" can provide a long arm to many inaccessible places, from picking cans off the top shelf to retrieving lemons that have rolled behind a counter.

· Is standing for long periods while cooking, or even talking on a wall phone, difficult? Mobile stools (with casters) can support 90 percent of the body's weight, while providing the same eye level as for a standing person.

· A long phone cord provides more flexibility. Better still, a "hands free" phone answers automatically on a preset ring, allowing you to talk without lifting a receiver. When the caller hangs up, the unit is automatically reset to take the next call, great for when the pot is being stirred, hands are in soapy water, or when it takes too long to answer before the caller hangs up.

· If a parent is in a wheelchair, a mirror mounted at an angle at the back of the stove allows him or her to see if a rear plate is red hot or if a pot is boiling.

· And for those who worry that water might be put on for tea and forgotten, make sure that your parents have a whistling teakettle.

· Most of us use a kitchen timer that we set to ring when cooking food needs to be checked. If there are problems grasping small objects, however, our parents may find these timers can be difficult to set. Big timers, which can be wall mounted, can be set with the palm of the hand turning the large numbers.

· When limited to one good hand for cooking, a "pan holder" that attaches to the stove with suction cups will hold a pot securely in place between two steel rods, allowing safe stirring with only one hand.

· Another easy product for those with the full use of only one hand is a strainer that locks over the pot. It will not fall off and the vegetables will not go down the drain.

- Reading familiar recipes may become more difficult as eyesight fails. Large-print cookbooks make good gift items, and a Plexiglas bookholder keeps the book open to the right page.

- An electric can opener is a simple solution.

- Many of us solve the lid-opening dilemma by passing the jar on to someone who looks stronger, but undercounter jar lid openers, requiring only one hand, or lever-type jar openers are less frustrating. They do the job with a simple twist.

- If the strength of our parent's grip has been limited by a stroke, arthritis, or some other condition, there are many utensils that can compensate. Utensil handles that are curved, weighted, or oversized can be of great help, as can palm straps that require no grip. Also fork/knife or spoon/fork combinations make cutting and eating easier. There is always the electric carving knife, but handle with care.

- Rimmed plates that provide a surface to push food against avoid spills and unnecessary embarrassment. They can be placed on grip pads that insure no slipping across the table.

By now you have the idea. Where there is a problem, there is a solution.

GARDENING HELP

Stepping out of the kitchen and into the garden, we can find ways that therapeutic yard work can continue, in spite of a parent's failing strength. A back-saver rake with a unique angle allows the gardener to stand upright, with a minimum of pulling effort. Garden shears with exaggerated handles make clipping flowers or weeds an easy task, and knee pads can soften the job of weeding.

Some other garden products save time and effort while preserving the sense of satisfaction in a job well done. For example, a leaf blower is relatively light and can clear a driveway in record time. Weed- and grass-clipping machines come with nylon cords that whip around to do the job without any need for bending. Water valves that must be tight to prevent leakage can be opened easily with plastic tap turners that fit on top of a variety of faucets. Finally, garbage cans on wheels make disposing of any mess easier.

More Help for Arthritic Fingers: Have you considered a giant push-button adapter that clamps over a regular push-button telephone to make dialing easier? How about a cardholder disk, or a card shuffler for parents who like to play? If a pencil grip does not offer enough help, perhaps a slip-on writing aid would. Conceivably, the most helpful of all would be to replace all round doorknobs with flat handles that do not require a strong grip and are easy to open.

BATHROOM ASSISTANCE

Bathroom products abound, since this is an area fraught with potential dangers for the frail. Most of us are aware of the need for nonslip pads in the tub, but railings, bathtub seats and stools, tub grab bars, raised toilet seats, and nozzle attachments allowing a shower while sitting in the bathtub are all safe ways of helping our parents prevent falls. Long scrub brushes with sponges at the end make terrific gifts—or how about a hairbrush with a Velcro strap that wraps around the palm of the hand?

In order to find a full selection of products on the market, you may want to collect several catalogues. Your local hospital equipment and supply store, which can be found in the Yellow Pages of the phone book, will have the most popular products for sale, but they also stock catalogues that show more unusual products that are not profitable to maintain in stock, but that can be ordered specially. And do not ignore NARIC under the information and referral section on page 158.

MOBILITY SOLUTIONS

As our parents age, it may become increasingly difficult for them to do simple tasks such as getting in and out of a chair. A remote-control channel changer for the television set, as well as remote-control lamp and radio devices, can save much frustration for a parent who has difficulty moving. And a portable cordless telephone could be a delight to your parent. The easy-lift chair has existed for many years, but perhaps your parents are not aware of other versions of long-legged chairs with increased seat height that allow them to sit and rise with a minimum of effort.

A cane is the first step in providing support for walking. There are many styles to choose from, and your parent could even make a fashion statement. This is a good stage at which to reevaluate the layout of the rooms in our parents' home to make sure there is plenty of space to walk through without being hampered by excess furniture. Any unstable pieces of furniture that might not support your parents' weight, should they lean on them, ought to be removed. Scatter rugs should be tacked down and lamps or other fragile objects that could topple over should be secured or removed.

If a walker is needed, it is even more important to have all doorways unencumbered so that the elder can be encouraged to exercise and is not dissuaded by tight passageways that make movement a formidable challenge. There is an array of accessories that can be attached to the walker that hold everything from eyeglasses to a bag of groceries.

Should your parent ever need a wheelchair, you might be pleasantly surprised at their maneuverability, flexibility, and portability. Of course, the need for a wheelchair may make a stair seat necessary, or a lift, depending on the construction of the home.

Twentieth-century engineering has made it possible for elders with walking handicaps to be able to cover distances in style with such products as electric scooters. Designed to mimic a golf cart, they are sleek and smooth and easy to operate. With baskets to hold purchases, they are also very functional. On some, the seat swivels and allows the elder to position himself or herself at a desk or dining-room table.

There are many products available, and we should become familiar with them to enable our parents to experience maximum freedom and independence for as long as possible.

Again, this is a time to remember that it is our parents' home, and though we are motivated by concern for their well-being, we must also show respect for their feelings by proceeding slowly with change and by involving them in the decision-making.

FOR MORE INFORMATION: For *Helping People to Help Themselves* and *Aids to Independence,* write: Health Care Products, Dixon, Inc., P.O. Box 1449, Grand Junction, CO 81502, or telephone toll-free (800) 433-4926; *Comfortably Yours, Aids for Easier Living,* 52 W. Hunter Avenue, Maywood, NJ 07607; (201) 368-0400 (this catalogue has some products, but is primarily clothing); *Enrichments, Helping Hands for Special Needs,* Brissell Health Care Corporation, 145 Tower Drive, P.O. Box 579, Hinsdale, IL 60521 (a wide variety of products, including aids for the home and communication aids).

## Safety Tips

Most safety is a matter of common sense, which is the same for our parents as for all of us. The only difference may be that our parents become more vulnerable targets for crime, as they are less able to defend themselves. The truth is that more older people die from falls in the home than from being mugged. But the perception of themselves as victims can be damaging. The sense of confidence that results from the proper precautions can be as helpful as the precautions themselves.

The following lists some of the easy ways in which we can help prevent our parents from becoming victims of crime, as well as assist them in avoiding common accidents in and around the home.

- Install smoke alarms.

- Reduce water heater temperature to prevent burns.

- Add handrails along hallways to aid an unsteady walker.

- Eliminate throw rugs, or make sure edges are tacked down.

- Keep staircases uncluttered to avoid tripping.

- Remove objects still in use from any high shelves in closets and cabinets to avoid the temptation of using a stepladder.

- Write out emergency phone numbers by each phone.
- Make sure the entry to the house or apartment is well lighted.
- Stairwells to attic and basement also should be well lighted.
- Check wiring throughout the house, particularly if parents have lived there for many years.
- Examine lamps for shaky bases and frayed wires.
- Make sure no electrical wires are camouflaged under rugs where they can become worn.
- In rural areas with no streetlights, install outdoor floodlights that are activated by darkness.
- Plug in night-lights, so your parents can see when getting up at night.
- Consider attaching glow tape (as used in the theater) to objects that need to be identified in the dark—light switches, for example.
- Have working flashlights available in the home and the car.
- Consider installing a burglar alarm—some have emergency buttons that alert the police, firemen, and/or ambulance.
- A watchdog can give a sense of security if it suits your parents' temperament.
- Install locks on all windows, dead-bolt locks on all doors.
- Good rapport with neighbors is always a plus.
- Never put a name and address on key chains.
- Do not hide keys near the house door.
- Consider having an automatic garage door and/or gate opener.
- Install a peephole in the front door.
- Use an initial in the phone book as opposed to a female first name.
- Have all deliveries stopped when parents are out of town.
- Arrange to have the lawn mowed, garbage put out on appointed day.
- Leave lights and radio on timers when going out at night.

· Suggest that your mother avoid carrying a shoulder purse that can pull her down if it is snatched.

· Insist on their fastening safety belts when riding in a car.

· Try to have your parents find a companion for outings to avoid walking alone.

· Have Social Security and retirement checks sent directly to the bank.

According to the experts, the most common crimes against the elderly are purse snatching, consumer fraud, theft of checks from the mail, and vandalism. With proper precautions and an alert attitude, our parents should never number in any of these statistics.

## Transportation

AUTOMOBILE MATTERS

Whenever adult children gather to share their concerns about caretaking, the issue of their parents' driving surfaces as an area of major concern. Everyone has a story about a near accident, and such incidents escalate the fear of letting parents drive. Many adult children simply refuse to allow their own children to drive with their grandparents when they feel that their parents' driving has become too dangerous. But that does not alleviate the fear for the safety of our parents. In America, the male ego seems to be inextricably related to his automobile. The car becomes an extension of his personality and a validation of his independence. Some women have the same love affair with their cars, but the attachment does not seem as permanent. Telling such a parent that he or she is too old to drive may be the equivalent in their eyes of saying that their independent life has come to a screeching halt! They will not relinquish the keys without a fight.

Some alternative transportation methods meet with less resistance than others. Perhaps one of the following solutions would be the right one for your parents.

1. Create a driving agreement. Ask that driving time be limited to daylight hours and to clear driving conditions, no rain, no snow.

2. Hire a driver for heavy traffic situations and for night driving to ease into a gradual takeover. This could be a perfect opportunity for good intergenerational contact, particularly if a grandchild lives nearby. The experience of the grandparent and the quick reflexes of the grandchild could create a terrific partnership. Scheduling might be the biggest hurdle.

3. Use taxis (or car service) for the same situations as the above with the eventual goal of replacing the car. There are valid economic arguments for this arrangement, as it is far less expensive than the total cost of running a car, when insurance, gasoline, maintenance, and repairs are considered. In order to overcome their parents' notion that the use of a taxi is a waste of money, or that taxis should be taken only when absolutely necessary, some adult children have convinced their parents to take the equivalent money that would have been put into the use of a car over the course of a month and put it in a "taxi fund." Knowing that the money is readily available breaks down some of the psychological resistance to taxis and restores a feeling of independence.

You also will find free taxi service to the handicapped in some areas. (San Francisco offers this to four thousand of its citizens, but budget limitations in 1987 left another five hundred on the waiting list.)

4. Use paratransit and public transportation alternatives. Here, some exploration of exactly what is available in your parents' area is necessary. Paratransit, which is transportation especially funded for the elderly and the handicapped, is available in some communities, but not all. If you live in one of ten counties in southeast Tennessee, for example, your parents will not have a problem. Through their human resource agency there are vans available to drive them anywhere in town for 35 cents one way. Just call the day before to say where they need to be picked up and where they want to go. In certain major metropolitan areas such as Atlanta, Georgia, some of the municipal buses are equipped to take wheelchair riders. An added incentive is that many towns offer specially reduced fares for senior citizens. In larger urban areas, there are often many programs that allow reduced rates or

151

free public transportation for seniors. Some of these programs are run through senior centers, where transportation to shopping centers is offered on a regular basis. Church groups are another source of possible transportation—for recreation as well as regular shopping needs. The trick is to get through to the right agency. Many of these programs are budgeted through the cities. City Hall is a good place to start your calls, or in the government listing pages at the front of the White Pages of your phone book, under "Senior Services." Ask specific questions and prepare to spend some time on the phone. Fielding this kind of bureaucratic runaround for our parents can be a big gift to them.

Whichever solution works for you, it is a good idea to start the habit now. It is important to short-circuit the notion that when your parents no longer drive, you will be the logical one to turn to for transportation. Many of us, as adult children, are so sympathetic to our parents' diminishing capabilities in this area that we make great promises to fill the void, thus putting unnecessary stress on ourselves while further diminishing our parents' independence. Finding solutions in which they can fend for themselves is the greatest gift that we can give them.

**Points to Remember**

· Identify housing possibilities for your well parents:
—living in their own single-family residence
—renting an apartment
—buying a condominium
—buying into a co-op
—buying a mobile home
—sharing their home with others
—moving into congregate housing
—moving into a life care community

· Find out about housing possibilities within their community. Lack of choice may warrant considering a move.

· Review the lifestyle choices that concern them the most, for example:
—financial security
—personal safety
—companionship
—privacy
—freedom from maintenance chores
—intergenerational contact
—communal support
—gardening possibilities

· Relate their lifestyle choices and financial means to available housing options.

· Review safety tips.

*Chapter 6*

# Reaching Out: Community Support Services

FINDING physical aids to help our parents is just one step in enabling them to be more independent. The next step may be to tap into community resources designed to provide a variety of services that help them to maintain this independent lifestyle. These resource services can be our partners in the caretaking responsibilities for our parents. Although caretaking has been a family duty for a long time—particularly within certain ethnic groups—as we have seen, it is obvious that the two-career couple and the single-parent family preclude full-time caretaking. We should consider the care of our parents a joint endeavor with church, synagogue, and community service organizations to maximize the possibilities for them. Here we shall review some of the most popular services that are likely to be available within your community. You should, however, explore beyond those mentioned, since wonderful new experimental programs are continuously springing up throughout the United States.

We stated earlier that there is more divergency among the over-sixty-five age group in America than in any other segment of our society. Some of our parents are years away from needing any of these services, and some of our mothers are married to older men who are showing the signs of aging much more than they themselves are. At what point do we, the adult children, determine that outside help is needed? Age certainly is not the determining factor. Nor is waiting for our parents to ask for help the solution.

154

We all know that our parents are quite likely to shield us from their own frailty or needs in an attempt to protect us, and to protect their own pride. Social workers and case managers tell us that knowing when to institute service programs can be one of the most difficult tasks for adult children. We, too, often suffer from denial of our parents' aging, while some of us indulge in overprotective behavior.

The real problem is finding a way to merge our needs and desired results with those of our parents. We may find an easier, quicker way to do something that would give us the satisfaction of knowing that we have solved a problem, only to discover that our parents enjoy the routine of the "old-fashioned" way. A home delivery grocery service, for example, may save our parents much effort, but it may also deny them the joy of the social contact involved with shopping for themselves. It could eliminate what might be the only exercise of the day, and possibly the only outside activity. For a parent fully involved with volunteer or other activities, however, a grocery delivery service might be the ideal solution. The balancing act is difficult and very individual.

The reason we worry so much about our responsibilities to our parents is that caretaking involves a complex set of decisions that relate to a constantly changing situation. There is no barometer to tell us if our choices are correct, and a happy ending is not guaranteed. Knowing that the enormity of the weight of our responsibility is understood by health care professionals can be a tremendous support for us. In other words, turning to community services for some relief may be as important for our own well-being as it is for that of our parents. There is no question that in the end, how well our parents fare is directly related to our own level of stress.

## Community Links

There are two community links that may be unknown to most caregivers. One is a result of technological advances, and the second fills a basic human need.

The most direct link for our parents to a community service is an actual implement that is worn around the neck of the elder with a panic button for help in emergencies. This button, available from Lifeline Systems, Inc., 1 Arsenal Marketplace, Watertown, MA 02172; (617) 923-4141, activates a home unit attached to the telephone, which automatically dials the community emergency response center. There are a number of other companies that offer similar products, some of which even have voice-to-voice home response systems ("Listen in Program," Mark Corporation, P.O. Box 1532, Westford, MA 01886) and some camouflage the transmitter in a necklace or bracelet ("Careline," William Agency, 45 Acorn Circle, 102, Towson, MD 21204). One program for the elderly and disabled run by the District of Columbia Government's Office on Aging has a system that is linked directly to major municipal fire department alarm centers. Often these systems are used by parents who live alone and who say that they wear the device for the peace of mind of their children!

A far more personal link to the community is provided for many elders through the Senior Companion Program funded by the national volunteer agency ACTION. Most senior companions serve the homebound elderly to help them with difficult chores, as well as provide a buffer against loneliness and isolation. The volunteers themselves are seniors, which often leads to developing friendships while providing a vital link to appropriate community services. Write to: ACTION, the National Volunteer Agency, Washington, DC 20525.

## Informational and Referral Services

Making the decision to use a community resource is a lot easier when we know what is available. The whole process of finding the right service can be frustrating and time-consuming. It is better to explore the possibilities in your community before the need for the service arises than to wait until a time of crisis, when it will be much more difficult to make an intelligent decision.

The information and referral services that are most likely to be available within most communities are these:

156

- The Administration on Aging has area agencies in most communities throughout the United States, including state units and over 672 area agencies. These are designated by the governor or the legislature of the state, and respond to all matters that relate to the needs of the elderly in the community. Local Area Agencies on Aging (AAA) have different names, so finding them may be a two-call task. The local government (City Hall) should be able to refer you to "Senior Information and Referral," or the correct name and number of your area agency. See the listing at the end of the book for the state AAA, which could also put you in touch with the local agency.

- The Administration on Aging, under the auspice of the Office of Human Development Services, Department of Health and Human Services, 200 Independence Avenue, S.W., Washington, DC 20201, publishes a bimonthly magazine, *Aging*, which has informative articles that focus on successful ongoing programs concerned with all aspects of aging throughout the United States. In addition to feature articles, this magazine lists new publications, news articles, and exchange experiences. A subscription costs $15 per year.

- Your local library is always a good source of lists of city, state and federal agencies. The local Department of Public Health publishes an annual information and referral guide called *Resources Guide of Services for Seniors* in some cities.

- Religious organizations often have their own extensive elder support systems. Check with your church or synagogue as to what is available through them, or look in the White Pages of the phone book under your religious preference to see the services listed, for example, the Catholic Committee for the Aging or Jewish Family and Children Services.

- Another place to seek information may be where you work. Corporate America, awakening to the needs and time restraints of its employees vis-à-vis elder care, is beginning to provide information and referral services (see chapter 11).

- Community umbrella organizations, such as the United Way, and community centers may be able to refer you to the appropriate help.

157

- Hospitals, particularly those with geriatric or rehabilitation centers, should have reliable information about helpful local organizations.

- The Yellow Pages generally provide listings of private as well as public services under "Home Health Services." Check these listings with your parents' doctor, hospital, social worker, or health organizations for their personal recommendations.

- If your parents are suffering from a specific ailment, contact one of the many national health-related organizations for help, such as the American Cancer Society, American Heart Association, Arthritis Foundation, American Foundation for the Blind, American Diabetes Association. Local chapters of these national organizations are found in communities across America. In addition to information on the diseases, they are also good contacts for finding support groups consisting of others who are facing a similar crisis.

- The National Rehabilitation Information Center (NARIC) is funded by the National Institute on Disability and Rehabilitation Research, United States Department of Education. NARIC, a rich source of information, is equipped to meet specific needs as they relate to understanding and coping with a particular disability. Call their toll-free number and a representative will listen to your situation and provide appropriate literature. As important as the literature are the product suggestions that are made to help our parents function with greater ease. For personal assistance call: (800) 34-NARIC.

- There are numerous national associations that elders can join that offer a variety of literature on all aspects of aging, from housing to insurance, from psychological support (how to deal with the death of a spouse) to travel. The American Association of Retired People (AARP) is by far the largest such organization. The $5 membership fee for members—fifty and older—entitles your parent to the bimonthly magazine *Modern Maturity,* the monthly news bulletin of AARP, and plenty of support literature and senior discounts. Write: AARP Membership, 1909 K Street, N.W., Washington, DC 20049. (See appendix 1 for names and addresses of other national associations.)

- There are also independent newsletters and magazines to which our parents, or we as caregivers, can subscribe. For example,

*Advice for Adults with Aging Parents or a Dependent Spouse* is a bimonthly newsletter that helps caregivers maximize the independence of their aging parents while providing information geared to minimize the stress of the caregiver. It focuses on practical day-to-day coping mechanisms. Write to: Helping Publications, Inc., P.O. Box 339, Glenside, PA 19038 ($14 per year at date of publication).

- The National Association for Home Care—for information about home care agencies, this national clearinghouse makes available for $2 a consumer's guide, *All About Home Care,* and a free guide, *How to Select a Home Care Agency.* Write to them at: 519 C Street, N.E., Stanton Park, Washington, DC 20002.

- Contact your local medical association or the gerontology department of a nearby medical school or university for referral to geriatricians, counselors, or psychologists. They also may be able to help you find assistance programs for your parents.

## Case Management

As adult children, we may be too emotionally involved or inexperienced to objectively and knowledgeably determine our parents' needs. Many of the organizations listed above have on staff case management workers whose job it is to evaluate our parents' situation. Often, this service includes a home visit. These evaluations are quite thorough, including assessment of psychological and social needs in addition to solving the usual physical problems. It is the case manager, for instance, who might recommend a senior companion for an elder who is in relatively good health, but who shows signs of loneliness. In another situation, a couple whose nutrition seems neglected might have a home-delivered meals program recommended.

One important service provided by the case manager is the constant monitoring of the situation with follow-up calls to make sure that the programs are doing the job. As anyone knows who cares for the elderly on a regular basis, putting a new program into place is just the first step. Making sure that the service is being properly provided and, more importantly, that the elder is accepting the service are two very important components.

If a case manager is not being used, it is important for the caregiver to periodically review the services provided. Jennifer was appalled at her parents' poor eating habits, and when a friend told her of Meals on Wheels, she was delighted with the simplicity of the solution. She arranged for two meals a day to be delivered to her parents' home. When Jennifer visited her parents a week later, she found stacks of trays of uneaten food. What Jennifer thought was the complete solution to the problem was only a partial one. The next step for Jennifer was to find out what her parents' objections were to the program and then to solve the new problem.

As the aging population has grown, so has the demand for case managers. Many nonprofit agencies and religious organizations have entered the case management field. The fee for case management agency services generally is based on a sliding scale. It is estimated that some two hundred private firms have entered the field in the past few years. These for-profit businesses vary widely in their costs, but the average caseworker charges are between $45 and $85 an hour.

A fairly new networking service is now available to serve those of us who are long-distance caregivers. When the caregiver lives too far away to be available at a moment's notice, it is a relief to know that a case manager can visit our parents, assess their needs, and refer us to the appropriate services, which can actually provide the necessary help.

With so many newcomers in the networking business, it is important to get good references and to carefully check their credentials. Your parents' doctor may be able to recommend a good service, or you can check with any of the informational and referral services listed above. Certain religious organizations have been successful in developing their own long-distance networking of case managers.

## Home Care Services

*Homemaker services.* Again, the key to proper help for your parents is understanding what their real needs are. If their health is fairly good but failing eyesight or energy has made household chores difficult, homemaker services may be all that are needed. As the name implies, these workers can do all of the household work that a homemaker does, in addition to grocery shopping, running errands, walking the dog, and perhaps even handling the household bills. The private sector and many nonprofit organizations provide this service, the latter on a sliding payment scale. The overworked caregiver can consider this a good delegation of responsibility, which frees personal time or provides time for more enjoyable pursuits with our parents.

*Home health care services.* The home health care service worker plays a different role. He or she provides care for all physical needs, including feeding, changing, dressing, bathing, toilet needs, and shaving. Under a doctor's or nurse's supervision, this care may include giving pills, eyedrops, insulin shots, and so forth. These services are particularly useful if a parent is recovering from a hospital stay or even if he or she is fighting a bout of the flu.

*Home-delivered meals.* Many agencies, as well as religious organizations, offer home-delivered meals. Meals on Wheels, one such popular service for hot and cold meals, is a federal nutrition program for the elderly that contracts out to local agencies, who actually administer it. Again, the fee is on a sliding scale, and the program depends on volunteers for delivery. Not only are the meals nutritionally balanced, but there are ethnic choices available based on the community needs. In addition, soft meals can be ordered for those with dental problems, and dietary restrictions are taken into consideration. This program can be used for as many as two meals per day, or to supplement your parents' needs—weekends, every other day. The White Pages in most communities list "Meals on Wheels," or you can contact your area agency on aging for this and other meal programs available in your community.

*In-Home Supported Services* (IHSS) is the largest publicly (federal and state) funded service to provide nonmedical help to the functionally impaired. This program allows the frail with very limited resources to remain in their homes, while IHSS pays for workers, or contracts with various agencies, to perform special services based on need with a maximum of twenty hours per week. Household services often include cleaning, cooking, laun-

161

dry, shopping. Personal care services may be for feeding, dressing, bathing, and even bowel and bladder care. Other services are paramedical, transportation to medical appointments, and protective supervision. Persons sixty-five or over, blind or disabled, and economically disadvantaged qualify for IHSS, provided they are not able to stay in their homes without such services. Call your local department of social services or Area Agency on Aging (AAA) for further information if your parents qualify, and persevere. Like most free programs, the price you pay is time.

*Miscellaneous home services.* With time at a premium for many of us, the world of commerce has made it possible to shop for practically everything from home. This convenience for the career worker can be a boon to our parents. A variety of home shopping catalogues can provide entertainment and service in our parents' living room. Or our parents can join the latest craze of shopping by television through the cable network channels. Most communities have stores with home grocery delivery, and take-out-food restaurants that deliver. Cleaning and laundry services also offer home delivery. One can bank by mail—a good safety measure—pay bills by phone (contact your local bank for this service), and, in some communities, take advantage of mobile clinics.

Communities differ in how they provide for their elderly. The information and referral sources in this book can help you to determine what unique services are available in your particular area. In certain communities—San Francisco, for instance—the fears of the elderly who hesitated to go out from home alone were somewhat allayed by the formation of the Police Department's Senior Escort Outreach Program. Any elder citizen of the community may call for an escort to accompany him or her for shopping, trips to the bank, to the Medicare office, or other errands. The program has expanded to offer recreational outings for small groups of elders, such as ferryboat rides and excursions to the park. Some communities offer Friendship Lines for the elderly, which provide daily telephone contact. If an elder fails to call in, a community worker will phone or otherwise make contact to assure the well-being of the elder. Check your parents' community to find out the options available to them.

## Mutual Support Groups

We have discussed in chapter 1 the reasons for support groups for the caregiver and how to find them. Support groups can be a great help to all members of the family. As the needs of those in stress are more openly recognized, support groups are forming in a growing number of communities. An estimated 450 to 500 local groups exist across the country, in addition to those affiliated with larger organizations. These include caregiver support groups, groups for the adult children of aging parents, outreach programs for widows and widowers, and support groups pertaining to a particular disease or condition such as Alzheimer's, cancer, or alcoholism. They allow people who have common concerns to share their feelings in a confidential and supportive environment. Support groups are often facilitated by social workers or clergy, who encourage the members to express themselves and to take care of themselves. Such groups often teach us new ways of coping, while networking with others in similar situations. The need to share our problems is so basic that, in the absence of formal groups, those with like concerns—such as widows—often gather on their own for mutual support.

Family counseling is also available through the community in both the profit and nonprofit sectors. Even close families can benefit from the objective advice of trained counselors during this unusually stressful time in their lives. The stresses of family caregiving affect everyone, often creating rifts among siblings, tension between husbands and wives, and a feeling of abandonment by the children of the caregivers.

FOR FURTHER INFORMATION: Check local sources, including the mental health association and "Social Service Organizations" in the Yellow Pages, or write to: Children of Aging Parents, 2761 Trenton Road, Levittown, PA 19056, or call (215) 945-6900. Send a self-addressed, stamped envelope for a list of CAPS support groups in other states, information on long-distance case management workers, the name of a local self-help group, or the price of a kit on how to start one.

## Points to Remember

· Investigate panic buttons to be worn for emergencies.

· See if a Senior Companion Program exists in your parents' community.

· Become familiar with all the information and referral services for caretakers.

· Alert your parents to the national associations for seniors, such as AARP.

· Institute home-delivered meals and homemaker services as needed.

· Explore home health care services.

· Learn about eligibility for In-Home Supported Services (IHSS).

· Discover what mutual support groups exist within the community.

# Chapter 7

# Money Matters: Financial Planning, Retirement, and the Paperwork of Aging

Financial planning is a lot more than dusty wills and trusts. It is taking a comprehensive overview of our parents' assets and future needs. Once we know the picture, and then thoughtfully factor in the desires of our parents, an overall strategy can be formulated to calm the difficult emotional, financial, and legal problems that inevitably ensue. Helping our parents to see and understand the benefits of sharing this responsibility with us will help to eliminate the added stress related to the sudden illness or death of our parents. Developing a plan together can also help create a real bond as we consider the option of our parents' early retirement and the economic problems created by the increasing possibility of an extended life-span.

Discussing this subject with our parents is never easy. It is an emotional interplay of psychological forces between parent and child. We, the children, often denying the inevitability of our parent's death or possible infirmity, avoid or delay resolving the issues. Our parents, avoiding the fact of their own mortality, and being reluctant to give up any kind of control, also put off discussing this with us.

Contrary to popular belief, good financial planning does not mean relinquishing control. It actually allows our parents to control their lives and finances until the very end, and it gives us the assurance that their wishes have been carried out. Proper financial planning will eliminate unnecessary emotional and financial costs to the family. It can also reduce taxes, provide proper medical coverage, avoid family conflict, and reduce probate costs and legal fees.

The matters of old-age division of property and burial arrangements can produce lingering anxiety for our parents. Experienced estate planners and probate attorneys tell us that once these matters have been decided, a real burden is lifted from the parent, as well as from the child who assists with this process. It becomes increasingly prudent to seek informed advice as to the many options now available in planning for our parents' future.

The first step in the financial-planning process is to become informed. That means gathering all the facts and knowing what the choices are. One could read forty books on trusts, taxes, finances, and the like and still not gain the skills to do it alone. What follows is information on some of the most likely areas of concern for the adult children of aging parents. This is an opportunity for us to familiarize ourselves with the various options that we will need to consider when attempting to help our parents in preparing for their future.

## Tax Considerations

Before your parents prepare their federal and state income tax returns, phone the IRS at 800-424-1040 and ask for copies of the following helpful booklets: #524—Credit for the Elderly; #554—Tax Information for Older Americans; #575—Pensions and Annuity Income.

You may also want to ask the IRS for the Tax Counseling for the Elderly (TEC) office closest to your parents' home. These volunteer TEC counselors are trained with the cooperation of the IRS and the Franchise Tax Board. Counselors are recruited by the American Association of Retired Persons and many are retirees with considerable tax experience. When we called in mid-March, we discovered that tax counseling was available from January 1 through April 15 and only one day a week at the center nearest our homes. All of the appointment times had been filled.

The volunteers were happy to refer us to other centers around the city, however, where we might get an appointment. We recommend, therefore, that you call as close to January 1 as possible to assure your parents of an appointment.

## Retirement

When Social Security legislation was passed in 1935, the age sixty-five had been commonly thought of as the "normal" retirement age. Today, however, most retirees leave work before they reach the age of sixty-five, according to a 1985 report of the Special Committee on Aging of the U.S. Senate. Eighty percent take the opportunity to retire when it is offered. Early retirement may now be a permanent fixture of the American lifestyle. Congress has sought to delay the retirement age, through the passage of the Social Security amendments of 1983. According to the National Commission for Employment Policy, research showed that a delay in Social Security benefits, which would be extended a full two years by the year 2027, would have a minimal effect on the age of retirement and would only raise the average retirement age by then by about three months.

These statistics contradict the popular notion that we will be working longer because we are living longer, healthier lives. They confirm that employers will have to come up with some rather enticing benefits packages if they are going to be able to keep their older workers.

While generally anticipated as the "golden years," the early years of retirement are often a period of frustration, depression, and difficult adjustments. When one's identity has been a function of what one does for so many years, the loss of a job, and more importantly the job title, can leave the retiree feeling stripped of his or her identity. The pattern of retirees becoming depressed or even sick shortly after they leave their jobs is a common one, but giving thoughtful consideration to the transition into retirement will help to eliminate this possibility.

Retirement is becoming an established institution that requires as much, if not more, careful planning than our school and our work years. The definition should be changed, for it now means the beginning of another quarter century of productive years. It takes on a different meaning for everyone. For some it is an opportunity to spend more time with the family or to travel. For others, it is a time to cultivate new hobbies or to give more time to those activities already enjoyed. Still others prefer part-time employment, a second career, political involvement, complete immersion in community affairs, or any of the many opportunities discussed in chapter 4.

Telling our parents about these activities may not be enough, however. A gentle push, perhaps in the form of an invitation to an activity after a lunch date with them, may insure their initial participation if they seem reluctant to follow through on their own.

In spite of the marvelous opportunities available and the example of many extraordinary elders before them, some of our contemporaries still hear the familiar complaint: "My mother is going crazy. My father retired from his job three months ago. Not only doesn't he have anything to do, but he wants my mother to stop everything and do nothing with him!"

The effect of a parent retiring can be devastating on family life. Understanding the stress that may be created with such a radical change in our parents' daily lifestyle is a major step in helping them cope. So much stress can be relieved simply by allowing a parent to vent his or her frustrations.

"If you want to get something done, ask a busy person" has been the motto of good delegators for years. When someone has too much time in which to do the activities of the day, less actually gets accomplished. Encouraging our parents to create a daily schedule is one way to avoid having the day escape with nothing to show for it. Whatever our parents choose, the old notion of spending these years rocking on the porch is not a valid option when one considers that retirement will extend for more than a quarter of a century for many of our parents. Planning for retirement is a key to making it happen.

A free pamphlet produced by the American Association of Retired Persons is a helpful guide for our parents who are planning for their retirement. Write: *Planning Your Retirement*, AARP, Fulfillment, P.O. Box 2400, Long Beach, CA 90801.

## Financial Issues

As crucial as deciding how one spends retirement days is deciding how to pay for these twenty-five (plus or minus) years of extra
days! This is as crucial for us as for our parents. Approximately
20 percent of the population is retired now. Sixty million Americans will be retired with the last of the baby-boomers. Let us
explore the financial issues our parents face.

REAL ESTATE

We know that older Americans have approximately $600 billion
tied up in equity in their homes. If our parents are fortunate
enough to own a home, they probably have substantial equity in
that home. This equity can represent a good deal of financial
security in their later years, and they do not have to break the
piggy bank (sell the house) in order to use the money. Some
methods for tapping this equity include:

1. *Sale leaseback.* This is a method of turning one's capital, which is
   tied up in the real estate of one's home, into cash without
   forfeiting the use of the property. The house is sold to a buyer
   and our parents sign a lease with the new owner allowing them
   to continue to live in the house for a specified time at a specified
   rental. Usually the lease states that it extends for the duration of
   the seller's life. This option has certain advantages and disadvantages. For example, the house is no longer in our parents'
   estate, but the money received is. Money invested from this sale
   can generate income. Now consider: Are our parents in an age
   range in which the increased income will affect their Social
   Security benefits? Be sure and get legal counsel.
2. *Reverse annuity mortgage.* This is a vehicle for creating monthly
   income for seniors by making use of the untapped equity in
   their homes. If an elder person is on a fixed income and cannot
   qualify for a loan but owns a home with substantial equity, a
   bank will write a loan based on the equity in the home and the
   owner's life expectancy. The amount of the loan will be paid out
   to the borrower in monthly payments, thereby giving the senior
   a monthly source of income. The elder maintains the right to

live in the home until death or sale of the property, at which time the bank settles the account with the estate.

These loans are not commonly made and are only available to date in thirteen states, although there is much action being directed toward legislative initiatives in senior advocacy groups, such as AARP, which is pushing hard for a reverse mortgage insurance demonstration project, in the hopes of assuaging lenders' and homeowners' fears of the risks of this little-tried funding vehicle. The key element of this federal demonstration project, according to AARP, will be the provision of FHA insurance to protect homeowners and lenders from default.

3. *Deferred payment loan plan.* A flexible plan designed to create available cash when needed. The equity value in our parents' home would be used as a line of credit, allowing them to draw from it as they need it. The interest on a deferred loan is allowed to accrue and is then added to the principal when the loan is repaid. The loan is due and payable upon death of the homeowner or sale of the property.

Considering the complexities of these transactions and their even more difficult interrelationships with estate planning, it is critical that your professional adviser be correctly chosen.

## Choosing an Attorney, Accountant, or Financial Planner

One should take a great deal of care in choosing a professional. It must be someone with whom our parents are comfortable, particularly since many of their generation have a mistrust of lawyers. We need to take the time to shop for the right person and the right location. It may take several trips to his or her office before the process is completed. We should consider that our parents may be planning to move, and estate planning must conform to the laws of the state of their residence. Poor Tilly and Mort spent $2,500 with a New York financial planner only to find that when they moved to Arizona (a community property state), their plan was unacceptable under Arizona law!

Most states have lawyer referral services listed in the Yellow Pages, and you may find this helpful. An initial consultation at which your parents can get a feel for the personality and experience of the attorney is usually available at a minimal charge. Many local bar associations have developed panels of attorneys experienced in "elderlaw," an emerging legal specialty.

Of course, our parents already may have had dealings with a professional whom they like. In that case, there are questions that must be asked. Is this person the right one for the job? Different areas of expertise must come together. The financial planner, for example, will summarize the assets with probable future income and make estimates. He or she can address such issues as maximizing return and controlling risk through portfolio diversification. An accountant may be useful to point out tax-saving opportunities and pitfalls. A qualified insurance agent understands the interrelationship of Medicare, Social Security, hospitalization and private insurance plans. His or her recommendations may be vital. In some instances, insurance proceeds can pay large estate taxes. Depending on the facts, a competent estate planner (a lawyer) may be required to draft complex trusts and/or wills.

The expertise of the professionals often overlaps. When choosing these individuals, put their qualifications ahead of friendship. You may also want to ask whether home or hospital visits can be arranged.

PREPARING FOR THE FIRST WORKING SESSION

Before the first visit there are a few questions that you may want to ask of the prospective attorney or financial planner to help with your selection:

- How long has he or she practiced in the present location? How long in the community?

- Where did he or she go to law school? What degree does the financial planner hold?

- What is his or her area of expertise?

- Ask for the names of several clients for references.

171

· Discuss and understand the fee structure before hiring the professional. It is customary that he or she confirm the rates in a letter to you. Are they competitive?

When preparing for the first visit, our parents should ask in advance what they will need to bring along. A summary of their retirement benefits, deeds that show precisely how our parents hold title to real and personal property (homes and cars), our parents' previous tax returns, any other wills or trusts that they have set up, their insurance policies, any outstanding loans, and a list of their assets and liabilities. They might also include a list of the areas they are interested in covering—wills, trusts, special needs trusts, conservatorship, power of attorney and durable power of attorney, gifting, special treatment of residence, division of assets, and so forth.

PERSONAL ESTATE PLANNING

Estate planning is good preparation. When it comes time to carry out any of these plans, particularly when they involve illness or death, it will be an emotionally difficult period and a good time to rely on advance preparation as well as close family, close friends, and the community for support. In addition to carrying out the wishes of our parents for the distribution of their estate, much estate planning should focus *in advance* on the possibility of long-term hospitalization and mental incapacitation. As we'll discuss in chapter 10, Alzheimer's and other dementias can be devastating to a family. Personal and real property belonging to a person disabled by severe brain damage cannot be transferred after the fact without enormous tax consequences to the estate. In considering all estate planning, how our parents hold title to their property and whether or not they make use of the laws of partition are of great importance. Consult a professional in the field for your parents' specific needs.

(NOTE: If your parents' finances do not permit them to hire an attorney for any of these issues concerning property, estates, wills, and trusts, there are programs that provide both legal advice and legal representation in court to elderly and low-income persons.

For information, contact the local bar association or the Area Agency on Aging.)

## Wills, Trusts, and Transfers

A will directs what is to be done with a person's money and property upon death. Without a will, all choice is gone and one's money and property (estate) will be distributed according to the laws of the state of residence. Our parents' wishes and what the legislature has decreed, in the event of intestacy (no valid will), are probably quite different.

Eric wanted his wife, Madeleine, to have his home and bank accounts upon his death. Because he used the wrong words on the deed to his home and the bank signature card, however, when he died intestate (without a will) the laws of his state of residency required that Madeleine get only one-half of his estate and their four renegade children share in the remaining half. Elderly, widowed Madeleine must now sell her home to pay off the estranged children.

If it is hard to broach the subject of wills with your parents, you might try bringing up the subject by discussing your own personal wills with them to solicit their advice. By breaking the ice in this way, your parents may be more willing to discuss their own wills. All wills should be revised periodically as circumstances change—new grandchildren, death of spouse, change in tax laws, and so forth.

### THE EXECUTOR

When writing their will, our parents will be asked to name an executor and an alternate in case their first choice is unable or unwilling to serve. This executor may be a friend or a family member. It is generally preferable that the executor be a resident of their state. The executor is responsible for the care and handling of the estate and can be held personally liable for the estate in the event his or her duties are not faithfully executed. Depending on the size and complexity of the estate, the task of the executor could range from simply signing a few forms all the way to running a complicated business and having to direct a team of lawyers, accountants, and specialized financial advisers.

Our parents should consider several questions when appointing an executor, and it is good for us to be aware of the complexities of the job as well, should we be asked to assume such responsibilities.

- Is the executor willing and able to assume these duties?

- Is the executor likely to be alive and well when the need arises?

- In most states, the executor is entitled to a fee equal to or sometimes greater than the lawyer's fee. Will the executor waive the fee?

- To insure the honesty and care required of the executor, most states require an insurance policy for him or her (a bond). The annual premium could be substantial. Are our parents significantly sure of the ability and the integrity of both the executor and possible alternate to waive the bond and save the premium?

A HOLOGRAPHIC WILL

A holographic will (written entirely in one's own handwriting) can supersede any printed will. It does not require a lawyer or a witness. The individual writing the will must expressly indicate in the document that it is a will, and it must be dated and signed. Some states no longer require that the date appear on the will. It is only important in those cases that the court can determine when the will was written. Some attorneys tell us that to be safe, date it. It is a good idea to date and sign each page and to include the time of day. The hour is particularly important if the individual is on any medication. If your parents are ill, one or several witnesses are advisable. The wording is important, because the intent is not enough. For example, "I wish to leave my house to my daughter" is not sufficient. "I leave my house to my daughter" is correct. Of course, there is no problem if the will is not contested, but just in case, it is better to have written it correctly.

Every state has its own variations on what constitutes a valid holographic will. In some states, writing on preprinted stationery

174

could invalidate the will. In other states, the addition of a witness or a notary signing the will could have it thrown out of probate court. Most people using holographic wills do so because the size of their estate is too small to warrant a lawyer's fees. Local bar associations, as a public service, are pleased to send a short statement outlining the dos and don'ts for holographic wills in each state. Unless the estate is small, consisting mainly of items of personal property, the few dollars saved by not using an attorney may be spent many times over if unforeseen problems arise. Competent estate attorneys are generally available at modest cost to the elderly. Do not hesitate to shop by phone when inquiring about the cost of a simple will.

THE "RIGHT TO DIE": LIVING WILLS

Public attention is increasingly focused on "right to die" issues, as advancing medical technology makes it possible to sustain, almost indefinitely, some vestige of life in dying patients. The term "right to die" refers to individual decision-making regarding the prolongation of life through the use of heroic measures. The instrument or legal provision that enables others to carry out a person's wishes regarding the nonuse of extreme life-sustaining measures is called a living will.

Many states have enacted statutes that enable persons to carry out their wishes in the event of brain death with life being sustained by machine. A living will is a signed, dated, and witnessed document that allows a person to state wishes in advance regarding the use of life-sustaining procedures during a terminal illness. This document indicates the appointment of someone else to direct care if the patient is unable to do so for himself or herself. It should be signed and dated by the person and two witnesses who are not blood relatives or beneficiaries of property. A living will should be discussed with the doctor and a signed copy should be added to the individual's medical file. A copy should be given to the person who will make decisions in the event that the older person is unable to do so. It should be reviewed yearly to make changes as needed. Be sure to check whether such instruments are valid in the state where your parents reside, and whether they can be effective for a given number of months or years.

The durable power of attorney, as it exists in California, is an even more effective legal tool to remain in control of one's medical treatment (see page 178).

TRUSTS

The trust is perhaps the most flexible and widely used legal device, both in estate planning and for redistributing or transferring property and assets for tax purposes. Trusts are fiduciary relationships created when the property of one person, "the trustor," is transferred to someone else, "the trustee," to be held for the benefit and use of a third person, "the beneficiary." Because it is flexible, a trust also may be an advantageous way for an individual or family to organize their property and assets to provide for future changes. Typically, the trustee "owns" the property transferred into the trust, although the ownership is not absolute. The trustee holds bare legal title to the property, which means that only the trustee can sell or mortgage the property or otherwise deal with it as if he were the absolute "owner." The trustee's actions must always be in the best interests of the beneficiary. Commonly, the beneficiary has the right to "possession" of the property or to some or all of the income generated from it.

The trust may be established in one of two ways.

The *living trust* (inter vivos) is established by a trust document that becomes effective during the life of the person creating the trust. A living trust is often used for probate avoidance because the property placed in this trust before the person dies is transferred to the beneficiary outside of probate. It is a widely and firmly held misconception that one should avoid probate at all costs. There are many instances in which it is far more advantageous and economical to go through the probate process. Again, see a competent estate-planning attorney.

As opposed to "common law states," for those "community property states" that have enacted laws allowing for the division of property for couples when one is receiving Medicaid, it is important to understand that in a living trust both spouses have access to all the assets. The law of division of assets regarding

Medicaid benefits strips one spouse of all assets, which is in contradiction to the wording of the trust. Provisions should be made within the body of the trust to accommodate the possibility of our parents exercising the division of property laws regarding Medicaid. (It is highly unlikely that anyone with the assets to create a living trust will be interested in qualifying for Medicaid, but it is worth noting.)

The *testamentary trust* is established by a will and does not become effective until the person dies. These trusts do not avoid probate, but are usually used as a way to reduce inheritance taxes, or to control bequests.

All states have laws governing trusts that specify the conditions upon which trusts may be established and that set out the duties of the trustees and the rights of the beneficiaries. The wide-ranging legal, financial, and tax implications of a trust can be extremely complicated. The trust should be considered only when its effect on a particular individual or the family's financial situation is fully understood. In other words, it is important that we consult with a qualified lawyer who understands fully our parents' particular needs.

### DIRECT TRANSFERS AND GIFTS

The larger the size of our parents' estate, the more reason to see an estate planner. If our parents are fortunate enough to have acquired a large estate, they may be well advised to seek methods of reducing the size of their taxable estate. One such method is making gifts to loved ones or charities during their lifetime. If the gift is legally completed before death, that property is no longer considered as part of the decedent's estate, thereby reducing estate taxes. The rules, however, are somewhat tricky, and substantial gifts may trigger the necessity of filing a gift tax return. A competent estate attorney should instruct our parents on these legal complexities.

### POWER OF ATTORNEY

A power of attorney is a written document in which a person (the principal) designates another person or persons (the attorney-in-fact) to act on his or her behalf in matters requiring legal action. A power of attorney can be revoked by the principal at any time and is revoked automatically if the principal subsequently becomes mentally incompetent or dies. Generally, the power of attorney is created to handle financial matters. Occasionally, one would give a specific power of attorney for only one transaction, for example, if our parents needed someone to handle a real estate transaction in their absence.

Bob had just died in San Diego, and his widow, Ann, was too upset to handle the details of purchasing a smaller home for her retirement near her daughter in northern California. Ann gave her daughter a specific power of attorney that enabled her to perform all legal acts necessary, but only for the purpose of acquiring that property.

DURABLE POWER OF ATTORNEY

In California in 1982, the law authorized a new type of power of attorney called the durable power of attorney. It is one that is effective even after the principal becomes incompetent. It is created by including the words "this power of attorney shall not be affected by the subsequent incapacity of the principal." What makes this such a unique legal instrument is that parents can be in control of their lives to the end by giving specific instructions ahead of time as to what medical treatment they do or do not want to receive regarding heroic measures and life-sustaining equipment, thus relieving relatives of a difficult decision.

The durable power of attorney as it provides for heroic measures does not exist in all states. This may be legislation that we would like to see enacted in our state if it does not already exist.

A *springing durable power of attorney* is one that becomes effective *only after* the principal becomes incompetent. It is created by including the words "this power of attorney shall become valid only after the incapacity of the principal." This durable power of attorney has a life-span of ten years. (Reference: *Estates: Planning Ahead*, Northern California Cancer Program, 1301 Shoreway Road, Suite 425, Belmont, CA 94002.)

If we choose to make use of a springing durable power of attorney, we need to verify that the state within which parents will be living at the time that it is to become effective recognizes its legality.

Note that the springing durable power of attorney does not require professional draftsmanship for the purpose of eliminating heroic medical measures. We should ask the local hospital for the sample form that they commonly use under these circumstances.

CONSERVATORSHIP

Another common method of assuming control over an incapacitated or disabled individual's personal and/or financial and medical affairs is through a device called a conservatorship. A conservator of a person can manage that person's food, clothing, shelter needs, and medical consent. A conservator of the estate manages the person's financial and legal affairs, can sign contracts, buy or sell property, pay bills, receive income, make investments, and do anything financially or legally that the conservatee could formerly have done for himself or herself. The conservator can also, by action of the court, terminate a power of attorney. The conservator acts under the supervision of the local county probate court. Anyone can choose to establish a conservatorship, even if he or she is competent. For example, an aging parent may choose to appoint her daughter conservator simply because she is tired of dealing with her complicated finances. All transactions done by the conservator must be taken with the best interests of the conservatee in mind. The sale or purchase of real property and the sale or purchase of stocks that are not listed on the stock exchange generally require court approval. Otherwise, most transactions, day-to-day payment of bills, and receipt of income do not require court approval. Detailed "accountings" must be submitted periodically to the court for approval, and they become a matter of public record.

If the conservatee is capable of making decisions regarding his or her own medical treatment, he or she may do so; if, however, he or she lacks the capacity to give informed consent for medical treatment, the conservator may make this decision without special court consent. The court may authorize the conservator to change the place of residence of the conservatee, but authority

179

cannot be granted to place a conservatee in a mental health treatment facility against her or his will without very specific court proceedings. Because confinement to a medical institution deprives the individual of his or her liberty, most states provide special hearing procedures to safeguard against improper or involuntary confinement.

A conservator, subject to court approval, has certain limited powers to make gifts from, or rearrange assets in, a conservatee's estate. However, conservatorships are not "estate planning" devices, and are not designed for use by a family or spouse who simply wishes to transfer or redistribute joint or community assets.

Any person may be appointed as conservator, but courts generally prefer a spouse or close relative. The conservator should always work under the guidance of the attorney retained for the conservatorship.

GUARDIANSHIP

Some states utilize guardianships, which are similar to conservatorships. Traditionally, guardianships have been established when a person is adjudged by a court as "incompetent." (In conservatorship proceedings, a person is not necessarily adjudged incompetent.)

One reason to choose a conservatorship over a guardianship, if available in your state, is so that the family may avoid the stigma of having a loved one termed incompetent.

FOR FURTHER INFORMATION: *The Essential Guide to Wills, Estates, Trusts and Death Taxes.* Alex J. Soled. Detailed information on these subjects. AARP Books, Scott, Foresman and Co., 1865 Miner Street, Des Plaines, IL 60016; $12.95 ($9.45 to AARP members), plus $1.75 for shipping and handling.

Or *Legacy of Love.* Elmo A. Petterle. A practical workbook, with solid information and the forms you need to keep track of all records for complete estate planning. Shelter Publications, Inc., P.O. Box 279, Bolinas, CA 94924; $12.95 plus $1.50 postage.

## Points to Remember

· Choose professional help carefully.

· Start financial planning as early as possible.

· Involve all interested parties in decision-making.

· Become aware of special tax options for elders.

· Assesss parents' current financial position and needs.

· Review ways to tap equity in home without selling.

· Be clear about what your parents want a will to accomplish, particularly regarding a spouse.

· Help choose a willing, trusted, capable executor.

## Chapter 8
# Social Security and Private Health Insurance

Social Security is the nation's method of providing a continuing income for its elderly as their earnings stop or are reduced because of retirement. Your local Social Security office, which can be located through your telephone directory's listing under "Social Security Administration" or "United States Government," will be of help in answering your questions regarding eligibility.

Social Security is not automatic. In order to insure these benefits, our parents must apply for them. The Social Security Administration suggests that you contact your local Social Security office if you are within three months of being sixty-five years or older and plan to retire, if you are unable to work because of an illness or injury that is expected to last a year or longer, or if someone in your family dies.

WHEN TO APPLY

When our parents retire, they may start receiving retirement checks as early as sixty-two. It is important that they apply for their monthly benefits no later than the last day of the month in which they want the benefits to begin. In most cases, benefits payable for months before the age of sixty-five can begin no earlier than the month in which they applied. If one of your parents has died recently, your surviving parent may apply in the month after his or her spouse's death and still get a benefit for the month of death. Generally, benefits can be paid only for those months during which the person is eligible throughout the entire month.

When retiring at age sixty-five, our parents can apply for Social Security up to three months before the month they want the benefits to start. This will help assure that they get their first payment on time. If our parents passed their sixty-fifth birthday and failed to apply for Social Security benefits, back payments can be made for up to six months before the month they apply for retirement or survivor benefits.

WHAT IS NEEDED TO APPLY

There are several items that are needed when applying for Social Security, including one's Social Security number, proof of age, marriage certificate (if applying for spouse's, widow's, or widower's benefits), W-2 form for the last year, or a copy of one's last federal income tax return if self-employed. The Social Security office will guide our parents in gathering any of the information they may not already have, so urge them not to delay applying because of missing information.

WHO CAN RECEIVE THE CHECKS?

Social Security checks may go to workers and their dependents when the worker retires, becomes severely disabled or dies. A divorced spouse who has been divorced at least two years can receive benefits at sixty-two whether or not his or her former spouse has retired and is receiving benefits, as long as the former spouse is eligible. A surviving divorced spouse can receive checks at age sixty if the marriage lasted ten years or more, or at age fifty if the surviving spouse is disabled.

Ordinarily, a widow or surviving divorced spouse loses her Social Security rights when she remarries. Benefits can continue, however, without any reduction to a widow or surviving divorced spouse who remarries after age sixty, or to a disabled widow or surviving divorced spouse who remarried after age fifty. If her new husband gets Social Security, a wife's benefit can be put on his record if it would be larger than the widow's payment.

There are certain rules about Social Security that are particularly relevant to women. There is Social Security protection for our mothers—protection over and above what she may already have through our fathers' work. Our mothers should know exactly what their Social Security coverage means to them. In addition, they should know how public pensions for government employees can affect Social Security benefits.

For further information regarding women's benefits, contact your local Social Security office and ask for the pamphlet *A Woman's Guide to Social Security*.

Arrangements can be made through your parents' local bank to have their checks sent directly to the bank for automatic deposit, thereby avoiding any delay of payments or loss or theft of checks. Contact your local Social Security office for information about direct deposit and ask the bank about this service.

HOW TO QUALIFY

Before our parents can get monthly cash benefits, they must have credit for a certain amount of work under Social Security. The exact amount of work credit depends on their ages. Having enough credit means only that they are eligible to receive checks. The amount of their check depends on their earnings over a period of years. The staff at any Social Security office will be glad to help our parents determine how much credit is needed and what amount of payment they may be receiving.

The federal government's Supplemental Security Income Program (SSI) provides a minimum monthly income to needy people over the age of sixty-five with limited income and resources. The federal government establishes the basic benefits, while most states add a state supplement. Your local Social Security office will help in answering questions regarding eligibility.

If your parents travel outside of the country for thirty days or more while they are getting Social Security checks, their absence from this country may affect their right to checks. In addition, if they go back to work and are under seventy years old, their earnings may affect their Social Security benefits.

# Medicare

Medicare is a federal health insurance program for elder Americans. Over thirty million Americans are covered by Medicare in the United States today, according to the Department of Health and Human Services. Medicare is designed to protect people sixty-five and over who, as they age, may require more health care. At the time when income is dropping and medical expenses are increasing, it was hoped that Medicare would ease the financial burden of our elderly. In 1965, however, when Medicare came into existence, older Americans were spending over 15 percent of their total income on health care. Today, with Medicare, the figure is still the same! The cost of health care continues to rise, and with it the confusion about Medicare coverage, claims, and Medigap insurance. Perhaps the following information will make this system seem a little less cloudy. For complete information, write for the Medicare handbook mentioned on page 190.

Medicare is handled by the Health Care Financing Administration, not by Social Security; however, the people at local Social Security Administration offices will take your parents' applications for Medicare, complete claim forms, and answer any questions about the program. Medicare payments are handled by private insurance organizations under contract with the government. Your parents should always ask if the person or organizations providing services for them are approved for Medicare payments.

WHEN TO APPLY

It is a good idea for your parents to apply for Medicare three months before their sixty-fifth birthday. Then their protection can start the month they reach sixty-five. If, however, they are not planning to retire at sixty-five, there are a few rules administered through the Equal Employment Opportunity Commission of which they should be aware.

For example, if your father is over sixty-five and working, or if he is not working and your mother (any age) is working, their employer (with twenty or more employees) must offer workers age sixty-five or older the same health insurance benefits they offer to younger workers. (Note that the rule is not the same for individuals sixty-five and over with permanent kidney failure, so contact your local Social Security office and ask for the pamphlet *Medicare Coverage of Kidney Dialysis and Kidney Transplant Services* if this particular problem relates to either of your parents.)

This rule affects our parents in the following way: they may choose to accept or reject their employer's insurance plan. If they accept the employer's plan, it will be their primary health insurance, which means that this plan will pay first for any covered health care service received. If your parents' employer's insurance does not pay all of the charges, Medicare may pay secondary benefits for Medicare-covered services. In other words, Medicare may pay some of the services not covered by their employer.

Your parents' employer should provide an explanation of their options (if either of your parents is over sixty-five) under the employer's health plan and how Medicare coverage is affected. The employer should also give your parents an opportunity to make a choice.

Your parents should also know that even though there is usually a penalty surcharge added to the Medicare medical insurance premium for signing up late for Medicare, there is no penalty in this case. This special rule gives your parents seven months to enroll in Medicare medical insurance, beginning when they stop working or when they drop the employer's plan.

Medicare is divided into two parts: hospital insurance and medical insurance. When they reach their sixty-fifth birthdays, your parents become eligible for Medicare, even if they are still working, as long as they have sufficient quarters of creditable earnings under Social Security.


MEDICARE HOSPITAL INSURANCE

Generally, the hospital insurance part of Medicare (part A) helps pay the cost of inpatient hospital care and certain kinds of medically necessary follow-up care in a skilled nursing facility. Some home health care and hospice care are also covered. There are many restrictions and conditions that are fully discussed in the Department of Health and Human Services pamphlet entitled *Your Medicare Handbook,* available through your local Social Security office. Medicare hospital insurance is available without charge to everyone who is automatically eligible for it. If you are eligible for Social Security, then you are automatically eligible for the hospital insurance protection when you are sixty-five. People who are not automatically eligible may enroll by paying a monthly premium for this coverage.

The medical part of Medicare (part B) helps pay the cost of the physicians' services based on an allotted amount per procedure (physicians may charge more); outpatient hospital care, including physical therapy and speech pathology services; eligible home health care; certain medical supplies, such as wheelchairs or walkers; and services not covered by hospital insurance. Everyone enrolled must pay a monthly premium, which will be automatically deducted from their Social Security check. When our parents apply for the hospital insurance, they will be enrolled automatically for the medical insurance part of Medicare unless they specifically reject it. If they do reject this coverage, they can sign up for it later during an annual general enrollment period, which is held from January 1 through March 31. The premium may be slightly higher and the protection will not start until July 31 of that year. (There are a variety of employer benefit plans with more extensive coverage than Medicare. Are your parents eligible for such a plan? If so, that should take first priority.)

HOW THE MEDICARE SYSTEM WORKS

In 1983, Medicare began using the Prospective Payment System (PPS) to determine how much to pay hospitals (except in Maryland and New Jersey) for each Medicare patient's hospital stay. Under the PPS, the government makes reimbursements to hospitals based on average costs for a specific illness. For example, when you enter the hospital for a particular surgery that has been determined to cost $4,000, Medicare will pay the hospital $4,000 for that particular surgical procedure. If that hospital spends more than this allotted amount to care for you, generally the hospital will still only receive the $4,000. You will not have to pay

187

the difference, since the hospital suffers the loss. If, however, a hospital spends less than the $4,000, the hospital gets the full payment and can keep the difference between that and the actual cost of the surgery.

With knowledge of hospital costs in your area, the government determines an average cost for every category of treatment. These categories are known as diagnostic related groups (DRG). DRGs are assigned by the insurance companies that administer hospital Medicare claims. Regardless of the medical complications, every Medicare patient receives only one DRG designation per hospital visit.

The DRG assignment has no bearing on Medicare reimbursements to the physician. (See chapter 3 for how doctor assignments work.) It is important, however, to remember that it is the doctor who controls the treatment during your parent's hospital stay, makes the diagnosis used to determine the DRG, and is the one who discharges the patients. Consequently, our parents' physician plays an important role in helping the prospective payment system (PPS) work to our parents' best advantage.

One other important part of this system is the role of the peer review organizations (PRO). The federal government pays the PRO to review Medicare patients' hospital treatment. This organization has the government's authority to review a patient's care from before hospital admission through discharge. If you believe that your parents' coverage is being terminated too soon or that they are not receiving the treatment they need, you may request a review of the denial notice decision by the PRO and appeal the decision. There is a time limit governing these procedures.

Any hospital or Social Security office can give you the name, address, and telephone number of the PRO in your state, or you can write or call Medical Review, Health Standards and Quality Bureau, Meadows East Building, 6325 Security Boulevard, Baltimore, MD 21207; (301) 594-1432.

(NOTE: If you have any reason to believe that a doctor, hospital, or other provider of health care services is performing unnecessary or inappropriate services or is billing Medicare for services that your parents did not receive, use the toll-free hot line that has been installed by the inspector general for the reporting of any evidence of such fraud, waste, or abuse of the Medicare program. The number is [800] 368-5779. In Maryland, call [800] 638-3986.)

The Medicare system of health care offers hospitals the incentive to keep costs down. It is too soon, however, to know if the system is benefiting the patients/consumers and if it is encouraging hospitals to be more cost efficient. Of course, everyone has a different opinion of this system's benefits. Concerns have been voiced because some patients are being denied admittance to hospitals when hospital officials are uncertain that the patient's stay will be declared necessary and Medicare reimbursement assured. Others contend that patients are being discharged too early from hospitals, "quicker and sicker," before their recovery is complete. It is with this in mind that our parents need to be informed about how this system works so that they may plan to use it to their best advantage.

Recognizing a void, the San Francisco Jewish Family and Children's Service, with funding from the Koret Foundation, is running a pilot program addressing the needs of the frail elderly who are prematurely discharged from the hospital. The Koret grant provides for social workers, who create a two-month individualized program for each recuperating frail elder in the community, linking them to the appropriate community services and thereby filling the financial gap created by lack of Medicare coverage.

MEDICAID

Medicaid is the federal government's medical insurance program for low-income Americans. Medicaid is available in every state, sometimes with a different name, through public assistance programs in counties and in cities, or through the public health office. (In California, it is called Medical.)

Medical expenses covered by Medicaid vary considerably from those covered by Medicare. The most startling difference between the two as they relate to the elderly is that long-term nursing home care is covered under Medicaid. There are strict eligibility regulations governing Medicaid, which precludes the possession of almost all personal assets.

189

FOR FURTHER INFORMATION: Contact the local Social Security office to ask for one of their many free brochures: *Your Medicare Handbook, How Medicare Helps During a Hospital Stay, A Brief Explanation of Medicare, Medicare and Prepayment Plans, Your Hospital Stay under Medicare's Prospective Payment System,* and *Medicare and Employer Health Plans,* for example, or write for: *Medicaid/Medicare, Which Is Which?,* U.S. Department of Health and Human Services.

## Supplemental, Medigap, Health, and Auto Insurance

According to the American Association of Retired Persons, over 60 percent of older Americans have some form of private health insurance to supplement Medicare. These supplemental policies, sometimes called Medigap policies, are intended to cover the difference in cost between the coverage that Medicare assigns and its deductible, and the true cost to the patient.

If our parents need help in deciding whether to buy private supplementary insurance, they can call any Social Security office and ask for the pamphlet *Guide to Health Insurance for People with Medicare.* The pamphlet is free and describes various kinds of supplemental insurance and explains how they relate to Medicare coverage.

Private health insurance policies for older Americans vary primarily with the kind of benefits they pay and the range of protection they offer. Insurance plans generally fall into two categories: "service benefit" policies and "indemnity benefit" policies, each with its own set of distinct advantages and disadvantages. Although many policies include benefits of both types, the major benefits of any one policy usually direct it into one category or the other. When talking with our insurance agent, it is important that we understand the differences and choose according to our needs. Private health insurance policies vary in the range of coverage offered, and it is no surprise that there is a direct relation between how much coverage your parents will get and how much they will pay. Types of coverage most frequently discussed with an insurance agent include first dollar coverage, limited benefit plans, specific disease coverage, and comprehensive coverage.

INSURANCE FRAUDS

Be cautious about the pressurized sales pitch, and the door-to-door scams. The elderly are traditionally vulnerable to those who prey on their fears. As reported by the Council of Better Business Bureaus, consumer fraud saw an increase of 12 percent in 1987. One popular packet of insurance for long-term health care is sold with the ploy that children would not have to be at financial risk if illness strikes, a worthy concern to our parents, but the small print indicates that the policy is only good for one year! When policies sound too good to be true, they usually are.

During the Senate hearings in 1987 for the passage of a catastrophic health insurance bill, many examples of insurance abuse were cited. One, as reported in the *Washington Post* in June 1987, was of an eighty-year-old woman who had been pressured into buying fourteen different insurance policies with overlapping coverage.

(NOTE: For detailed information on consumer fraud, write for a free copy of: *Before You Say Yes: 15 Questions to Turn Off an Investment Swindler,* M. B. Woods, Consumer Information Center, Pueblo, CO 81009.)

The best protection against such pressure is to ask your parents not to make any on-the-spot decisions regarding financial outlays. Ask that your parents allow their insurance agent, or ours, to examine any policies they are considering for purchase.

As we know, our parents' insurance choices are many. It is important they understand that Medicare alone will not be sufficient coverage. They may decide that Medicare with a supplemental Medigap policy is fine for them. They may choose Blue Cross/Blue Shield, continue a retirement health insurance policy through their place of employment, or choose a prepayment plan such as a preferred provider organization (PPO), a health maintenance organization (HMO), or a competitive medical plan (CMP).

HMOS AND PPOS

A health maintenance organization (HMO) is a private insurance company, such as Kaiser Permanente in California, whose monthly prepaid premiums entitle participants to an array of professional services, health facilities, and supplies. They have built-in twenty-four-hour care.

A preferred provider organization (PPO) is another form of private insurance in which doctors and hospitals are chosen from a "preferred" list of providers. A discounted fee is paid after using the services of these selected physicians and hospitals.

What is available in our parents' community will help in the decision-making process. In order to make a fair comparison, a list of specific questions follow concerning the nature of the coverage offered that can be a helpful practical guide when trying to choose the correct insurance:

- Is a physical exam required for coverage?

- Are prior health problems under immediate coverage?

- Is the coverage overlapping with Medicare?

- Is the policy guaranteed renewable? (This will protect you from not having coverage, but the premium can be increased.)

- Is the policy noncancelable? (This means that the insurance company must renew the policy and cannot increase the premium. Such coverage is very expensive.)

- What areas of nursing home day care and home health care are covered?

- Who fills out the claim forms?

- Will coverage provide for specific needs—hearing, vision, dental?

- Is coverage limited geographically?

- Are there health problems that are not covered?

- What are the elimination periods (the time lapse between the purchase of the policy and when the coverage actually begins)?

192

## PAPERWORK

There are those who are convinced that the paperwork involved in filing insurance claims was created to discourage the filing of such claims! The paperwork is cumbersome, but help can be found: through the local Social Security office, through free programs offered by many hospitals (Mt. Zion care account in San Francisco), through some senior centers and through private brokers who make a business out of helping seniors with the paperwork of aging. The staff at our parents' doctor's office can often be the first source of information as to what services are available for assistance in their community, and the Silver Pages (the senior Yellow Pages), the Yellow Pages, and the telephone directory may yield more contacts.

## AUTOMOBILE INSURANCE

The subject of our parents' driving is one of great concern to many adult children, and a topic which has been dealt with in some detail in chapter 5. For those whose parents are still very much among the well old and who enjoy driving, there may be special benefits that they should ask their insurance agent about. Automobile insurance at any age is becoming more and more expensive, and for the elderly, it becomes increasingly difficult to obtain reasonable policy rates.

## INSURANCE DISCOUNTS

Safe driver discounts are offered by a number of companies to drivers who have not had an accident over a specified period of years. Most insurance companies offer discounts and other credits to those individuals who drive short distances or infrequently. They also offer discounts when a person renews an insurance policy with the same company. Many automobile insurance companies offer discounts when one purchases other types of insurance policies, such as a homeowner's policy, from them as well. The American Association of Retired Persons (AARP) offers a defensive driver program called "Alive—Mature Driving

Program," and graduates from that training program, or other accredited driver improvement courses, may be eligible for credits toward insurance premiums.

GETTING THE MOST FOR YOUR MONEY

- Check to see if your parents qualify for any of the discounts (see above).

- Compare policies!

- Make the deductible higher.

- Evaluate cost of collision and comprehensive coverage with the actual cost of repairing your car. An old car with low book value may not qualify for enough repair money to make the premiums worthwhile.

- Do your parents have sufficient liability insurance to protect their assets?

- Make sure that payments do not overlap with benefits from medical insurance, so that duplicate coverage exists that will not be paid in the event of an accident.

- See if roadside services included in the policy are cost effective. Perhaps a specialized service, such as Automobile Association of America (AAA), would be better.

- Check renewability. Most states now have laws that make it illegal to cancel policies on the basis of age.

## Points to Remember

- Social Security is not automatic. Your parents must apply.

- Have monthly Social Security checks sent directly to the bank.

- Extended out-of-the-country travel may affect payment of Social Security checks.

- Additional earnings may affect Social Security checks, if your parent is under the age of seventy.

- Not all persons or organizations providing care are approved by Medicare insurance. Ask before receiving services.

- Medicare can be used as a primary or secondary health insurance.

- Parents become eligible for Medicare at age sixty-five if they have sufficient credited earnings from Social Security.

- Medicare has two categories: part A, hospital insurance; and part B, medical insurance.

- Medicaid is government insurance for low-income Americans.

- Medigap insurance supplements what Medicare covers up to the full cost to the patient.

*Chapter 9*

# When Parents Can No Longer Live Alone

THE family story goes that everyone had gathered at my father's house for Christmas dinner. It was the first time that all the children and grandchildren had been together all year. My grandfather, who was eighty-five and in good health, lived with my father. He came to the table in rare form, full of stories of Ireland and escapades he had had as a young "lad." Some of the grandchildren had never heard the tales and were fascinated, begging for more details. Too soon the meal was over, and my grandfather excused himself to go upstairs and take a nap. My grandfather died in his sleep that afternoon.

The dream for many of us is that our parents will continue to live independently until the day when they fall asleep, comfortable in their own beds, and simply do not wake up in the morning. The reality, of course, is rarely like this. Few elders remain totally independent after age eighty-five, and many need help much earlier. Often the degree of help needed is unclear.

What happens when our parents reach the point at which they can no longer survive without outside help? This shift from independence to dependence is often a gradual one, unless a crisis situation, such as a heart attack or a stroke, precipitates an immediate and dramatic change.

In chapter 6, we introduced community services and sources of information and referral that were recommended to help our parents who are still living essentially independent lives. Many of these same resources will be our greatest help in caring for our dependent parents. These community services that were started to make life easier for our parents may eventually become essential to their survival.

## Making a Decision

The hope is that before total dependency occurs for our parents, we shall have taken the time for family conferences, preferably *with* our parents, to decide on probable plans of action—ways to care for them when they can no longer care for themselves.

One of the biggest decisions to be made is who will be the one to take on the role of primary caregiver. Sometimes the choice is obvious, but often such discussions allow old sibling rivalries and unresolved child-parent conflicts to surface and cloud the issue. *All care issues will be easier to discuss with our parents' input, and before a crisis.* When the caregiving is to be assumed by the adult children, a good solution is to have one care for their parents' paperwork and finances, if needed, and another be in charge of all service arrangements, personal hygiene, and so forth. If there are multiple siblings living reasonably close by who are eager to help, then shifts of caring can be established, greatly easing the resulting stress. Arrangements can be shared so that long-distance children, unable to give or supervise any of the physical care, can contribute by handling much of the red tape by telephone.

Another important process as we prepare for our parents' increasing dependency is to determine where all their essential papers are kept, such as deeds, wills, trusts, and funeral plans. See chapter 7 for the details of paperwork preparation.

This is also the time to be clear about our parents' wishes for life-sustaining equipment and burial choices. Do they want to be cremated? Have they bought a family plot? Do they want a closed casket? Today, many of us carry driver's licenses that show that we are organ donors. Have our parents made such choices? The more that we know ahead of time, the more smoothly we can operate in time of crisis. Knowing that we are fulfilling our parents' wishes will make their deaths easier to bear.

We all know that family dynamics vary dramatically. For some, the discussion of death is not difficult, for others, it is extremely awkward to approach. In the early years of my marriage, I had a mental block about making a will. Whenever Howard suggested seeing a lawyer to draw up a will, I became overwhelmed with sadness and could not discuss it. His sympathetic reassurances that it was a mere formality did no good, but when Howard switched to humor my attitude changed dramatically. The ridiculous images he painted of the arbitrary distribution of my possessions made me see the absurdity of my position, and humor has been a part of such discussions in our family ever since. We laugh about which parts of our body would be accepted and which rejected by donor programs, and on trips we have been known to explore cemeteries looking for interesting or humorous epitaphs. Two family favorites are: "I told you I was sick!" and "Gone but not forgiven."

If your parents are unwilling to discuss decisions regarding death, you may want to try a new approach.

- Start the discussion with family decisions you have made with your own family, and it may be easier for your parents to express their wishes.

- If you feel comfortable with it, try humor—what others might say about you on your tombstone, what you would say about yourself, etc.

- Elicit the help of a third party, perhaps a family friend who has recently made such decisions. Often things can be discussed with outsiders present that are too difficult with just family.

- Ask the family lawyer to explain the importance of having an informed family in time of crisis.

- Suggest that they read the appropriate parts of this book or other books on the subject of preparedness.

ASSESSING THE SITUATION

For most of us there comes a time when we have to step in and institute necessary changes in our parents' lives. The right moment for this move is not always clear. As adult children, we are more likely to be concerned with their safety, while our parents hold tenaciously to their independence. There are some guidelines we can use to assess whether or not our new concern is warranted by actual need or whether it is a product of our own fears for a parent's well-being.

- Has your parent's health changed dramatically in recent weeks, months?
- Can he take care of his personal and hygiene needs, such as dressing, shaving, bathing?
- Can he prepare meals and feed himself?
- Can she pay her own bills?
- Can she function safely in her home, by climbing stairs, negotiating hallways, and using the bathrooms?
- Is he capable of taking his own medicines, eyedrops?
- Is she oriented? Can she call for help if needed?
- Is he continent?
- Is she demonstrating excessive forgetfulness or other signs of senility?

To get a complete assessment of the quality of our parents' lives, it is helpful not only to talk with them, but also to get input from their doctor, neighbors, and friends.

REVIEWING THE OPTIONS

When you have determined that changes must be made in our parents' lifestyle, it is time to see what is available for their particular circumstances.

The three principal choices are: (1) living at home with multiple support systems, (2) living in someone else's home, or (3) living in an institution.

Whether or not all three of these options will be available will depend in large part on our parents' medical and financial situation, what the community offers in the way of services, and to what extent family members can participate.

199

Understanding the particulars of your parents' medical condition is essential to making the appropriate choices. Serious health problems will take many of the decisions out of our hands and force us to choose services that can provide the necessary care.

What we may not understand is that ultimately we may have to decide what constitutes appropriate care. Most of us assume that doctors dictate treatment, but getting a second opinion often means getting a different opinion as to what course of action should be followed. It is then up to the family members to find out as much as possible about the medical problem our parents face and to decide, with our parents if possible, what should be done.

For those of us whose parents face illnesses with which we are unfamiliar, help is available to facilitate seeking out such information. Many hospitals, for instance, have educational tapes which can be borrowed, on various diseases and conditions, and some have established libraries on aging and age-related issues. There are national organizations for all major diseases (heart disease, Alzheimer's, stroke, cancer) and for major conditions (deafness, blindness); these can provide both literature and advice. If the condition is simply advanced age, there are other factors that need to be considered.

## Innovative Ways to Support Elders in Their Own Homes

Keeping an older parent in his or her own home who can no longer function alone is not impossible, especially if he or she does not need constant medical attention. Whether or not it is the desirable plan of action may be determined by how much the elder wants to remain there, the advice of the doctor, what community services are available to help keep him or her at home, and who is able to coordinate those services. Having close family with the desire and ability to work with the elder, and having available community resources, form the ideal combination.

The continuing expansion of services for the elderly is making this option feasible in more and more communities. Many of our parents, who just a few years ago would have been natural candidates for nursing homes because few community support systems

200

were in place, are now able to remain at home. In addition to the many services described in chapter 6—homemakers, case workers, home-delivered meals, specialized products, paratransit, and so forth—there are other services specifically created for the frail old.

## ADULT DAY CARE/ADULT DAY HEALTH CARE (ADHC)

As the name implies, adult day care is a daytime community program for the elderly with centers run by hospitals, nonprofit organizations, and community groups. This exciting alternative to the trauma and cost of placing our parents in nursing homes is a choice many are making, as it is quite clear that most frail elders cannot remain unattended at home during the day. Adult day care is a viable and comforting choice for frail parents whether or not they live alone.

The funding for these centers generally comes from a combination of state and city money, grants, corporations and foundations, with fees based on a sliding scale from zero to about $50 per day. In twenty-seven states, Medicaid reimburses for this type of care, which previously had to be received in an institutional setting.

By 1987, there were twelve hundred to fourteen hundred such centers nationwide, up from a mere dozen in 1970, according to the National Institute on Adult Day Care, part of the National Council on the Aging, a nonprofit service organization. The private sector also is involving itself in adult day care, as has the community.

Adult day care center participants can use these facilities as necessary, once a week or on a daily basis, usually determined by a case worker or doctor. The average is two to five days per week. Transportation through paratransit or through the centers themselves is generally provided. For an elder at home alone, this is a wonderful socializing opportunity, but it is much more than that. Centers provide such diverse services as hot meals, recreational outings, arts and crafts, music, rehabilitation exercise, shopping excursions, counseling and guidance, often including family members, and even facilities to take showers with assistance. An effort is made at these centers to involve the participants as actively as possible, often relegating the television set to a small corner or having none at all, thereby encouraging the elders to get involved with the activities of the day.

Adult day health care goes even further by providing medical attention. Centers generally provide speech, physical and occupational therapy, particularly geared to those patients rehabilitating after a stroke or as a result of premature hospital discharge. These early dismissals from hospitals, attributed to the current DRGs (see chapter 8), have created a major care crisis for the recovering elder patient. Often it forces adult children to take vacation time or extended leave from work in order to nurse a recovering parent back to health. Adult day health centers have done much to fill this need.

There are also adult day health centers that have begun to provide specific programs to respond to the needs of their Alzheimer's patients—and in urban areas there will undoubtedly be more specialization of services as the old old continue to represent a larger segment of the population. Some centers offer blood pressure screening, and in an attempt to further serve the community, some also offer family support group therapy.

An important factor of adult day health care is that it provides respite for the caregiver. Knowing that our parents have an opportunity for social interaction with good medical and rehabilitation attention enables caregivers to make use of some guilt-free time away from their demanding tasks. "It is not a baby-sitting facility," said one dedicated center director. "We hope to teach our patients to use what they have." For those of us combining caregiving with careers, adult day care can be absolutely essential.

As is the case with all services, it is important to become familiar with the particular center you are interested in. Visit once with an appointment and again unannounced, at another time of day. Ask questions, talk with the elderly, and see what your doctor and his or her nurse feel about the center. Prices, quality of service, and types of services vary greatly, as does personnel. Regulations differ from state to state. Some require licensing, others certification, while still others require neither.

An elder's eligibility for adult day health care is determined by health, not age. These centers are for those frail elders who need medical or rehabilitation services to avoid institutionalization. The services of the ADHC are authorized by the individual's physican, and they are reimbursable by Medicaid, or available on a sliding scale payment.

On Lok (Chinese for "abode of peace and happiness"), in San Francisco, is an innovative program of total comprehensive care with an extremely successful adult day health care center at its core. Based in the Chinatown district, On Lok provides the means by which over three hundred frail elderly can remain in their own homes. Started in 1972, On Lok has expanded the traditional adult day health care concept to include total care of the frail elder, overseeing everything from planning an individualized health care program to arranging the necessary hospitalization. An act of Congress in 1986 allowed On Lok a permanent waiver from standard Medicare and Medicaid reimbursement policies, which are done on a fee-for-service basis, and established a single monthly payment plan for each participant. This financial structure (similar to that of an HMO), its well-coordinated assortment of services, and its successful execution have made On Lok a model for total care centers in the developmental stage in almost a dozen cities across the country. For further information write: On Lok, 1441 Powell Street, San Francisco, CA 94133; (415) 989-2578.

San Francisco is a good city to look at when discussing adult day health care because of its innovative programs, resulting from the fact that the city has a disproportionate number of the elderly living there. Seniors number 15 percent of the population (50 percent more than the state average), and the city has responded with some unique services.

The San Francisco Adult Day Health Network (ADHN), of which On Lok is a member, represents a new approach to service delivery. Contributing their technical assistance, On Lok and Mt. Zion, another center that has been providing adult day health care in San Francisco since the late 1970s, joined hands with the

Adult Day Health Network to secure funding for an additional five Adult Day Health Centers in San Francisco. Since their beginning in 1983, the ADHN now coordinates their efforts not only to raise funds, but also for its marketing, to advocate for legislative change, and to provide transportation for patients.

This joining together secured twenty founders with grants of over $2.5 million. The ADHN continued successfully, with the support of the United Way acting as the service agent providing staff.

The network is available for seminars that advise on the development of similar programs elsewhere.

FOR INFORMATION: Contact The United Way in San Francisco, 1435 Market Street, San Francisco, CA 94102 (415) 554-2426.

If adult day care does not exist in your parents' community, there may be alternative community services for the frail old that we can make use of for daily support. When used in combination with earlier mentioned services (see chapter 6), resources such as the visiting nurses' association, home-delivered meals, health aids, and physical therapists may be sufficient support to allow a frail elder to live alone. The final component for making these services work is the vital coordination and follow-through that is generally done by an adult child, a spouse, or a case manager.

## Home Away from Home

Entire books could be written on the psychology of three-generational familial living. For some families, having a loved parent come live with them is no more of a decision than whether or not to send their children to school. It is a foregone conclusion. "When Mother is too old to take care of herself, she will come to live with us." If "coming to live with us" means a move across town, and there is ample space, this may be the answer. If it means moving across the state or the country, however, it may not be the best move for parent or adult child. Whatever the situation, serious thought should be given to such a move, so all parties concerned are as prepared as possible for the inevitable changes that will take place in their lives and their relationships.

MOVING IN WITH THE FAMILY

Examining the reasons for taking a parent into our own home is vital to the success of the arrangement. If we make such an offer out of guilt, for instance, but are lacking the psychological or physical stamina or the financial ability to make it work, such a move would be a big mistake. The decision not to have your parent live with you is not the same as saying that you no longer love them. It may be a greater love that is willing to take the criticism of others when one's parents' current location offers better care and facilities. Such a big decision requires as much input as possible, but we must remember that no one else's experience is quite like ours. Whatever the decision, we should not lose sight of the fact that if the relationship between parent and child is basically good, there is no reason to assume that it will change, but if it is rocky, we should not expect it to get better.

Outside counseling before making a move can be time well spent. Expectations should be discussed by all family members involved in the household. Some key points of discussion are:

- Can she or he eat the same meals as the rest of the family?

- How much privacy does each family member need?

- Who will have primary responsibility for the care?

- Will all family members participate in the needed care?

- Will you be able to go out at night?

- What will the finances of the situation be?

It is important that everyone understand what the progression is likely to be in the case of a particular illness, so that there are as few surprises as possible. Remember that the care described in chapter 5 to make your parents' home easy to live in will have to be implemented in your own home to provide the same mobility and safe conditions in their new home with you.

I was a child when my grandmother came to live with us. Although my mother was not the favored child—in fact, Ros had never had a close relationship with her mother—she was the only child in a position to care for her mother at home. My grand-mother was a spoiled woman, used to being the center of atten-tion, and we knew that her addition to our household would precipitate many changes.

Aware that the newness of the situation would soon wear off and that the children's offers to help would grow less frequent, my parents called a conference to discuss how each of us would participate in the schedule of caring for the frail new member of the family. It was certain that she would need lots of attention. A deal was struck and heartily agreed to by all of us; my sisters, Ruth and Carole, and I would be on duty for a week at a time and be paid as if it were a job. The duties were primarily to answer our grandmother's buzzer whenever she rang and to bring what she needed.

Our youthful energy saved Mother from climbing stairs a zil-lion times a day, and a week of one grandchild at a time allowed a relationship to develop between each of us and our grandmother, without the confusion of constantly changing faces at the door.

The money was our immediate gratification, but coming to know Grandmother and realizing that we were a major help to Mother were the lasting rewards that stay with us to this day.

If the decision is made to have our parents live with us, it is wise to do so on a trial basis for several weeks. This will enable you to assess if the family can live together. It is also the time to put the community services into action to see how well they function for our parents. Many of the services employed when a frail parent lives alone may make it possible for him or her to live comfortably with us.

RESPITE CARE

Begun in 1982 by the Washington, D.C., chapter of the National Council of Catholic Women, this community service was created specifically to give short-term relief to the family caregiver. A trained volunteer comes to the home for a few hours or days on a weekly or a monthly basis, giving the caregiver a break in the hopes of avoiding burnout. Although they are not trained nurses, these volunteers have had an initial training program to learn the basics of caring for a frail elder. They learn techniques in feeding, helping an elder walk, or aiding the patient in and out of a wheelchair. They know how to deal with an emergency, and, in general, learn the skills of being a caring companion. The training skills vary with the organization and the caregiver should specify the needs of her or his particular case. The Catholic pilot program was so successful that it has spread to almost two thousand parishes, and the concept has been adopted by many communities as well as other religious and health care service organizations.

Respite care can also mean away-from-home help on a temporary basis. If the family is going on vacation, for instance, and needs two weeks of good supervision for a parent, there are rest homes and board and care facilities that provide respite care. The kind of service available will depend on the medical condition of the elder. For those not continent or mobile enough for some facilities, hospitals are another possibility. Many are beginning to offer beds for respite care, and some have even built special housing for respite patients. The costs vary considerably.

For those of us whose parents do not wish to be cared for by anyone other than their children, and for the caregiver who feels that only he or she can do the job properly, making the decision to use respite care, even in the home, is not an easy one. Respite is strongly recommended, however, by most geriatric professionals. The stress of caregiving is enormous, and the caregivers who do not take proper care of themselves by taking periodic breaks risk becoming sick and not being able to care for anyone else. Often the caregiver is the last to recognize the need for respite. Waiting until we are too tired to continue does everyone a disservice. Scheduling periodic respite in advance is a way to insure that caregivers get the break that they all need to allow them to go on giving.

CREATIVE LIVING ALTERNATIVES

Home away from home for the frail elderly does not necessarily mean moving in with the family. The variety of nonmedical conditions that may prompt them to look for alternative housing suggests some creative solutions. If the death of a spouse, for instance, has made the elder afraid to remain alone, or if loneliness is the motivating factor, then the choice of housing does not need to include medical care. A careful review of chapter 5's discussion of housing alternatives may suggest a solution. An elder with a failing memory or even a weak heart may require a living situation that provides supervision and companionship, not medical attention.

*Foster care housing* is being provided through local agencies for those who qualify financially as well as physically. In foster care, the frail elderly live in private homes with families who have received special training and are under the supervision of the local agency. A parent in this situation would have to be able to function independently with limited supervision. The area agency on aging could tell you what is available in your community.

*Adult Family Care* is a program in Massachusetts funded by the state, together with private foundations, which has grown since its inception in 1979 from servicing one county to including almost the entire state. This project places frail elders, with their doctors' approval, in private homes in lieu of nursing home placement. The provider families are carefully screened, as are the homes themselves. Careful attention is also given to matching the elder with the family. This Massachusetts program is a successful example of intergenerational living outside of the immediate family, which other states are starting to imitate. It is strongly endorsed by the state Medicaid program, as the daily allotment for adult family care is considerably less than the payments Medicaid would be making were the elder in a nursing home. Those elders who do not qualify for Medicaid pay a flat fee ($17.50 per day at time of publication), which is still far less than comparable nursing services.

*Board and care homes (B and Cs) and residential facilities for the elderly (RFE)*, are sometimes referred to as *sheltered housing*. Under many different names, these facilities, when properly operated, can provide a homelike atmosphere where residents have private rooms but eat meals in the communal dining room. Available as an affordable alternative to housing for the frail elderly, these residences vary considerably in the services offered and quality of care because there is no uniform licensing regulation. Each state regulates its board and care facilities in any way it chooses.

208

Although all states now require that board and care homes be licensed, there are thousands of them still operating without a license. The number of B and Cs in the United States, therefore, is unknown. In California, however, a recent survey revealed over thirty-five hundred board and care homes certified by the Social Service Department, with basic standards for safety, sanitation, and nutrition.

These homes usually service a wide cross section of seniors, from those who have been discharged from hospitals but are too ill to return home to those who are homeless. Rent usually includes room and board, utilities, cleaning, and laundry, as well as daily attention. The manager is responsible for the care of the elders. Help can be as personal as getting in and out of bed, bathing, and dressing, but B and Cs are not considered medical facilities. Contact the Veterans Administration or the Area Agency on Aging for local recommendations, or your local Department of Health.

*Group homes* are emerging as another living alternative for the frail elderly. This is a situation in which several elders live together, either in a private home or an apartment, under the supervision of a case worker through a local agency. The social worker makes provisions for daily necessities such as shopping and cleaning, and she or he stays in close touch with the elders to see how the unit is doing, providing counseling when necessary. The Jewish community has been very active facilitating these kinds of living arrangements. Your religious organization or the area agency on aging could be of help in locating existing group homes in your parents' community.

## Points to Remember

· Decide who will be the primary caregiver.

· Agree on how caretaking roles will be divided.

· Be clear on who will pay for care.

· Find out where all essential papers are kept: deeds, insurance, wills, funeral plans, etc.

· Know the signs to recognize when parents can no longer live alone.

· Review the options:
  1. living at home with multiple support systems;
  2. living with someone else;
  3. living in an institution.

· Assess the quality of the adult day care and adult day health care available.

· Identify what community care is available to help, as discussed in chapter 6.

· Determine whether moving in with an adult child is an option for your parents.

· Explore what respite care is available.

· Consider the availability of alternative housing: foster care, board and care homes, group homes.

*Chapter 10*

# Institutions: Long-Term Health Care

ACCORDING to the Senate Special Committee on Aging, 5.6 million Americans over sixty-five, or one in five older Americans, need long-term care. Most of them receive the care they need at home, while 1.4 million Americans are in nursing homes today.

## Nursing Home Residents: Who Are They?

Only 5 percent of all Americans over sixty-five are institutionalized today. Not surprisingly, the percentage rises with age. Sixteen percent of all eighty-five and older Americans, the old old, are in nursing homes. Americans eighty-five and over are the most rapidly increasing segment of our population, and it is projected that by the year 2000 there will be over two million nursing home residents. Seventy-three percent of nursing home residents today are women, and many of them do not have children. Over 50 percent of nursing home residents suffer from mental or behavioral problems, often due to Alzheimer's disease or other forms of dementia. The average age of residents is seventy-eight, and the average stay is two and a half years.

### ABOUT THE INDUSTRY

The nursing home industry is in a state of flux. It is big business, becoming the fastest-growing sector of the health care industry in the last ten years. Eighty percent of the sixteen thousand nursing homes in the United States are controlled by for-profit businesses. A quarter of a century ago, only half a billion dollars were spent on nursing home care. According to the *Mayo Clinic Medical Essay* of May 1987, there were $32 billion spent in 1984, with a projection of $60 billion anticipated for 1990. Although the additional monies spent should indicate better-quality care, this is not always the case.

As of this writing, there are 14,500 certified nursing homes throughout the country that participate in the Medicare and Medicaid programs. Nine thousand are skilled nursing facilities—providing around-the-clock care. The remaining 5,500 are primarily intermediate-care facilities. There are an additional 1,500 homes that are not part of Medicare or Medicaid.

Investigators for the U.S. Senate's Special Committee on Aging, while investigating only certified skilled nursing facilities, found that one-third of nursing homes did not comply with federal regulations. In many cases (one in ten), the picture was pretty grim, including maltreatment, neglect, and unnecessary deaths. The majority, however, do provide good care for our elderly. This simply means that we must inform ourselves as thoroughly as possible in order to choose wisely. One source of accurate information is the Ombudsman Program in your area, which can tell you if any complaints have been filed against the homes you are considering.

In 1978, as a result of the nonuniform, poor conditions found in many nursing homes, the Older Americans Act of 1965 was amended to include the establishment by each state of a long-term care Ombudsman program. Ombudsman is basically a watchdog program designed to protect the rights of the residents of nursing homes and other long-term health care facilities, by investigating and resolving complaints affecting their health, safety, and welfare. Residents and members of their families can report their problems, in confidence, to the Ombudsman volunteers who visit the nursing homes regularly. If warranted, the Ombudsman can assist in getting legal help.

ALZHEIMER'S DISEASE PATIENTS

According to the *Congressional Record,* more than a million and a half Americans are affected by Alzheimer's disease, a surprisingly common disorder that destroys certain vital cells of the brain. In one-third of all American families, one parent will succumb to this disease. It is the fourth leading cause of death among older Americans.

In addition to the devastating emotional price of supporting a family member suffering from Alzheimer's disease, the financial toll is in excess of $32 billion annually, spent by families to care for their loved ones.

Alzheimer's is a progressive disease, and in the early stages, when a victim is not exhibiting symptoms, he or she may act perfectly normal—to the point that the family has trouble believing that it will get worse. Denial in the initial stage can rob the family of the initiative to make the preparations necessary to cope with the oncoming total dependency, a deterioration that may take from three to as many as fifteen years. Characterized by loss of memory, physical deterioration, incontinence, an inability to communicate, disorientation, and, frequently, a change in personality, this disease can be devastating to a family.

A very dear friend of my family died a few years ago from Alzheimer's disease. Happily, my children had had a chance to know her when she was well, and so they understood my love for Charlotte. It is fascinating to me how we adjust to new circumstances in life and get pleasure from such different things. Charlotte had been wonderful to me and I always wanted to do something special for her. It was hard to find gifts that meant very much, although she had the knack of always making you feel they were special. I was thrilled, therefore, to be able to bring joy to Charlotte's life on an otherwise bleak day. My great happiness came when I walked into her room with my daughter, knowing that she would not know me anymore—but her face lit up at the sight of Nicole, and she held tightly to her hand for a long time. We were never sure who she thought Nicole was, but we knew that her presence had given Charlotte real pleasure, and it made us all extremely happy.

A greater national awareness of Alzheimer's disease has stepped up research efforts with the hope that the additional interest and concern will soon result in medical advances to combat this terrible disease. Meanwhile, the best advice for the families of an Alzheimer's patient would be to join one of the many support groups organized to help you cope.

FOR FURTHER INFORMATION: There are over 160 chapters of the Alzheimer's Disease and Related Disorders Association (ADRDA) across the nation and an additional 1,000 support groups for the caregivers. You may write them at 70 E. Lake Street, Suite 600, Chicago, IL 60601 or call toll free: (800) 621-0379 ([800] 572-6037 in Illinois).

Also, *The 36 Hour Day*, a family guide for caring for persons with Alzheimer's disease, related illnesses of dementia, and memory loss in later life. Nancy L. Mace and Peter V. Rabins. Baltimore: Johns Hopkins, 1982. Now available in paperback.

## When We Must Move

Keeping our parents independent as long as possible, with the help of community resources as needed, is a major goal of this book. Studies have supported what we intuitively have always known, that the longer our parents can remain in their own homes comfortably, the better off they are. For most of us, the decision to place a parent in a health care institution is a very difficult one even when it is best for them. We often associate such assignment with abandonment of our parent and failure on our part to effect a better solution. As we become responsible for much older parents, however, the likelihood of facing major physical disabilities increases, and few of us are equipped to handle twenty-four-hour treatment at home. When all alternative housing possibilities with attendant services have been explored and none can fulfill the specific requirements of our aged parents, it may be time to investigate nursing home facilities. If our parents reach the stage of needing around-the-clock care, and there is no way that we are financially or physically able to provide such care, a nursing home may be the most realistic and efficient answer.

According to government figures, consumer out-of-pocket expenses for nursing home care in 1986 are projected at 16 billion—about half the nation's total nursing home bill. The rest of the expense will be paid by Medicaid, Medicare paying under

2 percent of nursing home cost, and less than 1 percent of nursing home cost picked up by private insurance.

In spite of all that has been written about the exorbitant costs of nursing home care, when home care means employing twenty-four-hour supervision, it can become more expensive to keep a parent at home than to pay the typical $20,000 to $35,000 annual fee for nursing home care. This is usually the case when parents are still living alone. For the children of aging parents, this financial reality compounds the already difficult emotional and moral dilemma of choosing to place a parent in a nursing home. These soul-searching decisions must be made by each family within the context of what is possible for them. When nursing home placement is clearly the best decision under the circumstances, it becomes time to give up the guilt and make the necessary arrangements.

As a result of the fact that 90 percent of nursing home beds are filled, and there is an estimated shortfall of 250,000 beds nationwide, it is important to explore nursing home possibilities before they are the last resort. If a parent has a progressive disease, for instance, we should inform ourselves of the choices available in nursing home care well before it is needed.

Nursing homes fall into two basic categories:

1. *A skilled nursing facility* (SNF) is an institution that provides around-the-clock medical care through registered nurses, licensed practical nurses, and nurses' aids. A convalescent home or convalescent hospital is one example of an SNF. These SNFs are used by patients recovering from a hospital stay or those needing specialized medical treatment, for short or for long-term care. They offer physical, restorative, speech, and other therapies. It is important to note that only after hospitalization does Medicare cover the cost of the skilled nursing facility, and even then the coverage is limited to a stay of 100 days. Medicaid, however, pays for skilled nursing care (see chapter 8 for discussion of Medicare and Medicaid).

2. *An intermediate care facility* (ICF) is an institution with less complete medical staffing. Although around-the-clock medical care is not provided, at least one nursing shift per twenty-four hours is mandatory. Those elderly no longer needing the intense

care of a SNF, but who are incapable of living independently, generally move to an ICF. Note, too, that Medicaid also covers intermediate care, but Medicare does not.

A locked, or L, facility is necessary for some conditions of the elderly. Advanced Alzheimer's, for instance, or other dementias may require locked doors so that the patients do not wander off. Some SNFs offer locked facilities, but many do not. This may be an important consideration, depending on your parents' circumstances. Psychiatric hospitals or state hospitals are alternative choices.

Suzanne went through the agonizing decision with her mother to place her father in a nursing home. He was suffering from Alzheimer's and had become abusive to her mother. Up to this point, wandering off had not been a symptom of his disease and Suzanne never checked with the nursing home to see if it had a locked facility. It was not until he had settled in that her father began to wander, and the nursing home was unable to contain him. Both Suzanne and her mother had to face the agony of choosing another home, this time one with a locked facility, once again disrupting her father's life.

HOW TO CHOOSE A NURSING HOME

- Keep the parent involved in the decision as much as possible. If both parents are still alive, but only one is to be placed in a nursing home, much of the decision-making will be ours. Our well mother or father will be more apt to defer to us because of the extreme emotional stress involved.

- Obtain a list of all facilities available in your area. These lists are available through the state or county health department or through the local Ombudsman organization. (Consult the White Pages of the telephone directory.) The Yellow Pages will list local nursing homes. Your local hospital is another source of information.

- Gauge access to the facility for the family. Consider the family's transportation situation. What distances are practical enough to allow easy visitation? What is the availability of public transportation, parking facilities, and so on?

216

- Does the nursing home have a permanent or a provisional license? This information can be obtained by contacting the state or area nursing home Ombudsman.
- Seek good counsel.

The social workers attached to most hospitals are a good source of hands-on information regarding nursing homes. They are usually very familiar with the staff and how the facilities are run, particularly those social workers who are discharge planners.

Our parent's doctor would be one of the first to be consulted, but we may find that they are not always as knowledgeable as the social worker.

The clergy often visit nursing homes regularly and may be another good source of referral. Religious organizations can help with referrals, and they often have their own nursing homes.

Do not ignore the experience of friends, particularly those who have recently placed a loved one in a home. Although all cases and personalities are different, it can be quite helpful to know what unpleasant hurdles others have faced, or what pleasant surprises they have encountered.

- Does the nursing home accept Medicare patients and will it allow a patient to stay on if his or her resources diminish to the point of becoming eligible for Medicaid? Your local Ombudsman can help you to become familiar with your state's laws concerning this issue. Find out if the nursing home follows state regulations.
- Visit! Once a facility has been recommended, it is important to visit the nursing home, both to ask questions and to assess the atmosphere, the attitude of the staff, and the attitude of the patients. If it is a well-run, caring nursing home, such characteristics will be reflected in the attitude of the residents and visitors.

Understanding what a good nursing home provides will make us better judges of whether or not it suits our needs. A facility that is spotless, with manicured grounds and residents quietly watching television, may be aesthetically pleasing to the visitor, but not half as appealing to the residents as a noisy, active facility with people shuffling about in the halls and on the grounds.

Questions one should answer before choosing a home:

- Are there any vacancies? How long is the waiting list?

- Are the residents sedated?

- How are visitors restricted? Are patients and visitors given privacy? Are provisions made for conjugal visits?

- What is the aide-to-patient ratio? How many hours of training have they had? (Draft federal regulations would require eighty hours of training. None is required by law as of this writing.)

- How frequent is the staff turnover?

- Is the nursing home licensed?

- Is the food attractive? Is there variety in the menus? Are personal tastes and religious requests respected along with dietary controls?

- What is the cost? What is included—personal laundry, grooming, medical supplies?

- What insurance is accepted?

- Who takes care of the patient's personal finances?

- What belongings may be brought into the home? Furniture?

- Are any activities arranged for the bedridden?

- Are patients turned over enough to avoid bedsores?

- How does the nursing home provide for regular medical attention? Do doctors make regular visits? Dentist? Optometrist? Podiatrist?

- How are roommates chosen? What is done when personality conflicts arise?

- Is there a facility for worshiping? Are clergy available?

- What is the procedure for discharge? Refunds?

- What arrangements are there for telephone, newspaper delivery, radios, and televisions?

- Is there a social worker on staff?

- Do they provide for patients who need hand feeding?

- Do they provide care for incontinent patients?

218

- How do the residents look? Are they well groomed, fingernails and hair clean? Are the men shaved?

- Is the staff courteous?

- Is there an activities calendar posted for participation?

- Is reading material available? In large print or tapes?

- Are there strong, offensive odors in the home?

- Do the residents look alert?

- Does the staff refer to residents by name?

- Does the staff treat residents as adults or as children?

- Have efforts been made to create a more homelike atmosphere?

KNOWING YOUR RIGHTS

Nursing home reform is a hot issue of the eighties and with the swelling nursing home population as we approach the end of the century, it will become even hotter. The difficulty in giving advice is that with the variances of the fifty states, there is little consistency of policy. Through recent legislation in most states, however, there are very specific rights that must be assured to all nursing home residents. Knowing what these rights are in your state could help you assure the best possible comfort, both psychological and physical, for your parents. Contact your local Ombudsman Long-Term Care Program for a complete list of patients' rights. Some State Department of Health Services, Licensing and Certification divisions produce consumer guides to nursing homes, and the Area Agency on Aging can provide you with appropriate government publications.

FINANCIAL INFORMATION IN PREPARATION
FOR ENTERING A NURSING HOME

1. Power of attorney. Upon entering a nursing home, your parents will usually be asked to grant someone a power of attorney to be responsible for seeing that all the bills are paid (see chapter 7).

219

2. Medicare eligibility. It is important for our parents to know if they are eligible to receive Medicare. If the nursing home tells them that they are not eligible for Medicare, they should request, under their rights, that the nursing home send Medicare a "no-payment" claim. This claim will cause Medicare to respond with a written denial that our parents can use to appeal, in the hopes of reversing the decision. Over half of the appeal decisions are reversed. There are time limits within which one must appeal.

Medicare does not pay nursing home custodial care. Medicare will pay nursing home care, however, under two conditions: (1) the patient must have spent three days in a hospital and enter the nursing home within the following thirty days, and (2) the patient must be in need of skilled nursing home care.

3. Medicaid and division of assets. Our parents should be aware of whether or not the state within which they are residing provides for the division of assets, when qualifying for Medicaid, when one spouse is admitted to a nursing home. Some states do.

In California, when entering a nursing home a married couple's assets are automatically divided. When the spouse in the nursing home spends his or her assets down to $1,800, that spouse will then qualify for Medicaid (called Medical in California). Family residence, car, and home furnishings are exempt from division and benefit the spouse outside the nursing home.

Medicaid administrators will include assets that have been transferred out, within two years of applying for benefits, as remaining a part of the applicant's estate. It is very important, therefore, to keep proper financial records, and to do as much advance estate planning as possible.

Check with an attorney or the Social Security office to be sure of patients' rights under the law. Federal court legislation is now pending that will help to make clear the regulations regarding Medicaid. Most lawyers are unfamiliar with Medicaid rules and asset preservation. We should ask our parents' attorney, if he or she is unfamiliar with these laws, to supply our parents with the names of consultants from the American Bar Association Commission on the Legal Problems of the Elderly, or write: American Bar Association, 1800 M Street, N.W., Washington, DC 20036. The Area Agency on Aging or the local Legal Services offices can also be of help.

MAKING THE TRANSITION EASIER

Placing a parent in a nursing home, as difficult as it may be, does not have to signal the end of a close relationship. We can help our frail parent to make the transition by discussing the fears and apprehensions we both may have and by making his or her new surroundings as familiar as possible. Bring plenty of favorite objects, including pictures, to personalize the new room. We should also try to stay and have the first meal with our mother or father, and get to know those who will be most directly in charge of his or her care. Not only will frequent visits help in the adjustment, encouraging visits from other family and friends will help our parents to continue to feel included. And we can always, when physical conditions permit, take our parents out for the day. A family picnic is an excellent setting for intergenerational interaction.

As their physical abilities diminish, the sensual pleasures that our parents experience from little things can be greatly heightened. We are often told of the joy derived from watching a beautiful sunset, or the pleasing sensation of the warm water of a shower over their bodies. What this should mean to us is that a hug is more valued than ever. Perhaps taking the time to thoroughly brush our mother's hair, or to give our father a nice back rub, are gifts more important than flowers or a card.

Our children should be prepared for any unsightly changes in our parents so that they are not afraid to be close. Having a hand held by a grandchild during a visit can produce a great deal of pleasure.

MAKING VISITS MORE SUCCESSFUL

For some of us, making the decision to place a parent in a nursing home was easy compared with the emotional strain of visiting. Our feelings of guilt are often mixed with the sadness that we have nothing to say to each other. The following list of the most pleasurable ways to stay involved with each other was compiled through the many suggestions of nursing home staff and residents:

- Bring flowers that your parent can help arrange in a vase.

- Bring children. There are usually areas out of the flow of traffic where they can play.

- Bring other family members for birthdays and holidays so that your parent can feel a part of the family.

- Bring letters from family members and read them aloud.

- Bring tape recordings of conversations from family members to play together, and record one to take home.

- Bring current pictures of family members and old albums that you can relive together.

- Bring magazines and newspapers and read them aloud. Often they are available from the resident library.

- Bring record albums that can be played in the common area.

- Bring a picnic lunch to eat outside, or inside if the weather is poor. This is a good time to talk about recipes and perhaps compile a family recipe book.

- Bring projects that can be worked on together, such as needle-point or a jigsaw puzzle.

- Bring holiday cards for your mother or father to send. You can address them and help with the notes, if necessary. This is a good way to insure them more mail during the holidays.

- Decorate your parent's room for each holiday. Involve the grand-children in this project.

- Go for walks together.

- Take your mother or father out for a drive, and stop somewhere for a treat to eat.

- Join your parents in activities run by the home such as bingo, singing, etc., so they can show off their family.

- Give your mother or father a manicure and hand massage, maybe while watching a television show together, or while talking of things you did that week.

· Ask for your parent's advice when making family decisions. Keep him or her psychologically involved with all that is going on at home.

When you cannot visit:

· Phone.

· Send letters or postcards.

· Send flowers.

· Send "care" packages.

· Send pictures.

## On Death, Dying, and Funerals

The issues of death and dying and how to prepare for them are complex. Religious values, personal truths, and wishes of the family may all vary. As a culture, we tend to ignore death, and doctors traditionally think of it as a failure. Today, thanks to the early works of Elisabeth Kübler-Ross, a pioneer in the study of dying, and to those who have followed her lead, we have more understanding of the needs of the dying person. The fact that there is a pattern to the psychological acceptance of death had been generally ignored, with the feeling that "of course they are depressed, they are dying." Now we have some guidance in helping a dying loved one. The denial, the anger, the depression, and the grief are stages through which our patience and support can help them progress.

### COMMUNICATION WITH THE DYING

Statements that acknowledge the seriousness of the condition while still expressing hope can be of great value and promote honest dialogue. Often the patient is anxious to discuss his or her feelings only to have the family insist, "You certainly are not going to die. Now I don't want to hear that kind of talk." The cue as to what you should discuss with your dying parent should be taken from him or her. If there is a reluctance to discuss death on

223

the patient's part, it should not be forced. There should be honest answers from family and doctors and plenty of loving attention. If they want to be alone, that, too, should be respected. It may be hard not to take it personally, but they may need that time to adjust to their condition. Be sure that they know you are available whenever they need you.

Understanding that death is a very important part of life gives us a new perspective. We begin to think of it not as an end but as part of a process. Those of a religious nature may be reassured by the popular, simple observation—dying is of divine origin, which means it is absolutely safe.

FOR FURTHER READING: *On Death and Dying* or *Death, the Final Stage of Growth,* Elisabeth Kübler-Ross (New York: Collier Books, 1969); *Living When a Loved One Has Died,* Earl A. Grollman (Boston: Beacon Press, 1977); *Who Dies?* or *A Gradual Awakening,* Stephen Fevine (New York: Doubleday, 1982).

INSTRUCTIONS REGARDING DEATH

For the purpose of nursing home/hospital selection, it is important to know ahead of time what measures you, or your well parent, expect to follow in the case of imminent death. Chapter 7 discusses the "right-to-die living will" and "durable power of attorney." Both are legal vehicles that affect whether or not "heroic" measures should be taken for purposes of resuscitation. It is important to know what the policy of the nursing home is regarding this issue and to make your parents' wishes known to immediate staff and friends as well as to the doctor.

Ann and her mother had discussed death openly and her mother had been adamant that she did not want any heroic measures taken to sustain life. She felt so strongly about the matter, in fact, that she left instructions with her doctor to this effect. Unfortunately, neither she nor her doctor were present when her mother suffered a major stroke in a restaurant with her friends. Ann's mother was resuscitated by the paramedics who were called, and she was put on life-sustaining equipment almost immediately. Although technically brain-dead, Ann's mother survived for another year with the help of machines, a year of great expense, pain, and guilt for Ann, who somehow felt responsible for her mother's sad condition. Had Ann's mother told her friends of her wishes, the family might have been spared this year of pain. There are no simple answers in this age of technological advances.

## HOSPITAL POLICIES FOR THE DYING

The moral issues, as well as the religious implications, involved in life-releasing measures make these decisions ones that hospitals and doctors cannot make alone. The legalities of removing a brain-dead patient from life-sustaining equipment can be very complicated, sometimes requiring legal action. Religious and legislative leaders are grappling with this sensitive issue.

Meanwhile, hospitals vary considerably in their treatment of the dying. Some hospitals use a variety of inconspicuous codes by the patient's name to differentiate the means of patient resuscitation. Rather than reflecting a callous attitude, these systems simply show the confusion resulting from lack of proper guidelines that hospitals face today, given the technology they possess to keep bodies alive long past the time when nature would have let them die.

The Joint Commission on Accreditation of Hospitals has asked hospitals to come up with formal policies to determine when doctors and nurses should refrain from resuscitating the terminally ill: DNR—do not resuscitate. New York's Task Force on Life and the Law puts that state in an easy position to reply since it has already recommended such guidelines to the state legislature.

Previous patient consent can alleviate the burden of decision-making by others in such a time of crisis.

## HOSPICE

When death is imminent (six months or less), and the patient and family have accepted its inevitability, hospice can be of valuable help. Funded by Medicare, and also privately funded, hospice is a coordinated program of services, including pain control and counseling, which allows the family to care for the dying patient at home. The patient's doctor usually is a main part of the hospice team, changing his curative approach to one of pain and symptom management. Social workers, nurses, aides, volunteers, and clergy work in tandem with the family to allow the loved one the dignity of a pain-free death in his or her own home, surrounded by family.

If these circumstances are similar to the situation of one of your parents, you may want more complete information about the hospice programs and how they work. The National Hospice Organization tells us that over 65 percent of their patients are elders—sixty-five and older. They have roughly fifteen hundred programs across the United States caring for the needs of 100,000 dying patients annually. Write to them at 1901 North Fort Myer Drive, Suite 901, Arlington, VA 22209 or call (703) 243-5900.

---

What to do when a parent dies:
  · If the death occurred at home, call your doctor or the coroner to pronounce your parent dead.
  · Call family and dear friends. Some may need time to get there and you will need support.
  · Call the funeral home. They get the necessary permits and death certificates and come for the body.
  · Call your parent's minister, priest, or rabbi, if there is to be a religious service.
  · Call the attorney who will be handling the estate.
  · Notify the local newspapers of the funeral notice. A biographical blurb about your parent, and a picture if he or she was active in the community, can be prepared ahead of time.
  · Send in any insurance claims.

Reading this list now may save many anxious moments later by having the information ready that you know you will need—important telephone numbers, names, and papers.

---

FUNERAL ARRANGEMENTS

The greatest gift to any family is to have one's funeral desires specified ahead of time. Many parents have bought burial plots and have written instructions concerning everything from the service to the kind of casket. We have known for twenty years my mother's wishes, but, lest we forget, Ros has gone over them with the mortician she chose. It has been a source of teasing over the years, but it is actually a present the whole family will appreciate.

There are an increasing number of options available as alternatives to the traditional funeral. The expense (between $2,000 and $3,000, exclusive of burial), shrinking land space in urban areas, and the desire of many to further the knowledge of medical science have all contributed to the choices.

- Traditional funeral—most costly. This is still the most popular, and legislation has been passed to help fight unnecessary expenses incurred at a time of grief and cloudy thinking. Funeral homes are now required by law to disclose all costs—even over the phone, so that comparison shopping is possible—and to make them available in writing when requested. You need not be intimidated by the caricature of the mortician leaning over the grieving widow and saying, "Of course, you want only the best for your husband." The best could be a mahogany casket lined in satin for thousands of dollars.

   The costs include:

   Transportation of the body from the place of death to the funeral home and later to the service and the burial plot.

   Coffin. This can make a big overall difference with substantial variety in price and style.

   Embalming. This preservation technique that replaces all body fluids is not required by law, but is recommended for an open casket and in hot climates.

   Paperwork. This includes death certificates, burial permits, obituary notice (if done by them). Death certificates are usually $3 to $5 each, and they are necessary for the filing of insurance papers, real estate dealings, stocks, and any other transaction for which proof is needed for a change of name of ownership from the deceased to another party.

   Use of the funeral home for viewing and/or a memorial service. If the service is done elsewhere, there may be fees associated with the clergy.

- Cremation. This increasingly popular alternative has simplicity and reduced costs in its favor. The body is taken to a crematory where it is reduced to ashes so that no burial plot is needed, although the urn of ashes can be buried in a cemetery or placed in a special building with a bronze marker. Many people prefer to scatter the ashes on a mountaintop or over a favorite lake. (Check state law for restrictions.) All the other expenses associated with death remain basically the same.

· Donation of body. Many people feel little attachment to the body after death and are happy to donate it for educational purposes. The cost is minimal and often the cremated remains will be returned to the family, if so requested. Call the anatomy department of the nearest medical school for further information. The requirements and needs vary from school to school. Write: U.S. Department of Health and Human Services, Washington, DC 20201 for the pamphlet *How to Donate the Body or Its Organs,* publication no. (NIH) 79-776. You will also receive a Uniform Donor Organ Card. (Also note, the deceased's next of kin must agree to the donation or it becomes invalid, so talk it over.)

· Direct disposition. This method speeds up the process by taking the body directly to the cemetery or the crematorium. This may be a particularly sound choice if your parent died away from home and memorial services are to be held elsewhere.

FOR FURTHER INFORMATION: Continental Association of Funeral and Memorial Societies, 2001 S Street, N.W., Suite 530, Washington, DC 20009; (202) 745-0634 (they publish a pamphlet that lists local funeral societies throughout the United States); Cremation Association of North America, 111 East Wacker Drive, Chicago, IL 60601; (312) 644-6610.

## Points to Remember

- Make plans right away if a dementia is diagnosed—well before the symptoms precipitate a crisis.

- Learn how to choose a nursing home and what key questions to ask.

- Understand the financial commitment and the rights of the patient.

- Plan the transition with as much family involvement as possible.

- Consider the guidelines for successful visiting experiences.

- Know ahead of time what steps the nursing home or affiliated hospital will take in case of death.

- Review "right-to-die living will" and "durable power of attorney."

- Explore hospice services: If death is imminent, particularly from cancer or other progressive disease, these services for a pain-free death at home may be preferred by the patient and the family.

- Review all funeral options. To avoid being pressured, consider taking a friend with you when making funeral choices, or get costs over the phone.

*Chapter 11*

# The Wave of the Future: Corporate, Social, and Legislative Changes

"A measure of our success as a Nation is how we take care of our young and our old."

*Hubert H. Humphrey*

"Anyone who thinks that we've reached the end of the longevity rainbow simply hasn't been paying attention to developments in medicine. Just imagine what a cure for cancer could do to the need for senior housing, nursing homes and life care centers."

*Hicks B. Waldron*
*Chairman and Chief Executive Officer, Avon Products, Inc.*

WE'VE discussed how we as caregivers are sandwiched be-tween our many responsibilities—giving time and care to our children, our spouses, our careers, our community involvements, and our aging parents. We've also said that the great majority of caregiving in America is done by women—wives, daughters, and daughters-in-law. One major part of the equation that has altered the picture of how America traditionally cares for its elderly is that women are now an integral part of the workplace. They are not as readily available to give care. This does not mean that they are not the ones still taking on the greatest responsibility for the caregiving; it means that the caregiving job for them is more stressful than ever before. The amount of time spent caregiving can, in some cases, be equivalent to a second career for a woman, and there are no clear role models to follow.

Although today the work force is comprised primarily of white American-born males, by the end of the century, only 15 percent of the entrants into the work force will be white males, according to a study conducted by the Hudson Institute of Indianapolis for the U.S. Labor Department. This altered profile will include, in increasing numbers, women, who are predicted to account for two-thirds of the job-seeking work force by the year 2000.

The Hudson survey confirms previous studies in predicting that the majority of new jobs will be in the service industries. They go on to say that unemployment will continue to be highest among low-skilled workers, with more opportunities for educated employees.

The prevalence of divorce in our society, one of the factors that has thrown many women into the work force as primary wage earners, has also resulted in fragmented families. The women are often left with less immediate support in their caregiving tasks than ever before, and sometimes they have more people for whom they are concerned, for example, former mothers-in-law or fathers-in-law.

The stress of the caretaking role is exacerbated by the fact that our mobile society has moved some of us many miles from our parents. This has made family communications more awkward, even if a sibling lives close to where his or her parents are. Knowledge of what resources are available in time of crisis, or for long-term care, becomes more crucial as the distance increases. Good sources of information and referral, therefore, are of primary importance.

## Caretaking and Corporate America

The economic impact of this complex situation is beginning to be recognized by corporate America. Just as the business world woke up to the fact that good child care is of primary concern to many of its employees, business is becoming aware of the dependent care crisis of its employees vis-à-vis their aging parents. "Company support for elder care is likely to become the new pioneering benefit of the 1990s," says expert Dana Friedman of the Conference Board, a well-respected business research organization in New York City. She feels that it will be more readily received than child care issues because elder care is a

231

more acceptable problem in the workplace, since the executive decision-makers are more likely to have aging parents than to have preschoolers.

Chapter 1 tells us that many adult children will spend more time caring for aging parents than they do for their children. This statistic is not lost on industry. Employees who spend so many hours caring for their aging parents display a loyalty and sense of responsibility that are the very characteristics valued by employers. Business cannot afford to lose these workers, who are increasingly difficult to replace. As a result of the fact that the baby-boom generation is already in the workplace and the pool of younger potential employees is growing smaller, finding entry-level employees is a growing concern for American businesses.

Nor can business afford to lose the time required by the caregivers for making calls during working hours to community resources, to their aging parents, and to otherwise deal with the caretaking of their parents. Another concern to business is that the worker's productivity is additionally affected when his or her concentration is diverted by the stresses of caregiving. This increases errors and inefficiency. Caretakers are more prone to depression and stress and often use more medical benefits than their co-workers. Lateness and increased absenteeism are additional concerns to business.

Some companies are beginning to feel that the natural solution is for business to become a partner with these valued employees in the managing of their caretaking responsibilities. Allowing more-flexible work schedules could create some daytime hours when phone calls could be made, for instance. Corporate pressure on health agencies to stay open later in the evening is another way of aiding the caregiver. Most valuable of all, perhaps, would be for business to become the source of the needed information and referrals, which the new caregiver has to ferret out for herself or himself, and which takes so much time.

First, of course, business must be aware of the problem. In 1985, an employee survey by **The Travelers Companies** revealed the concern of those employees related to the caregiving of elderly parents. According to the survey, one in five of the Travelers' employees age thirty and older provides some form of care to an older person. Eight percent of those employees spent thirty-five hours or more per week on caregiving tasks.

Caregiving employees provide an average of 10.2 hours per week of care for an older relative. For females providing care, the average jumps to 16.1 hours per week. One of the unexpected results of the survey was to find that the task of elder care began at such a young age for a number of the employees. Thirty-one percent were in the thirty-to-forty age group. As reported in the June 1986 issue of *Business and Health,* James Davis, then vice-president of The Travelers' corporate personnel and administration department, said, "One of the results of our aging population is that increasing numbers of employees are caring for an older person and, in some cases, for their own children as well. Travelers believes that heavy caregiving, coupled with work and other family responsibilities, can affect job performance and that by identifying caregivers' needs, the company can help those employees meet their responsibilities as well as build a more productive work force."

The Travelers Employee Caregiver Survey found their employee concerns were for more information on:

| | |
|---|---|
| Community resources | 80% |
| Public or private insurance coverage | 78% |
| How to choose community resources | 77% |
| Specific illnesses | 71% |
| Home care | 67% |
| Questions to ask a physician | 64% |
| How to choose a nursing home | 64% |
| Educational workshops and tips for caregivers | 57% |
| Support groups for caregivers | 45% |

As a result of the survey, The Travelers was anxious to respond to the needs of their employees. Their first step was to hold a Caregiving Fair at which they brought in twenty community agencies who were invited to discuss their services with the employees. Included were home health care, counseling, adult day care, lifestyle alternatives, long-distance caretaking, and caregiver support groups. Next, The Travelers instituted lunch-time seminars with speakers knowledgeable in the caregiving field. Some discussions included how to communicate better within the family and understanding how we age. The company made use of in-house television screens for videotapes on various aspects of elder care. The overall informational program was further supported by the creation of a library on elder care, and the in-house newspaper began publishing articles on elder care. The final step was to develop a caregiving support group that continues to meet weekly during the lunch hour.

This multipronged experimental approach to assisting The Travelers employees at their home offices in Connecticut was well received. The convenience of the program added to its success and word-of-mouth communication among the employees helped the program to grow. The Travelers noted that once an employee uses an assistance service program, other programs are more likely to be used by that same employee.

Perhaps the most successful part of The Travelers Companies'experience was the fact that results from the survey drew national attention to this dependent care issue in the workplace. At the same time, a number of other corporations were experimenting with assistance programs of their own.

**Pepsico, Inc.** has emerged as a recent corporate leader in creating special benefit programs to deal with eldercare. According to Shan Burchenal, benefits planning manager for Pepsico, the average age of their employees is well under forty. Pepsico feels, nonetheless, that caring for elder parents will become an increasingly important employee issue for United States industry, and one that should be faced now.

Phase one of their employee support program regarding elder-care was put into effect in early 1986. This "cafeteria" program included:

1. Workshops with information and discussion for personal action plans.

2. A resource guidebook created with great sensitivity for understanding the aging process and presenting a practical reference of resources for the caretaker.

3. A telephone hot line set up for specific questions from caretakers, providing anonymity.

4. A pretax reserve account for medical expenses, referred to as a "benefits plus" plan; this plan allows the employees to set aside money from earnings before taxes into a special reserve account set up by the company to pay for medical and dependent care expenses, provided very specific conditions are met.

Phase two, which went into effect in 1987, has a stronger concentration on education and information. In addition to the original services, there are more discussion groups that focus on emotional rather than factual matters, while other groups deal specifically with the financial aspects of caregiving. The second annual health fair had a special section on eldercare to make the employees more aware of local support systems. One of the problems, according to Burchenal, is that people tend to ignore the information until they themselves are in a crisis situation. "We hope to make them better prepared to handle a crisis by helping them to know what is available ahead of time."

**Ciba-Geigy, Con Edison,** and **Mobil Oil** tried to sensitize their employees to the issues of eldercare by hiring an outside consultant to present lunchtime seminars entitled "You and Your Aging Parents."

**The Procter and Gamble Company** has taken a different approach. Through its FlexComp program, it helps its employees by providing nontaxable reimbursement of in-home and day care expenses incurred for elderly dependents.

**IBM** estimates that 30 percent of its employees have some responsibility for elder care. Recognizing the emotional and physical stress that caretaking exerts in the workplace, IBM implemented a nationwide corporate Elder Care Referral Service in February of this year for its employees and retirees. Work/Family Elder Directions, Inc., of Watertown, Mass., developed the ECRS network of 175 community-based organizations for IBM and will administer the program.

ECRS is the first corporate elder care program to be established nationwide and it is significant to note that the network will be available for use by other companies, both on a local and a nationwide basis, later this year.

The options for employees seeking elder care depend primarily on what services exist within a given community. Elder Care Referral Service is able to help IBM employees to become aware of the possibilities and to make educated choices by providing:

- Access to information on local elder care from a single source
- Consultation to discuss employee's specific family needs
- Referrals to elder care providers
- Material to help make appropriate choices
- Follow-up contact to insure that employee needs have been met

**Southwestern Bell,** as with many of the Bell Telephone systems, believes that the issue of caregiving employees has a direct and deepening influence on business. According to John E. Hayes, Jr., Southwestern's president and CEO, "It is a sound business decision to get involved with eldercare." He believes that what was once a family matter has become a major national issue.

The three-part awareness program installed at Southwestern Bell is called "Caregiving, the Challenge of Eldercare." It consists of:

1. A resource manual.
2. An audiotape entitled "I Care." This advice and reassurance program for the caregiver is designed for maximum flexibility in fitting any worker's schedule. It is available in cassette form for a car or portable tape player.
3. A television documentary "We're Not Alone," narrated by Colleen Dewhurst. This program reaches outside the immediate employee group. It airs on PBS and is available for use by community groups.

For information on fees and copies of the videotape, audiotape, and manual, write: "Caregiving: The Challenge of Eldercare," 7 Nowell Farme Road, Carlisle, MA 01741, or call (617) 371-0518.

**Campbell Soup** of New Jersey, which has a vested interest in the growing elder population from a products marketing point of view, has a heightened awareness of the demographic shift in the age of America's population and is, therefore, one of the early corporations to respond to the needs of its caretaking employees. The company is making available, through its employee benefits program, the family care leave policy. This allows workers up to a three-month period of time off within a twenty-four-month period, without pay, to care for a seriously ill immediate family member, including parents. The company continues support for benefits during this leave, and assures the worker of the same or comparable job upon return.

**Hallmark Cards, Inc.,** is another corporation that has knowledge of the changing demographics and sees older Americans as an emerging consumer group.

Hallmark's corporate philosophy in assisting their employees with caregiving tasks is to make use of qualified resources already in place within the community. In their Kansas City corporate home office, for instance, they have contracted with Family and Children Services, through the United Way, to provide necessary services for their employees. The three primary services are:

1. Telephone case assessment

2. Consumer materials mailed to the employee, and

3. Written follow-up by the provider

Hallmark also makes available a pretax reserve account for dependent medical expenses through their Flexible Benefit Plan (FlexPlan). Furthermore, this plan also includes reimbursement for out-of-pocket health care expenses not usually covered by insurance, such as eyeglasses and contact lenses, hearing aids, and health care travel expenses. Specific qualifications must be met in order to be eligible for these benefits.

Clearly, this is only a beginning. It is significant that major corporations with nationwide employment are starting to talk about the dependent care of elder parents as an issue of great concern. There are many other businesses, large and small, that have recognized the problem and have begun programs to do something to relieve caregiver stress for their employees. The University of Bridgeport in Connecticut, through its Corporate Eldercare Project, funded by the United States Administration on Aging in 1985, has been doing extensive studies on the care-taking role and its effects on business. In its briefing book, *Issues for an Aging America: Employees and Eldercare,* are listed some of the businesses that have taken the corporate initiative to offer elder care support to their employees. While all of these corporations have information or referral services, the following have proceeded a step farther by offering programs for flexible benefits, easing time constraints, formal community linkages, or counseling: **Blue Cross and Blue Shield of Indiana, Champion International, Honeywell, Inc., Levi Strauss & Company, McNeill Consumer Products, People's Bank of Bridgeport, Connecticut, Pepsico, Inc., Pitney Bowes, Inc.,** and **Remington Products.**

No company will be able to solve all the complex problems that the caregiver faces, but as Jack Carter, director of Dependent Care Programs for IBM, stated in an interview with Dana Friedman of the Conference Board, "It seems that the universal thread that holds everyone together in a sea of issues is the need for information." At this stage, the employer often knows as little as the employees about caregiving needs. As a result of early corporate initiatives, however, some companies are already emerging as strong partners who, together with their employees, have taken the first important step in looking for solutions.

We have taken the time to outline some specific programs that are now in place in corporate America because it is we, the adult children of aging parents, who are in a position to advocate many of these changes. Some of us are the ones who sit in the board rooms, but most of us are valued employees who may be spending less and less time concentrating on our jobs while we spend more and more time seeking solutions to our concerns for our parents' care. Knowing what other companies are doing, particularly in the area of information and referral, may be enough incentive to get a program started at our place of employment. Feeling that we have a sympathetic ear at work, as opposed to having work be the place where we must sneak in phone calls whenever we can, should go a long way in relieving some of the stress of caregiving.

Talking with the management team at work is a good place to start, particularly if there are a number of women in your firm. Talk to other employees, especially those who are caring for an elder or those married to a caregiver. If you are able to provide substantial information from data you have been able to collect, it may be easier to sell your ideas for change to management. Emphasize the pluses of taking the caregivers' needs into consideration—less time on the phone, less absenteeism, and so forth. Companies are always looking for ways to save money—show them how. Point out how other companies are responding to the needs of the caregivers. When it comes time to plead your case, be prepared with documentation, your requests, and copies of your reports for everyone. The issue is one of caring for our country's elders and an appeal to management should cause no damage to your career.

A simple first step to initiate is to request that your company order and distribute the booklet *Where to Turn for Help for Older Persons.* Produced by the United States Administration on Aging, this pocket-sized guide is a layman's directory to resources for older persons for any community in the nation. Businesses are encouraged to imprint their company logo on the cover of this resource booklet and make it available to all of their employees on a national, regional, or local scale. The cost of this caregivers' guide is $1.75 per copy. Write to: Superintendent of Documents, United States Government Printing Office, Washington, DC 20401, stock number 01706200139-1. Camera-ready copies can be obtained for reprinting by writing to: Caregivers' Guide, U.S. Administration on Aging, 330 Independence Avenue, S.W., Washington, DC 20201.

## Employing Older Workers

Although it is still too early to know the extent to which corporate America will be involved with the caretaking issue, much creative thinking is taking place today. Government, private industry, and care providers are coming together to help produce a collective response. The consensus seems to be that an integral part of how we can best care for our elderly is to help them live productive lives in the mainstream of society for as long as possible. Social scientists used to tell us that it was natural for the elderly to remove themselves from active involvements in life as they aged.

The overwhelming feeling of gerontologists today, however, is that the best medicine to assist the elderly in staying happy and well is to allow them opportunities to continue to contribute to society. For many, this means helping them stay employed. Although employee benefit programs concern themselves primarily with caretaking of the frail elderly, keeping our parents independent for as long as possible will postpone this caretaking task, not only for the adult children, but for corporate America as well. A bumper sticker seen recently in the Pocono Mountains in Pennsylvania said it well: "Hire an older worker, it's good business!"

The question of what is going to happen in the future with our growing pool of older workers coupled with a decreasing source of younger workers is not clear. Nor do we have a good understanding at this point of the nature of the jobs that will be available as technology continues to change. When we were children, writing to our pen pals, never did we conceive of the notion of writing our letters on a screen that would correct all our spelling errors and then spew out the letter on the recipient's screen all the way across the country. By the same token, we can only guess at the variety of jobs demanding less strength and more skill that might be perfect for us during our older years. Today, however, our parents may find themselves caught in an era in which mergers are eliminating some jobs before workers are ready to give them up and technology has not yet created a variety of new jobs for the future.

The advantages of hiring older workers are not lost on everyone. As a group, they are more dependable and more flexible than their younger co-workers. The following vignette, as published originally in the *Detroit Free Press* in March 1987, and reprinted by the Travelers Corporation, shows the value of the older worker to corporate America:

> When Hartford, Ct. was hit by a big snow storm in January, personnel officials at the Travelers Co. looked out over their ranks of desks and computer terminals and discovered that only one of their "unretired" workers—their elderly, part-time workers—had not made it in.

Among the younger employees from a temporary-help service who were supposed to be there on that snowy morning, the absence rate was substantial.

Senior workers have a wide range of experience to share, and often imbue young workers with good work habits. Another bonus of hiring these valuable employees today is that they attract a peer consumer group.

One forward-thinking program that is being tested is **The Travelers Corporation**'s "retiree job bank," through which seniors can find part-time positions. Travelers "unretired" workers are allowed to work up to 960 hours per year, without loss of Travelers retirement income. A response to the bank of 350 Travelers retirees was not enough to fill the company demands. In order to help publicize this program, the company gave a large "unretirement party" and opened its doors to all seniors in the area, whether or not they had previous affiliations with Travelers. Today, the total retiree job bank pool of "unretired" workers numbers close to seven hundred.

**McDonald's** McMasters program is an example of the need of business for service employee positions filled by the older worker. It is a program designed specifically to find, train, and hire workers fifty-five and older to work at McDonald's fast-food restaurants. Although this food service market may not be challenging enough for many retirees, it does offer others an opportunity to remain integrated in society while earning a salary, and it has the flexibility of offering part-time employment for those who do not want a full-time commitment.

Operation ABLE—Ability Based on Long Experience—is another approach to employment designed to match the job with the specific skills of older workers. Based in Chicago, it is a joint effort of private foundations, government agencies, and several Chicago corporations. This very successful program, serving five thousand job-seeking elders a year, helps the older individual market himself or herself. This concept of community cooperation has been repeated in a number of cities across the nation, including San Francisco, Los Angeles, and Boston.

241

AGEISM IN THE WORKPLACE

In spite of the strides being made by some forward-thinking people, there is still an insidious problem facing many of our parents in the workplace—ageism in corporate America. Those companies who have not yet awakened to the significance of the population shift and its economic impact on business will be caught short—literally, of employees—if they do not become savvy soon. There is a pressing need for business to see older workers in a new way, for we can no longer afford the waste of human potential that occurs every time an older worker is passed over for advancement or forced out of a company early. Valuable people are being lost and the cost of replacement is high. Turnover expenses include recruitment, orientation, training, and loss of experience—and that is assuming there is a pool of qualified workers from which to choose. Age discrimination cases are becoming increasingly popular in our nation's courts, making such practices unprofitable in yet another way. The sad part is that some of the discrimination is not a result of malice, but of ignorance—not understanding the capabilities of our senior population. That is something we, the adult children, should be able to change!

The plight of the older worker is poignantly presented in a new twenty-nine-minute "awareness" film called *Working Late*. Produced by Woody Clark Productions in San Francisco, this true-to-life portrayal of prejudice in the workplace was commissioned by the U.S. Administration on Aging and is hosted by Elliott Gould. A few copies should be available for viewing through the Area Agencies on Aging, or copies can be purchased by your company or civic organization from Woody Clark Productions, Inc., 943 Howard Street, San Francisco, CA 94103; (415) 777-1668.

ENTICEMENTS NOT TO RETIRE

The irony of the situation is that when the decade comes to an end and business begins to face the serious shortage of entry-level workers, it will not be enough to simply allow older workers to stay on. Employers will have to offer direct incentives to retain their over-sixty employees. As we have read in chapter 4, there are many exciting opportunities awaiting the healthy, retired crowd. The numbers of those who choose to remain employed are not very high, nor will they increase until business understands the changes that are needed to entice them to stay. Certainly, more flexible work hours, financial rewards for delayed retirement, more part-time work with benefits, and accrued pension benefits, even after the age of sixty-five, will be in order.

## New Businesses Addressing the Elderly

The concerns and interests of the elderly are new targets for our entrepreneurial dollars. Today's business, keenly aware of changing demographics, is looking to the senior population as a greatly expanding source of income by supplying them with more services, opportunities, and products. As a result, new for-profit businesses are opening, and established businesses are redirecting their marketing efforts in order to address this rapidly growing consumer group. With the erosion of heretofore accepted stereotypes, services to the frail elderly are being joined by many new services for the well old.

We have mentioned the influence that the growth of the elder population is having on architecture, elder law, medicine, and education, in addition to business. The possibilities for new businesses, new products, new services, and a repositioning of existing products are developing as rapidly as the new interests of the aging. When the legs of the tennis-playing, marathon-running baby-boomers begin to ache, for instance, someone better have built enough golf carts to drive them around the courses!

*Physical fitness:* One entrepreneur, from Cedar Falls, Iowa, understood the need for physical fitness activities geared to the fifty-plusers and started a program called "Take Time." The exercise regime is a back-to-basics method, done at a leisurely pace set by the participants. Early publicity brought a slew of enthusiastic responses and the originator hoped to sell ninety franchises by the end of 1987, according to the January 1987 issue of Kiwanis magazine.

*Products:* An example of new focus for their products is demonstrated byCampbell Soup in their new line of single-portion, sodium-free soups. Many elderly live alone, and many are

243

restricted in their salt intake. This successful new product is the direct result of recognizing a need in the "mature" market and responding to it.

*Real estate:* The field of real estate is not untouched by the rush to earn a share of the dollars available in this new market. Nursing home syndications are being promoted as vehicles for diversifying money back into this fastest-growing segment of the real estate industry, and many established corporations, including a number of major hotel chains, are shifting their focus and entering the field of elder housing. Avon is an example of this diversification into the elder market.

Hicks B. Waldron, chairman and chief executive officer of **Avon**, addressed the Northeast Gerontological Society in 1987, pointing out that

> the aging of America offers opportunities to the broad range of American businesses.
>
> With our acquisition of the Mediplex Group, Avon moved into the nursing home field. We operate more than a dozen long-term-care facilities with almost twenty-one hundred beds. This is a designated growth area for us. We are currently developing nine additional long-term-care facilities with twelve hundred beds. And, because we can't build nursing homes as quickly as our plan calls for, we're looking for acquisitions, but frankly the quality of those available haven't been up to our standards. We won't settle for less.
>
> Another growth area for us is congregate living facilities, which are not to be confused with old folk's homes. These are apartments for the active elderly. There are about 700,000 congregate living units in the country, but demand is expected to grow at about 8 percent a year, four times the population growth.
>
> About 18 months ago, we acquired Retirement Inns of America, which operates eight facilities with more than seven hundred living units. We have four additional units under construction with another seven hundred units and we plan to start ten more projects this year. These inns have dining facilities, arts and crafts rooms, and recreational facilities. Our residents range in age from 55 to 101. The average age of our new residents is 80.

Clearly, Avon sees "the graying of America" as big business!

*Retailers:* Sears, Roebuck & Company is a forerunner of the merchandising trend to entice the older consumer with its "Mature Outlook" program. This buying club for seniors fifty and older offers price cuts on their merchandise. It is one of many advertising tactics Sears is using to attract this growing segment of the population.

In June of 1987, Hallmark Cards instituted "The Best Years" promotion with a new series of retirement and anniversary cards for older audiences. They depict grandparents in shorts and tennis shoes, silver-haired couples in running suits, and elders in situations that reflect an active, vibrant involvement with life.

*Magazines:* The dollars represented by elder Americans are being wooed from all sides. When quizzed as to the most popular magazines in America today, how many would cite *Modern Maturity*, a publication of the American Association of Retired Persons? It ranks third in circulation of all magazines in the United States. One and two? *Reader's Digest* and *TV Guide.*

*Pharmaceuticals:* Publications are only the tip of the iceberg for AARP. Their pharmacy ranks as the world's largest private mail-order drugstore, filling six million prescriptions a year as a service for their over twenty-six million members.

*Insurance:* The industry is very much a part of the aging business and, through **Prudential**, AARP's members pay millions each year for group health care insurance. **Aetna Life & Casualty** has introduced a policy through which grandparents can insure the education of their grandchildren, and Amex Life Assurance Company, a subsidiary of **American Express**, offers long-term health care for people sixty-five and older. (See chapter 8 on medical health insurance.)

*Service businesses.* Today, many businesses are stepping in where they see an opportunity to make a profit by providing those personalized services for the elderly that were once provided exclusively by church, nonprofit, and community organizations.

- **Kelly Girl**, for instance, is providing, through a subsidiary, home care service for the elderly in addition to their traditional secretarial services.

245

- **Avon**, which we have already cited for its elder housing developments, is one of the largest providers of home health care services in the United States. Avon's Health Care Services Division markets hospital equipment for the home, such as beds and wheelchairs as well as oxygen and respiratory therapy and infusion care for nutrition and pain management.

- **H & R Block**, famous for its tax business, has entered the field as well.

- **The Visiting Nurse Service of New York City** has added to its ninety-three-year-old history of charitable services a for-profit business, providing the same services for a fee: home care, companionship, and related help.

The role of the social worker also is expanding into the private sector. The old stigma that social workers only served those who could not deal with their own problems, and who had very limited resources, has changed. Today, we are admitting that we need help caring for our aging parents and many of us are paying for the services of social workers who have moved into the private sector. For some caregivers, the time demands of our jobs and the distance from our families have taken caring out of the realm of the family and put it squarely into the service market.

The private sector has responded with enthusiasm to this new service need with over two hundred such businesses in existence today. There is now a National Organization of Private Geriatric Care Managers, and several states, including Massachusetts and New York, print their own directories. Although most of these care management organizations work within their states, many are set up to network in the handling of long-distance caregiving.

## Innovative Nonprofit Service

The nation's largest health care philanthropy, the **Robert Wood Johnson Foundation**, is involving itself in the delivery of health services to the elderly (and disabled) through various programs. One of the most innovative is its Service Credit Banking Program for the Elderly. Six sites nationwide are funded under this project. This innovative program allows the elderly to barter for services. Likened to the functioning of a blood bank, the Service Credit Banking Program enables volunteers to administer supportive services within the community to elders in need of assistance. The volunteer "banks" credit for his or her time. The credits can then be used by the volunteers for like services for themselves or for whomever they assign as the recipient, whether in their hometown or in another participating city, when they need them.

"The basic concept is as simple as the circle: purchasing power earned today by providing service is expended for receiving services produced by others at a later date. Volunteers earn service credits for the work they do providing respite care and homemaker care for the elderly. Then people spend those service credits to purchase respite care or homemaker care for themselves or for someone in their family. But that is just the beginning. All kinds of variations on the basic cycle are possible," according to Edgar S. Cahn, consultant to the Robert Wood Johnson Foundation and originator of the service credit banking concepts.

In an attempt to take this program nationwide, a limited initiative has been undertaken testing its feasibility in five states: Missouri, Massachusetts, New York, Florida, California; and the District of Columbia. This initiative provides for as many as six grants of up to $200,000 paid out over a three-year period for the support services needed. Should the tests prove successful, consideration may be given to expanding the effort to additional sites.

The idea of a workable bartering plan has captured the imagination of many who see the tremendous need for services among the elderly, during a time when help care costs are soaring and federal help programs are undergoing dramatic budget slashes. How to integrate such a system into our economy raises many questions—accountability for time given and received, backed by accredited nonprofit organizations, tax implications, liability, organizational details, and so forth—but whatever the hurdles, it is this kind of forward thinking that must take place if America is to overcome the national health care crisis. Making efficient use of its human resources in caring for its burgeoning elder population is a positive first step.

## Media Response to an Aging America

Business is not the only segment of our society to focus attention on our growing older population. Media sources have approached the "story" of aging from many angles. Nursing home abuses have become known to hundreds of thousands of Americans through sensational exposés in the printed media as well as in television and radio stories. Any attempted change in Social Security benefits or Medicare cutbacks receives immediate coverage, and legislation affecting retirement age is always hotly debated in the news. What is changing about media coverage is the knowledge and sensitivity with which the subjects are handled.

Major metropolitan newspapers such as the *Washington Post* and the *Los Angeles Times* have reporters on assignment to cover stories that have specific significance for the elderly. Local senior newspapers exist in almost every state, often in rural areas, where these newspapers are considered the major source of information concerning local events and news.

Cyril F. Brickfield, former executive director of AARP, stated in the June 1987 *News Bulletin* that AARP, along with the National Press Foundation, co-sponsored a seminar for journalists to learn more about every aspect of the aging of our society. Eighteen reporters from major newspapers, radio, and television stations were selected by the foundation to attend a three-day seminar in Washington, D.C., where they discussed a wide range of public policy issues with experts in the field of aging.

Mr. Brickfield went on to report the creation of Maturity News Services (MNS): "An independent news service underwritten by AARP and staffed by an experienced team of journalists. MNS will provide daily and weekly newspapers throughout the United States with authoritative, factual, unbiased reporting on major issues affecting America's 50-plus population. This up-to-date news and analysis of developments in Washington and throughout the country will be distributed to newspapers through The New York Times News Syndicate."

So much attention being focused on the elderly brings with it the promise of improvement in the way that American society sees and treats its oldest citizens. We, as caretakers, know that the family is still a primary force in caring for our aged. A basic change in society's attitude toward our elderly, however, would be a great help to our parents and to us as caregivers. With greater exposure should come a greater show of respect for the abilities and experience of the elderly, and a more open attitude in discussing the debilitating physical conditions requiring long-term care which so many of them eventually face.

## ADVERTISING

A dramatic change is taking place in the advertising industry. The bloom is off the rose as far as the "yuppie" market is concerned. The numbers are still high, but their pocketbooks are not open. With heavy mortgages, educational and child care expenses, they have less disposable income than previously imagined by Madison Avenue experts.

Welcome to the new "age of the aged"! "The fifty-five plus population earns $800 billion a year and accounts for half of all U.S. discretionary spending power. In striking contrast, the young control only twenty percent of that total," reported the Conference Board's 1985 study entitled *Mid-Life and Beyond*. This kind of specific information on the growing mature market has triggered a swell of advertising campaigns directed toward those desirable dollars.

Just as mature images are becoming more valuable tools for business advancement (younger men on Wall Street are wearing nonprescription eyeglasses to look older, which is assumed to translate into looking more powerful), so are mature-looking actors and actresses being chosen to spearhead new product campaigns. Bob Hope, George Burns, Phyllis Diller, Betty White, Joan Collins, Burt Lancaster, Rodney Dangerfield, Ed Asner, June Allyson, and Danny Thomas are but a few of the mature "stars" who have become product spokespersons. Even more dramatic in this recent shift to sell to the fifty-plus audience is the casting of older unknowns in television commercials, magazine, newspaper, and billboard ads for the selling of products not generically related to aging, for example: financial investments, long-distance phone companies, breakfast cereals, cookies, and so forth.

TELEVISION

Programming on television is beginning to offer some realistic portraits of elderly characters, complete with sexual needs. Good viewer response will insure more of this kind of offering. "Golden Girls" and "Our House" are good starts in the right direction.

The made-for-television movie starring Helen Hayes and Fred Astaire entitled "A Family Upside Down" went a long way toward fostering understanding of the dilemmas facing even the most loving of families when one is struck with a heart attack and can no longer live alone. This film dealt sensitively and practically with the need for feelings of self-worth and independence, even in the frail old, while sympathizing with the many stresses of caregiving.

"Mercy or Murder," starring Robert Young, created the same audience understanding for the frustration that the afflicted, as well as the caregiver, might feel. This time the television special dealt with the insidious destruction of family relationships when one member is afflicted with Alzheimer's disease.

"Between Two Women," starring Colleen Dewhurst and Farrah Fawcett, was another made-for-television movie about what happens when a domineering, unloving mother-in-law is left helpless as a result of a stroke, and the total responsibility for the caretaking falls to the disliked daughter-in-law. "Are you shielded from nursing her by some stupid male privilege?" screams the exhausted caregiver to her husband.

These true-to-life portrayals, cast with major stars and aired on prime-time television, do a great deal toward making us aware of what crisis can do to an unprepared family. They highlight the need for thoughtful discussion within the family before a crisis arises. They also remind us that no human involvement is without the potential for great personal growth. As with the caregiver, Valle, in "Between Two Women," we can amaze ourselves at the great love we develop for the invalid we nurse, even as we hate the circumstances that hold us captive.

We should make television networks and sponsors aware of our enthusiastic response to the programming they present that helps promote greater understanding and respect for our elders.

FILMS

Films provide yet another outlet for the development of new definitions for aging Americans. Few are not thrilled with the performance of the late Jackie Gleason in *Nothing in Common,* directed by Garry Marshall, as they watch the love develop between him and his reluctant caregiving son, played by Tom Hanks. It is a wonderful vehicle to expose our own children to the responsibilities of caregiving. *On Golden Pond* captivated us with the realistic performances of two screen giants, the late Henry Fonda and Katharine Hepburn. The intergenerational relationship with their step-grandson, which bridged close to seventy years, pulled at our heartstrings, and chords of empathy were struck with many in the audience as the grown daughter, played by Jane Fonda, struggled for her father's approval.

The thrill of these and other movies that feature mature actors is that producers are realizing they are not box office flukes. America is awakening to its full potential by not ignoring the talents of its elder citizens. *The Whales of August,* starring ninety-year-old Lillian Gish and co-starring seventy-eight-year-old Bette Davis, is a unique undertaking because it does not have any younger-generation characters. Vincent Price and Ann Sothern round out this cast of geriatric superstars under the sensitive direction of Lindsay Anderson. The beauty of such a film is that it allows the audience to see the strong personality differences among the cast, thus negating the myths that maintain that all old people act a certain way. *New York Times* film critic Vincent Canby called it "a cinema event."

## Advocacy Groups for the Aging

Many of us have loud voices with which to criticize "the system" in discussions on potential political reforms, but we feel less confidence when the time comes to act. In spite of our successes as a generation, there is still a sense that the legislative process is large and complex and that we as individuals can do little to alter the outcome of any single piece of legislation. Our strength remains in acting as a group. For those whose parents may be interested in direct political action, there are a number of lobbies that address the issues of older Americans, and, indirectly, the issues of the caretakers. Most of these organizations are headquartered in Washington, D.C.. They often have local offices, staffed by volunteers, but trying to make local contact can be frustrating. Look in the government listing pages at the front of your telephone directory for senior citizen services and senior information. For full information on political lobbies, you can write to the national lobby associations, some of the most popular of which are listed below:

**AARP**—The American Association of Retired Persons, with its twenty-six million members, is the largest and most powerful voice for older Americans in Washington. It is a nonpartisan organization whose members must be fifty years of age. Membership is $5 a year. Address: 1909 K Street, N.W., Washington, DC 20049 (see chapter 6, page 158).

The **Gray Panthers** is one of the most innovative of the lobby groups. Although it deals with all the traditional issues of the aged, it believes that all issues of concern to America, including hunger and world peace, are issues of concern to the aged. Membership is open to every age and this organization is particularly sensitive to intergenerational needs.

Aware of the powerful impact of television and advertising as major factors in our perception of people, Media Watch was created to alert members to negative stereotypes of both the old and the young. Their efforts have led the National Association of Broadcasters to add age to sex and race as criteria in making programming choices. Address: 3635 Chestnut Street, Philadelphia, PA 19104.

**The National Council on Aging** was founded in 1950. NCOA cooperates with other organizations to promote concern for older people and develop methods and resources for meeting their needs. This broad-based organization is involved in everything from maintenance of a fourteen-thousand-volume library on aging to conducting research and demonstration programs on problems of older people. Address: West Wing 100, 600 Maryland Avenue, S.W., Washington, DC 20024.

**ASA—American Society on Aging** was founded in 1954 as the Western Gerontological Society. This is the only established national organization in the field with its origins and headquarters in the West. It is involved in networking, training, educating, and publishing, as well as advocacy work at the local, state, and federal levels; membership is open to elders, professionals in the field, organizations, and interested laypersons. Address: 833 Market Street, Suite 512, San Francisco, CA 94103; (415) 543-2617.

**OWL—The Older Women's League** was established to address the economic and health problems that women face as they age. Membership is roughly twenty thousand across the nation, and their advocacy focus consists of seven basic issues including family care giving and remaining in control until the end of life. Motto: "Don't agonize—organize!" OWL, 1325 G Street, N.W., Washington, DC 20005.

It should be noted that politicians assume each letter received on a given issue represents a much larger number of constituents who feel the same way, yet did not write. In other words, our individual letters may have more clout than we imagine. If we know of a piece of legislation that we favor, we should not hesitate to drop a note to our state senators and representatives for state issues, and to our U.S. senators and representatives for issues before Congress.

## Silver-Haired Legislatures—Legislative Action for Seniors

In Missouri in 1973, the first Silver-Haired Legislature was formed in America. Now, twenty-three states boast such senior forums for political debate, some with slightly different names—Old Hoosier Assembly in Indiana, Legacy Legislature in Montana, and the California Senior Legislature. To share tactics, develop lobbying skills, and plan strategy, there is a National Silver Haired Congress that brings all the states together.

Silver Haired Legislatures (SHL) focus attention on issues of particular concern to the elderly, which are often acted upon by their state assemblies. The structure of the legislatures and their effectiveness vary from state to state. In California, the state legislature created the California Senior Legislature to advise state government on issues affecting the elderly. It is comprised of eighty assemblypersons and forty senators, each elected for a two-year term. Seventy-five percent of the legislation it has sponsored has been signed into law.

This is an area in which senior clout is on the rise. As the senior power base grows and more states take the lead from those who have had the greatest legislative successes, these SHLs should have a growing impact on state politics, thus adding to the influence of elders across the nation. With power often comes respect. These legislative vehicles will contribute to changing the image of senior Americans. New respect is coming their way.

Even those seniors who do not participate in a senior legislature or an advocacy group are exercising their growing power at the ballot box. Figures from the U.S. Census Bureau show that the number of potential voters in America over sixty-five outnumbers those in the eighteen–to–twenty-four age group for the first time since eighteen-year-olds received the right to vote. Coupled with their population growth is the patriotic tradition instilled in our seniors, resulting in a much greater proportion of their group exercising the privilege to vote, while younger, less politically interested voters remain absent from the polls.

The significance of this shift is having an effect on Congress. There is a heightened emphasis on Capitol Hill for legislation addressing issues for the elderly.

FUTURE LEGISLATION

There are literally hundreds of pieces of legislation under consideration, both on the state and federal levels, with varying amounts of support. It will take our country's strongest leadership, assuming both moral and fiscal responsibility, to produce the laws and guidelines we need as a country to face our aging crisis successfully. The following are just a few of the changes already being discussed, which we might see put into law in the coming years:

254

- Legislation for Medicare to offer its own Medigap insurance

- Legislation extending Medicare and Medicaid to include outpatient drugs and respite care

- Legislation extending health insurance benefits to cover long-term care at home as well as in nursing homes

- Legislation requiring business to provide unpaid work leave for employees to care for sick parents: (HR 925) Family and Medical Leave Act

- Legislation requiring employers to provide mandatory health insurance coverage for employees

- A chronic catastrophic (as opposed to acute) health bill

- Portable pension legislation, which will allow employees to take benefits with them from one job to another in order to accumulate better retirement packages

- Legislation expanding the services of hospice

- Legislation providing tax incentives for the caregivers

- Protection against spousal impoverishment

- Laws enacted to protect against elder abuse

- Property tax relief for elders

# Conclusion

IT is generally agreed that there are five basic elements needed to assure a happy life: good health, a home, people who care about us, something to do, and money. As we age, we often fall victim to the loss of one or more of these components of happiness. As children, these needs were first provided for by our parents. Now it is we, the adult children, who face the responsibility of providing one or more of these needs for our parents.

In this book, we have addressed each of these aspects of life, as redefined in the life of our aging parents. Our special focus has been to direct our peers toward the most effective ways of helping our parents recognize, provide, and plan for the inevitable changes in their lives. As an outgrowth, we have learned what lies ahead for us.

We are aware that the perception of the "graying of America" is changing to the more elegant "silvering of America" as the older population's self-image grows stronger. We, the adult children, are thrilled with the growing opportunities for our parents. We are thrilled because their lives are being improved and because we are developing a more positive image of what our own old age can bring.

However, some experts feel that the biggest crisis America has ever faced is about to happen: the aging of its baby-boom generation. Seventy-six million baby-boomers are approaching middle age right now, and when the last of this number retires, we will

256

have over sixty million retirees in this country. The older half of the population will outnumber the young for the first time in the nation's history. Who will pay for their care? Without careful fiscal planning as a nation, the medical and home care expenses resulting from this population shift could bankrupt our current health care system.

The ideal would be to create an environment in which the frail elderly are assured of medical care for their final years and do not have to face the prospect of poverty and social alienation. Congress is currently tackling the catastrophic health care issue, but without real success. The catastrophic care bills that have been considered to date of this writing have been fairly limited in scope, dealing primarily with long hospital stays for the sick old with specific ailments. For the approximately 800,000 frail elderly in that category, such legislation is a great help. But for the remaining twenty-four million to twenty-eight million Medicare recipients, however, most of whom are more likely to face chronic, long-term care needs, no government financial relief is in sight.

The private insurance industry is also grappling with health care solutions for the elderly. Answering a call for help, a number of companies are now offering long-term health care coverage to limited groups. As we've noted, Travelers, Prudential, Metropolitan Life, and Blue Cross of Washington and Alaska are some of the corporations experimenting with coverage in this crucial area of need. Some of their programs are offered only on a trial basis, however, and in all cases the premiums vary greatly with increasing age.

Addressing the issue of long-term health care may well turn out to be America's greatest challenge. To solve the crisis, we must combine the resources of business, government, and a concerned population willing to contribute its time and energy to advocate for change, and then participate in its resolution.

A bright future will not happen on its own. It is true that the unknown aspects of our futures cannot be anticipated, but this book has stirred our thinking concerning those areas of our lives about which something *can* be done. Now is the time to bear in mind the prophetic saying, "We reap what we sow." Our chances of realizing twenty-five years of productive life after age sixty are greatly enhanced if we plan for them now.

Ours is a generation that has been written about since we were born. In numbers came strength. We knew what we believed and we went for it. We were the ones who made Vietnam an unpopular war; we made it all right for a father to witness the birth of his child; we pulled every social issue imaginable out of the closet. Our job is not yet finished. Before the door slams shut, it is our responsibility to be sure that our parents, and we ourselves when the time comes, are cared for, nurtured, and respected by a society we will have taught to revere its elders.

# *Appendix 1*
# **Resources**

Administration on Aging
Department of Health and Human
  Services
200 Independence Avenue, S.W.
Washington, DC 20201
(202) 245-0724

Alzheimer's Disease and Related
  Diseases Association (ADRDA)
70 E. Lake Street, Suite 600
Chicago, IL 60601
(800) 621-0379
([800] 572-6037 in Illinois)

American Association of Homes for
  the Aging
1129 20th Street, N.W.
Suite 400
Washington, DC 20036
(202) 296-5960

American Association of Retired
  Persons
1909 K Street, N.W.
Washington, DC 20049
(202) 872-4700

American Cancer Society
4 West 35th Street
New York, NY 10001
(800) 4-CANCER

American Health Care Association
1200 15th Street, N.W., 8th Floor
Washington, DC 20005
(202) 833-2050

American Heart Association
7320 Greenville Avenue
Dallas, TX 75231

American Lung Association
1740 Broadway
P.O. Box 596
New York, NY 10019

American Society on Aging
833 Market Street
Suite 512
San Francisco, CA 94103
(415) 543-2617

Children of Aging Parents
2761 Trenton Road
Levittown, PA 19056
(215) 945-6900

Consumer Information Center
P.O. Box 100
Pueblo, CO 81002

Gray Panthers
311 South Juniper Street, #601
Philadelphia, PA 19107
(215) 545-6555

NARIC
National Rehabilitation Center
4407 Eighth Street, N.W.
Washington, DC 20017
(800) 34-NARIC

National Association for Home Care
519 C Street, N.E.
Washington, DC 20002
(202) 547-7424

National Council of Senior Citizens
925 15th Street, N.W.
Washington, DC 20005
(202) 347-8800

259

## Aging Parents and You

National Council on the Aging, Inc.
600 Maryland Avenue, S.W.
Suite 100 West Wing
Washington, DC 20024
(202) 479-1200

National Home Caring Council
235 Park Avenue South
New York, NY 10003
(212) 674-4990

National Hospice Organization
1901 North Fort Myer Drive,
Suite 902
Arlington, VA 22209
(703) 243-5900

National Senior Citizens Law Center
2025 M Street, N.W.
Suite 400
Washington, DC 20036
(202) 887-5280

OWL—The Older Women's League
1325 G Street, N.W.
Washington, DC 20005

# *Appendix 2*
# State Agencies on the Aging

**Alabama**
Commission on Aging
State Capitol
Montgomery, AL 36130
(205) 261-5743

**Alaska**
Older Alaskans Commission
Department of Administration
Pouch C-Mail Station 0209
Juneau, AK 99811
(907) 465-3250

**Arizona**
Aging and Adult Administration
Department of Economic Security
1400 West Washington Street
Phoenix, AZ 85007
(602) 255-4446

**Arkansas**
Office of Aging and Adult Services
Department of Social and
   Rehabilitative Services
Donaghey Building, Suite 1428
7th and Main Streets
Little Rock, AR 72201
(501) 371-2441

**California**
Department of Aging
1020 19th Street
Sacramento, CA 95814
(916) 322-5290

**Colorado**
Aging and Adult Services Division
Department of Social Services
1575 Sherman Street, Room 503
Denver, CO 80203
(303) 866-3672

**Connecticut**
Department on Aging
175 Main Street
Hartford, CT 06106
(203) 566-3238

**Delaware**
Division on Aging
Department of Health and Social
   Services
1901 North DuPont Highway
New Castle, DE 19720
(302) 421-6791

**District of Columbia**
Office on Aging
1424 K Street, N.W.—2nd Floor
Washington, DC 20011
(202) 724-5626

**Florida**
Program Office of Aging and Adult
   Services
Department of Health and
   Rehabilitation Services
1317 Winewood Boulevard
Tallahassee, FL 32301
(904) 488-8922

261

**Georgia**
Office of Aging
878 Peachtree Street, N.E.,
    Room 632
Atlanta, GA 30309
(404) 894-5333

**Guam**
Public Health and Social Services
Government of Guam
Agana, GU 96910

**Hawaii**
Executive Office on Aging
Office of the Governor
1149 Bethel Street, Room 307
Honolulu, HI 96813
(808) 548-2593

**Idaho**
Office on Aging
Statehouse, Room 114
Boise, ID 83720
(208) 334-3833

**Illinois**
Department on Aging
421 East Capitol Avenue
Springfield, IL 62701
(217) 785-3356

**Indiana**
Department of Aging and
    Community Services
Consolidated Building, Suite 1350
115 North Pennsylvania Street
Indianapolis, IN 46204
(317) 232-7006

**Iowa**
Commission on Aging
Jewett Building, Suite 236
914 Grand Avenue
Des Moines, IA 50319
(515) 281-5187

**Kansas**
Department on Aging
610 West 10th Street
Topeka, KS 66612
(913) 296-4986

**Kentucky**
Division for Aging Services
Department of Human Resources
DHR Building—6th Floor
275 East Main Street
Frankfort, KY 40601
(502) 564-6930

**Louisiana**
Office of Elderly Affairs
P.O. Box 80374
Baton Rouge, LA 70898
(504) 925-1700

**Maine**
Bureau of Maine's Elderly
Department of Human Services
State House, Station #11
Augusta, ME 04333
(207) 289-2561

**Maryland**
Office on Aging
State Office Building, Room 1004
301 West Preston Street
Baltimore, MD 21201
(301) 383-5064

**Massachusetts**
Department of Elder Affairs
38 Chauncy Street
Boston, MA 02111
(617) 727-7750

**Michigan**
Office of Services to the Aging
P.O. Box 30026
Lansing, MI 48909
(517) 373-8230

**Minnesota**
Board on Aging
Metro Square Building, Room 204
Seventh and Robert Streets
St. Paul, MN 55101
(612) 296-2544

**Mississippi**
Council on Aging
Executive Building, Suite 301
802 North State Street
Jackson, MS 39201
(601) 354-6590

**Missouri**
Division on Aging
Department of Social Services
Broadway State Office
P.O. Box 570
Jefferson City, MO 65101
(314) 751-3082

**Montana**
Community Services Division
P.O. Box 4210
Helena, MT 59604
(406) 444-3865

**Nebraska**
Department on Aging
301 Centennial Mall South
P.O. Box 95044
Lincoln, NE 68509
(402) 471-2306

**Nevada**
Division on Aging
Department of Human Resources
Kinkead Building, Room 101
505 East King Street
Carson City, NV 89710
(702) 885-4210

**New Hampshire**
Council on Aging
14 Depot Street
Concord, NH 03301
(603) 271-2751

**New Jersey**
Division on Aging
Department of Community Affairs
363 West State Street
P.O. Box 2768
Trenton, NJ 08625
(609) 292-4833

**New Mexico**
State Agency on Aging
La Villa Rivera Building, 4th Floor
224 East Palace Avenue
Santa Fe, NM 87501
(505) 827-7640

**New York**
Office for the Aging
New York State Plaza
Agency Building 2
Albany, NY 12223
(518) 474-4425

**North Carolina**
Division on Aging
708 Hillsborough Street, Suite 200
Raleigh, NC 27603
(919) 733-3983

**North Dakota**
Aging Services
Department of Human Services
State Capitol Building
Bismarck, ND 58505
(701) 224-2577

**Northern Mariana Islands**
Office of Aging
Department of Community and
   Cultural Affairs
Civic Center
Susupe, Saipan, Northern Mariana
   Islands 96950
Telephone numbers 9411 or 9732

**Ohio**
Department on Aging
50 West Broad Street—9th Floor
Columbus, OH 43215
(614) 466-5500

**Oklahoma**
Special Unit on Aging
Department of Human Services
P.O. Box 25352
Oklahoma City, OK 73125
(405) 521-2281

263

**Oregon**
Senior Services Division
313 Public Service Building
Salem, OR 97310
(503) 378-4728

**Pennsylvania**
Department of Aging
231 State Street
Harrisburg, PA 17101-1195
(717) 783-1550

**Puerto Rico**
Gericulture Commission
Department of Social Services
P.O. Box 11398
Santurce, PR 00910
(809) 724-7400 or (809) 725-8015

**Rhode Island**
Department of Elderly Affairs
79 Washington Street
Providence, RI 02903
(401) 277-2858

**(American) Samoa**
Territorial Administration on Aging
Office of the Governor
Pago Pago, AS 96799
011-684-633-1252

**South Carolina**
Commission on Aging
915 Main Street
Columbia, SC 29201
(803) 758-2576

**South Dakota**
Office of Adult Services and Aging
Kneip Building
700 North Illinois Street
Pierre, SD 57501
(605) 773-3656

**Tennessee**
Commission on Aging
715 Tennessee Building
535 Church Street
Nashville, TN 37219
(615) 741-2056

**Texas**
Department on Aging
210 Barton Springs Road—5th Floor
P.O. Box 12768 Capitol Station
Austin, TX 78704
(512) 475-2717

**Trust Territory of the Pacific**
Office of Elderly Programs
Community Development Division
Government of TTPI
Saipan, Mariana Islands 96950
Telephone numbers 9335 or 9336

**Utah**
Division of Aging and Adult Services
Department of Social Services
150 West North Temple
Box 2500
Salt Lake City, UT 84102
(801) 533-6422

**Vermont**
Office on Aging
103 South Main Street
Waterbury, VT 05676
(802) 241-2400

**Virginia**
Department on Aging
James Monroe Building—18th Floor
101 North 14th Street
Richmond, VA 23219
(804) 225-2271

**Virgin Islands**
Commission on Aging
6F Havensight Mall
Charlotte Amalie, St. Thomas,
  VI 00801
(809) 774-5884

**Washington**
Bureau of Aging and Adult Services
Department of Social and Health
  Services
OB-43G
Olympia, WA 98504
(206) 753-2502

**West Virginia**
Commission on Aging
Holly Grove—State Capitol
Charleston, WV 25305
(304) 348-3317

**Wisconsin**
Bureau of Aging
Division of Community Services
One West Wilson Street, Room 663
P.O. Box 7850
Madison, WI 53702
(608) 266-2536

**Wyoming**
Commission on Aging
Hathaway Building, Room 139
Cheyenne, WY 82002-0710
(307) 777-7986

# About the Authors

EUGENIA ANDERSON-ELLIS has had a lifetime involvement in business and public relations, making numerous television and lecture appearances. An active member of community organizations, she chaired the Atlanta Women's Political Caucus, served on a special task force of the American Cancer Society, and currently serves on the Board of the Mental Health Association of San Francisco. A world traveler, Ms. Anderson-Ellis studied at the Sorbonne and was graduated from St. Lawrence University. She, her husband, and two daughters make their home in San Francisco.

MARSHA DRYAN was a co-founder and former vice-president of First National Mortgage Company in California. She has been elected to several boards of directors and has been actively involved in a variety of major philanthropic organizations. The recipient of many awards and honors, including the United Jewish Appeal National Young Leadership Award, she lives in San Francisco with her three children.

Additional copies of *Aging Parents and You* may be ordered by sending a check for $10.95, plus $1.50 postage and handling of the first book and $.50 for each additional book, to:

MasterMedia Limited
333 West 52nd Street
Suite 306
New York, NY 10019
(212) 246-9500

The authors are available for keynotes, half-day and full-day seminars, and workshops. Please contact MasterMedia for availability and fee arrangements.

# Other MasterMedia Books

***The Pregnancy and Motherhood Diary: Planning the First Year of Your Second Career,*** by Susan Schiffer Stautberg, is the first and only undated appointment diary that shows how to manage pregnancy and career ($12.95 paper).

***Cities of Opportunity: Finding the Best Place to Work, Live and Prosper in the 1990's and Beyond,*** by Dr. John Tepper Marlin, explores the job and living options for the next decade and into the next century. This consumer guide and handbook, written by one of the world's experts on cities, selects and features 46 American cities and metropolitan areas ($13.95 paper and $24.95 cloth).

***The Dollars and Sense of Divorce,*** by Dr. Judith Briles, is the first book to combine practical tips on overcoming the legal hurdles and planning finances before, during, and after divorce ($10.95 paper).

***Out the Organization: Gaining the Competitive Edge,*** by Madeleine and Robert Swain, is written for the millions of Americans whose jobs are no longer safe, whose companies are not loyal, and who face futures of uncertainty. It gives advice on finding a new job or starting your own business ($17.95 cloth).

## WATCH FOR THESE MASTERMEDIA BOOKS

***Beyond Success: How Volunteer Service Can Help You Begin Making a Life Instead of a Living,*** by John F. Raynolds III and Eleanor Raynolds, CBE, is a unique how-to book targeted to business and professional people considering volunteer work, senior citizens who wish to fill leisure time meaningfully, and students trying out various career options. The book is filled with interviews with celebrities, CEOs, and average citizens who talk about the benefits of service work ($19.95 cloth).

*Managing It All: Time-Saving Ideas for Career, Family Relationships, and Self,* by Beverly Benz Treuille and Susan Schiffer Stautberg, is written for women who are juggling careers and families. Over 200 career women (ranging from a TV anchorwoman to an investment banker) were interviewed. The book contains many humorous anecdotes on saving time and improving the quality of life for self and family ($9.95 paper).

*Criticism in Your Life: How to Give It, How to Take It, How to Make It Work for You,* by Dr. Deborah Bright, offers practical advice, in an upbeat, readable, and realistic fashion, for turning criticism into control. Charts and diagrams guide the reader into managing criticism from bosses, spouses, relationships, children, friends, neighbors, and in-laws ($17.95 cloth).